The Future of Employment Relations

Also by Adrian Wilkinson

The Sage Handbook of Human Resource Management (*edited with Bacon, N., Redman, T., & Snell, S., 2009*)

The Oxford Handbook of Participation in Organizations (*edited with Gollan, P., Lewin, D., & Marchington, M., 2010*)

The Handbook of Comparative Employment Relations (*edited with Barry, M., forthcoming*)

Handbook of Labour Unions (*edited with Gall, G. & Hurd, R., forthcoming*)

Work and Employment Relations in the 21st Century (*edited with Townsend, K., forthcoming*)

Also by Keith Townsend

Working Time Transformations and Effects (*with Russell, R., Peetz, D., Houghton, C., Allan, C., & Fox, A., 2003*)

Method in the Madness: Research Stories You Won't Find in a Textbook (*edited with Burgess, J., 2009*)

Research Handbook on Work and Employment Relations (*with Wilkinson, A., 2011*)

The Future of Employment Relations

New Paradigms, New Developments

Edited by

Adrian Wilkinson
Centre for Work, Organisation and Wellbeing, Griffith University, Australia

and

Keith Townsend
Centre for Work, Organisation and Wellbeing, Griffith University, Australia

palgrave
macmillan

First published 2011 by
PALGRAVE MACMILLAN

Palgrave Macmillan in the UK is an imprint of Macmillan Publishers Limited,
registered in England, company number 785998, of Houndmills, Basingstoke,
Hampshire RG21 6XS.

Palgrave Macmillan in the US is a division of St Martin's Press LLC,
175 Fifth Avenue, New York, NY 10010.

Palgrave Macmillan is the global academic imprint of the above companies
and has companies and representatives throughout the world.

Palgrave® and Macmillan® are registered trademarks in the United States,
the United Kingdom, Europe and other countries.

ISBN: 978–0–230–24094–0

This book is printed on paper suitable for recycling and made from fully
managed and sustained forest sources. Logging, pulping and manufacturing
processes are expected to conform to the environmental regulations of the
country of origin.

A catalogue record for this book is available from the British Library.

A catalog record for this book is available from the Library of Congress.

10 9 8 7 6 5 4 3 2 1
20 19 18 17 16 15 14 13 12 11

Printed and bound in the United States of America

Contents

Part III   Employment Relations and the Society

Tables and Figures

Tables

Figures

Acknowledgements

Many chapters in this book stem from an International Workshop on the Future of Employment Relations held at Griffith University in August 2009. We would like to thank all participants at that workshop for their involvement and support. This workshop and the ensuing book would not have been possible without the financial support from Griffith University through an 'International Workshop Award'. Most importantly, we would like to thank Joanne Pascoe and Clare Inwood, the administrative team at the Centre for Work, Organisation and Wellbeing, for their excellent assistance in organizing the workshop and making it a success.

We also wish to acknowledge the authors who were not at the workshop, but who wilfully contributed to what we think has become a worthwhile contribution to understanding the changing nature of research around work and employment relations. We would like to thank Teresa Chase and Georgina Cohen for their editorial support in the final stages of completing this publication. Finally, we would like to recognize the support from Virginia Thorp and her team at Palgrave Macmillan in bringing this book to publication.

About the Editors

Adrian Wilkinson is Director of the Centre of Work, Organisation and Wellbeing at Griffith University. Prior to his appointment at Griffith University in 2006, he worked at Loughborough University in the UK where he was Professor of Human Resource Management from 1998 and was also Director of Research for the Business School. He has worked at Manchester School of Management, University of Manchester Institute of Science and Technology.

He has written on many aspects of employment relations. His recent research has encompassed employee participation and voice, high performance work systems, and comparative and international employment relations. He has written nine books, over a hundred articles in refereed journals as well as numerous book chapters. His books (with co-authors) include *Making Quality Critical* (1995), *Managing Quality and Human Resources* (1997), *Managing with TQM: Theory and Practice* (1998), *Understanding Work and Employment: Industrial Relations in Transition* (2003), *Human Resource Management at Work* (4th edn, 2008), *Contemporary Human Resource Management* (3rd edn, 2009), *The Sage Handbook of Human Resource Management* (2009), and *The Oxford Handbook of Organisational Participation* (2010).

Keith Townsend is Senior Research Fellow in the Centre for Work, Organisation and Wellbeing at Griffith University. From 2005 to 2008 he was employed in the School of Management at Queensland University of Technology. Prior to that he held various roles in the Department of Industrial Relations at Griffith University and practitioner roles in private enterprises.

His research interests include employee misbehaviour and understanding the differences between organizational policies and employee experiences. He has published more than 50 refereed journal articles and scholarly book chapters. His recently published books include *Method in the Madness: Research Stories You Won't Read in Textbooks* (2009) and *Edward Elgar Handbook on Work and Employment Relations* (2011).

Contributors

Chris Brewster is Professor of International Human Resource Management at Henley Business School, University of Reading, Berkshire.

Annette Cox is Associate Director, Workplace Performance and Skills at the Institute for Employment Studies, Brighton.

Graham Dietz is Lecturer in Human Resource Management and Organisational Behaviour at Durham University, England.

Tony Dobbins is an IRCHSS Research Fellow and Lecturer in HRM at Bangor Business School, University of Bangor, Wales.

Tony Dundon is Senior Lecturer in Employment Relations and HRM at the School of Business and Economics, National University of Ireland, Galway.

Ina Ehnert is Substitute Professor for the Chair of Sustainable Resource Management at University of Bremen, Germany.

Ann Frost is Associate Professor of Organisational Behaviour at the Richard Ivey School of Business, University of West Ontario, Canada.

Marc Goergen is Chair of Finance at Cardiff University, a research associate of the European Corporate Governance Institute, and a fellow of the International Institute of Corporate Governance and Accountability based at the Law School of the George Washington University, USA.

Kari Hadjivassiliou is Principal Research Fellow at the Institute for Employment Studies, Brighton.

Richard Hall is Professor of Work and Organisational Studies and Associate Dean – Research at the Business School at the University of Sydney, Australia.

Ashlea Kellner is a PhD candidate and Research Associate in the Department of Employment Relations and Human Resources at Griffith University.

Gill Kirton is Professor of Employment Relations and HRM at the Centre for Research in Equality and Diversity, School of Business and Management, Queen Mary University of London.

Stephane Le Queux is Senior Lecturer in the School of Business at James Cook University, Australia.

David Lewin holds the Neil H. Jacoby Chair in Management, Human Resources and Organizational Behavior in the UCLA Anderson School of Management, and is President-Elect (for 2012) of the Labor and Employment Relations Association (LERA).

Mick Marchington is Professor of Human Resource Management at Manchester Business School.

Rose Martin is a research officer at the Institute for Employment Studies, Brighton.

Akinwunmi Martins completed his Master's in Human Resource Management at the University of Durham in 2010. He is currently working for CPL Scientific Publishing.

Dennis Nickson is Professor and Head of the Department in Human Resource Management at the Business School, University of Strathclyde, Scotland.

David Peetz is Professor of Employment Relations at Griffith University, Australia.

James Richards is Lecturer in Human Resources Management at Heriot-Watt University, Edinburgh.

Rosalind Searle is Senior Lecturer in Occupational Psychology at the Open University and Hon. Senior Fellow, City University's Centre for Performance at Work.

Diane Van Den Broek is Senior Lecturer and Honours Co-ordinator in Work and Organisational Studies at the Business School, University of Sydney, Australia.

Chris Warhurst is Professor in Work and Organisational Studies at the Business School, University of Sydney and an Associate Research Fellow of scope at the Universities of oxford and cardiff.

Theresa M. Welbourne is a research professor at the Center for Effective Organizations, Marshall School of Business, University of Southern California, President and CEO of eePulse, Inc. (www.eepulse.com), and Editor-in-Chief, *Human Resource Management*.

Geoffrey Wood is Professor at the School of Management, University of Sheffield, and Honorary Professor of the University of Witwatersrand and Visiting Professor at the Nelson Mandela University, South Africa.

1
New Directions in Employment Relations

Keith Townsend and Adrian Wilkinson

It is difficult to argue with the notion that the world of work is changing. The change can be slow, for instance the manner in which some industrial sectors adopt new 'people management' practices, or rapid, like how technology is altering the way work is performed throughout the industrialized world. We have witnessed a fundamental sectoral shift in employment away from manufacturing and the public sector – sectors that are characterized by formalized employment relations (ER) and human resources (HR) systems, high levels of trade union membership, and larger employment units – towards the more informal, relatively union-free, and smaller employment units of the service sector. We have also seen other trends – such as moving call centre work overseas. The changing nature of employment has major implications for the management of people and for the systems of HR utilized. Working patterns have also changed during the past 30 years, so that the classic or 'old' image of work as principally male, full-time, and permanent is no longer a useful guide.

People are also changing. There is a wide range of research that is available through diverse disciplines elucidating how people are changing in their preferences for types of work, their involvement in unions and other collectives, and what they seek from their work and non-work experiences. However, one thing remains a constant through these changes: the great majority of our population must work to sustain their existence.

It is within the context of this constant and these changes that we bring together this collection of chapters to reconsider important aspects of work, the employment relationship, and organizations. We focus on some relatively neglected areas in the field of employment relations or others where we believe a new perspective is of value. We

1

have not imposed a label on authors that could be seen as arbitrary or geographically specific, as industrial relations, employment relations, and human resource management mean slightly different things across the globe. However, each author has been given the freedom to use the label that they feel is most appropriate given their context. We hope that, in some way, this book will encourage debate and contribute to developing research agendas well into the 21st century. Our book is divided into three parts: *Managing People in Organizations*, *New Perspectives on Employment*, and *Employment Relations and Society*.

We begin Part I with a contribution from US scholar David Lewin, who considers the implications and limitations of high performance human resources (HPHR) research (Chapter 2). The development of indices of HPHR in relation to business performance (via quantitative studies) has been a mainstay of much of this research. Key findings of HPHR research relate mostly to HR best practice and its impact on 'business performance', however this might be measured. Yet there are substantial limitations to the body of HPHR research, including the lack of secondary data sources regarding HR practices, the dearth of longitudinal studies performed, and survey 'selection bias' towards only those parts of the company that experience 'best practice' HR. Further, much HPHR research makes normative assumptions about employer/employee goal congruence and is generally indifferent to issues of employee 'voice' and conflict. These limitations suggest that HPHR does not offer a reliable 'new paradigm' for studying the employment relationship.

In Chapter 3, Gill Kirton points out that traditionally, industrial relations (IR) research paradigms, focusing on labour/management relations and bargaining, have seen gender, equality, and diversity as 'non-core' issues. While there has been increased union interest recently in introducing diversity issues into the bargaining framework, these issues still tend to sit somewhat uneasily with unions. Management is even more unlikely to bring these issues to the bargaining table. However, they may introduce diversity/equality into the workplace via HRM (human resource management) models, including diversity management. The development of diversity policies is often unpalatable to unions as it emphasizes the business case and is essentially a management tool. The author suggests that, if diversity management and similar tools are *not* brought into the bargaining sphere by unions, equality and diversity will remain management 'projects' designed ultimately for corporate benefit. IR research, with its focus on bargaining, conflict, voice, and resistance, should recognize diversity management in order that equality and diversity issues remain 'owned' by workers.

Another enduring tradition in employment relations research has been the assumption that the employment relationship consists of a two-party employer-employee contract. In Chapter 4, Mick Marchington, Kari Hadjivassiliou, Rose Martin, and Annette Cox argue that many modern employment relationships have three or more parties, with the worker employed by one firm, but managed by, and performing service at (and for the benefit of), another. This can complicate and/or enrich the relationship. In this chapter, public–private partnerships, supply chains, partnerships, and agency work are considered. While some generalizing is possible (controlled market economies tend to see better outcomes for workers in multi-party arrangements; high-skilled employees fare better than low-skilled employees), 'low road' or 'high road' employment relations in these arrangements depend on a variety of factors. These include national setting, the short- and long-term purposes of the arrangement, the type of industry, the length of the arrangement, the relationship between the firms, and union presence and intentions.

Following the notion of complex employment relations across organizational boundaries, Ashlea Kellner, Keith Townsend, and Adrian Wilkinson investigate an important but neglected area of workplace studies (Chapter 5). The last decades of the 20th century saw a significant increase in the spread of franchises as a form of organization. While the disciplines of marketing, law, and accounting have provided a comprehensive analysis of what 'franchise firms' look like from their disciplinary silo, the employment relations component of franchises has been completely overlooked. As a means of addressing this shortfall, this chapter provides an understanding of what ER looks like within franchise organizations.

Part II draws on some new areas in the employment relationship, and attempts to re-examine some enduring debates. In Chapter 6, Theresa Welbourne sifts through a vast volume of literature, both from a scholarly and from a consultant standpoint, on employee engagement. Questions about 'new bottle – old wine' are evident when defining what 'engagement' means; however, slightly more concerning is that 'engagement's' intrinsic worth has been largely presumed. Throughout this chapter, Welbourne suggests that, instead of considering only the 'how' of employee engagement, employers and others should also give thought to 'what' workers are being engaged in, and 'why'. Role-based research provides a framework for employers to determine the suitability of employee-engagement techniques. Five broad employee roles are identified: core work, entrepreneurial work, team member work, learning and developing work, and organizational citizenship work. The comparative utility of these roles (for the identified outcome of company success, however measured) can be identified when they are considered simultaneously. A blanket adoption of employee-engagement practices without identifying which roles employees are best 'engaged in' may be counterproductive. Welbourne suggests that employee-engagement practices may also need to be refocussed in order to take better account of the impact of increased engagement on workers.

In Chapter 7, Keith Townsend and James Richards claim that the current theoretical frameworks for studying employee actions require revision. As the authors point out, there are a range of employee actions, including what have traditionally been referred to as consent, misbehaviour, resistance, organizational citizenship behaviours, and more, that have been viewed through various disciplinary lenses. These approaches include industrial sociology, industrial relations, human resource management, and organizational behaviour and have often portrayed the employee actions too simplistically, as dualistic – for the benefit of either the firm, or of the employees. Townsend and Richards suggest that a revised conceptual framework that considers the diverse and sometimes contradictory behaviours of employees is required. Actions of individual workers, work teams or union collectives may be simultaneously productive and disruptive or somewhere in between these two ends of the spectrum. Further, employee motivation for action does not always translate into actual outcomes. Contrary to mainstream organizational behaviour theories, those employee actions traditionally perceived as 'non-conforming' are not always detrimental to productivity, just as 'conformist' actions are not (in both employer perception and reality) always beneficial to the firm. New theories of employee action must contain more nuanced explanations which go below the surface.

Maintaining our focus on employees, Chris Warhurst, Dianne van den Broek, Dennis Nickson, and Richard Hall suggest in Chapter 8 that the management of employees' physicality or corporeality (their looks and presentation) and the alignment of looks with corporate image is increasingly common in the highly feminized service economy. Using labour-process theory, the authors examine how 'aesthetic labour' is utilized to achieve corporate goals. As aesthetic labour becomes part of the wage-effort bargain of the employment relationship, there emerges the potential for a new type of discrimination – lookism. Through service industry employer surveys in Australia and the UK, the authors find that employers focus heavily on appearance (clothing, make-up, looks, body language) in recruitment decisions and in the management of staff. The research presented suggests an increase in the number of complaints by both women and men over discrimination on looks. This leads the authors to suggest a rethink about employee gender and looks, the importance of (and potential discrimination on the basis of) 'aesthetic labour', and how this appears to apply across genders.

Wrapping up this section is Chapter 9, which considers trust within the employment relationship. More specifically, Graham Dietz, Akinwunmi Martins, and Rosalind Searle consider the role of human resource managers and policies in establishing and maintaining trust in the employment relationship. According to the authors, 'trust' exists when there is a combination of a perception about the other party's *ability*, a belief in the *benevolence* of their intentions, and evidence of *integrity*. HR managers interviewed saw their role as creating the conditions for trust to thrive. HR personnel can assist in maintaining trust between parties through ensuring clarity around employer inducements and employee expectations, establishing employee voice mechanisms, ensuring the equitable application of standards, and developing transparent communication processes. HR managers' perception of the employment relationship impacts the strategies they use to foster trust. Where HR managers take an overly unitarist approach to understanding employer and employee interests, trust may be compromised when short-term commercial difficulties require management to deviate from express or implied promises.

In the final section of this book, we take a more macro view of employment relations and the role it plays in society. Leading this section is a chapter from Tony Dobbins and Tony Dundon, who examine the practical experiences of modern forms of workplace partnership and consider the case of Ireland (Chapter 10). Since the 1970s, various forms of non-traditional workplace partnership, from productivity bargaining and industrial democracy to recent HRM practices, have been introduced in both liberal market economies and coordinated market economies. Ireland's 'permissive voluntarist' liberal traditions and its lack of regulations underpinning firm-worker partnerships have meant that management is rarely compelled to uphold partnership commitments. This is so even where such partnerships are supported and promoted by state institutions. Case studies show that strong (voluntary) local-level partnerships are open to collapse given the state's vulnerability to international market competition. The authors suggest that states with greater regulatory support for workplace partnerships create an environment of 'beneficial constraint'. Here management and workers experience relatively risk-free incursions into their traditional spheres in order to maximize both productivity and wellbeing.

Two of the 'hot topics' within the global political environment throughout the first decade of the 21st century have been sustainability and the global financial (or economic) crisis. In Chapter 11, dealing with the latter of these hot topics, David Peetz, Stephane Le Queux, and Anne Frost consider the role played by states, by company HR and remuneration policies, and by unions in the recent global economic crisis. Corporate remuneration systems that rewarded short-term, high-risk behaviours meant that any costs associated with such risks were borne by the firm, and ultimately by society when such firms collapsed. Corporate culture as well as labour legislation meant that workers in the United States in particular faced wholesale termination rather than redeployment or alternative forms of employment. Union responses to the crisis ranged from bargaining for novel alternatives to redundancy to increased alignment with international social justice and trade union movements. While state responses (including corporate bail-outs, stimulus programmes, and amended unemployment schemes) were generally strong, policies of minimalist labour regulation meant that labour markets were unable to tolerate recessions. The authors make some interesting observations on the validity of 'self-correcting markets' and other neo-liberal hypotheses.

Ina Ehnert provides insight into the importance of notions of sustainability for HRM theory and practice (Chapter 12). Definitions of 'sustainability' (ecological, social, and economic) are myriad and have a variety of (sometimes conflicting) implications for HRM. 'Substance-oriented' approaches, where businesses strive to develop long-term, completely self-sustaining systems for accessing and developing their human resources, appear preferable to 'ethical' or 'efficiency'-related constructions of sustainability. Four key elements of a model of 'Sustainable HRM' are proposed: (1) exploring long-term, short-term, and side-effects of organizational decisions, (2) broadening the notion of 'success' to consider ethical and economic measurements, (3) fostering self-sustaining internal and external sources of human resources, and (4) continuously balancing the tensions of efficiency, sustainability, social responsibility, and economic rationality. The chapter concludes that more research is needed to establish clear conceptual models for interpreting the linkages between sustainability and HRM.

In Chapter 13, Chris Brewster, Marc Goergen, and Geoffrey Wood argue that industrial relations practices and union/bargaining regimes have changed in a non-uniform manner throughout the world. Explanations that rely on the notion of 'rational actors' for this non-uniformity have generally prevailed within research. In these explanations, different strategic decisions by rational actors trying to maximize their wealth are responsible for the uneven nature of systemic change. The authors canvass alternative institutional explanations for this non-uniform variance in IR and in union influence in particular. While institutional explanations have been used to account for *homogeneity* among states' IR systems, they have traditionally been excluded from explaining systemic *differences*. Institutional theories have been utilized only insofar as they provide explanations of restraints on the actions of rational individuals. Survey data demonstrate that, contrary to rational actor theories, countries with similar legal, electoral or political institutions do not necessarily experience uniform systemic change. Differences in states' relationships with institutions, and the complementary (not hierarchical) nature of institutions, provide compelling explanations for persistent variations in national IR practice.

Part I

Managing People in Organizations

2
High Performance Human Resources (HPHR)

David Lewin

Introduction

The phrase 'high performance human resources' (HPHR) is generally taken to refer to human resource management (HRM) practices that have positive effects on the performance of an enterprise, typically a business enterprise. During the past 20 years, a substantial body of research literature that apparently provides strong quantitative evidence of the positive contributions of sets or bundles of certain HRM practices to business performance has emerged.[1] Whether causal, this literature developed during a period in which HRM practices ostensibly became considerably more strategically focused and considerably less operationally focused. This transition – some would say transformation – is to some extent reflected in the supplanting of the older 'personnel management' by the newer 'human resource management'.[2] Nevertheless, one can question whether and to what extent HPHR constitutes a new paradigm for the management of people in organizations and for the employment relationship more broadly.

Precursors of contemporary HPHR research

During much of the 20th century, employment relationship research focused on unionization, union-management relations, and, in particular, the effects of unions on businesses.[3] Some researchers concentrated on documenting and analyzing the effects of unions on certain aspects of management, including hiring and staffing (or 'manning') practices, work shifts and assignments, discipline and due process, compensation practices, and layoff practices – or, in other words, terms and conditions of employment (Chamberlain, 1948). Qualitative research methods tended to characterize this body of research, and the dominant conclusion drawn from it was that unions narrowed the scope of management's decision-making authority and control, and to some extent shared that authority and control. A portion of this research analyzed the effects of unions on productivity and therefore had a somewhat more quantitative bent than that of the research dealing with union impacts on management authority and control (e.g. Hartman, 1969). A main conclusion drawn from this research was that unions, for the most part, had positive impacts on business productivity. On the whole, this literature also had a normative cast in which collective bargaining was portrayed favourably, unions together with management and government were the key actors in a well-developed industrial relations system, and the overall impacts of unions on business were positive even as managers often complained about union incursion into and about the narrowing of their decision-making authority and control (Dunlop, 1998; 1958). Hence, this industrial relations literature stands as a precursor to more recent research on HPHR.

At about the same time, another body of research focused squarely and more narrowly on the union impacts on wages. Unlike the union impacts on management literature, however, this body of research was grounded in a strong, widely accepted theoretical base, namely, neoclassical price theory, which meant, in turn, that this research was the province of labour economists. Guided by well-known microeconomic assumptions about product and labour market competition, factor mobility, information availability, and especially market equilibrium, labour economists produced a large body of quantitative research estimating the effects of unions on wages (Rees, 1977). In some industries, such as supermarkets and apparel, this 'union effect' was found to be relatively small, while in other industries, such as construction and steel manufacturing, it was found to be relatively large. This body of research also had a certain normative bent in that any positive effects on wages were, for the most part, judged to be anti-competitive because they resulted in higher costs to (unionized) businesses than would have otherwise prevailed (Friedman & Friedman, 1962). A minority view, which claimed that the higher costs resulting from unionism were roughly offset by enhanced productivity under unionism, nevertheless similarly reflected a normative bent (Freeman & Medoff, 1984). Later, labour economists expanded their studies to measure the effects of unions on fringe benefits, and still later on businesses' capital investment, research and development (R&D) expenditures, and profitability.

The main findings from this research were that unions had positive effects on fringe benefits, meaning that as with wages they raised benefit costs to employers, and had negative effects on capital investment, R&D expenditures, and profitability (Hirsch, 2007). These findings were then used to explain the subsequent large decline in private sector unionization in the US and in other nations.

The larger implication of this labour economics literature, however, is that it can be said to have spurred HRM researchers to focus on quantitatively measuring the impacts of human resources (HR) practices on business performance, especially because these practices were increasingly applied to non-union workforces.[4] Key to this HPHR research was the development of indices of HR practices that measured the extent to which such practices were of the high involvement type. Operationally, HR indices were constructed on the basis of responses to questions (i.e. items) that were included in surveys of samples of business firms and/ or establishments, with a typical establishment being a manufacturing plant. These samples were drawn from populations of publicly traded firms because data on the financial performance of these firms were available from secondary sources, thereby permitting analyses of the relationships between HR practices and business performance. In this research, one or another measure of business performance served as the dependent variable similar to the way in which wages (or wages plus benefits) served as the dependent variable in labour economists' studies of the union impact on pay. But rather than unionism serving as the main independent variable, HPHR research incorporated one or more indices of HR practices as the main independent variable(s).

To illustrate more specifically, in some of this HPHR research overall company financial performance, measured by return on investment (ROI), return on assets (ROA), and even stock price and/or market value, was modelled as the dependent variable (Huselid, 1995; Huselid, Jackson & Schuler, 1997). In other studies, the financial performance of business units of conglomerate or diversified companies was modelled as the dependent variable and was measured by ROI, ROA, and/or revenue per employee (Mitchell, Lewin & Lawler, 1990). The bulk of HPHR research, however, has focused on manufacturing plants (i.e. establishments) in which the main business performance measures – dependent variables – are productivity, product quality, plant (or line) up time, and labour costs (Appelbaum, Bailey, Berg & Kalleberg, 2000; Ichniowski, Shaw & Prennushi, 1997; Dunlop & Weil, 1996; MacDuffie, 1995; Arthur, 1992). The automobile, steel, and apparel industries have been featured prominently in this strand of HPHR research. A small number of HPHR studies have focused on service type establishments, typically field sales and service offices of large companies in the telecom and insurance industries (Batt, 1999). In these studies, revenue growth, quality of service, and customer satisfaction often served as dependent variables, i.e. as measures of business performance. Hence, an important contribution of contemporary HPHR research is its multi-level, multi-faceted modelling and measurement of business performance.

Another important, perhaps singular, contribution of contemporary HPHR research is the extensive use of primary research methods to develop indices of HR practices. Unlike much business performance data, which can readily be gleaned from a variety of secondary sources, systematic data on the HR practices of business (and non-business) firms are unavailable from secondary sources and must therefore be obtained directly from businesses. For this purpose, HR researchers have designed numerous survey questionnaires and interview protocols and administered them to within-industry and cross-industry samples of firms and establishments, with executives and managers serving as the survey respondents (e.g. Delaney, Lewin & Ichniowski, 1989). While these samples have been developed in what might most accurately be termed bottom-up fashion and have not been synthesized into an over-riding nationwide survey or database (comparable to national databases on firms' financial performance) featuring time-series replication, they have nevertheless enabled HR researchers to produce quantitative esti-mates of the effects of HR practices on business performance and to do so in numerous industry, company, and establishment settings. Moreover, this research has been conducted in a wide variety of North American, European, and Asian nations, which means that it has a strong global cast (e.g. Boxall & Macky, 2009; Lee & Johnson, 1998; Morishima, 1991). In this respect, contemporary HPHR research is broader and deeper than the research conducted in prior eras by indus-trial relations specialists and labour economists.

Key findings and implications of HPHR research

To researchers, a main or key finding rarely stands alone and is typically subject to caveats about sampling and generalization, the moderating effects of other variables, and the limitations of extant research designs and analytical methods. To practitioners, by contrast, a key finding from a particular body of research is often taken as dominant, without qualification, and is used to shape policy and practice (Rynes, Gilul

& Brown, 2007). With regard to contemporary HPHR research, a key finding is that certain 'high involvement' (or 'high participation', 'high commitment', or 'empowerment') HR practices are positively associated with – or contribute to – business performance. To illustrate, Huselid (1995, p. 667) concludes that 'a one-standard deviation increase in [High Performance Work Practices] is associated with ... $27,044 more in sales and $18,641 and $3,814 more in market value and profits, respectively'.

This and related empirical findings have been taken by HR practitioners in particular and business executives and managers more broadly to mean that there is a set of HR 'best practices' that, when applied, will enhance business performance. What are these practices? They are as follows: 1) employment security, 2) selective hiring, 3) teamwork and organizational decentralization, 4) high pay contingent on organizational performance, 5) extensive training and development, 6) reduction of status differences, and 7) information-sharing with employees (e.g. Pfeffer, 1998, 1994).

These HR practices are claimed to have their strongest positive effects on business performance when treated and applied as a set (or bundle or package) rather than individually. Indeed, some researchers argue that any one of these practices applied alone will have little to no effect on business performance – or, in other words, a 'one off' HR practice initiative is unlikely to be successful in terms of enhancing business performance (Pfeffer & Veiga, 1999). Furthermore, say these researchers, a short-term application of the full set of HR 'best practices' will be unlikely to have positive effects on business performance. Only when these practices are applied and sustained for the longer term will they be likely to enhance business performance. Apparently, however, only a relatively small minority of businesses follow this long-term HR best practices application, either because their executives and managers do not believe the HR-business performance research connection or because they are too strongly oriented towards the short-term performance of their businesses. But this also means that the large majority of businesses have the potential to enhance their performance if they can overcome the factors that inhibit or prevent them from adopting and sustaining the full set of HR best practices.

Limitations of contemporary HPHR research: selection bias

Given this reasoning about the untapped potential of putatively performance-enhancing effects of HPHR practices as well as the dominance of HPHR research in the extant literature on human resource management and on the employment relationship more broadly, it is important to assess the limitations of this research.[5] The first of these limitations may best be described as 'selection bias'. It refers specifically to the tendency of HPHR researchers to focus on that segment of a company's workforce to which 'high involvement' or 'best' HR practices are applied. This segment can be thought of as the 'core', and expenditures on HR practices that are applied to this core are often described as investments – investments on which there is a positive economic return (Lewin, 2008a). From this perspective, the core workforce is managed as an asset.

With this selection bias in play, HR indices have been constructed so as to measure the extent to which firms (or establishments) use high involvement HR practices to manage their workforces. While there is typically some variation within and across firms in the extent to which such HR practices are used, this variation is relatively narrow, ranging from modest or moderate usage to high or very high usage. Therefore, all firms appear to engage in some use of high involvement HR practices, and HPHR researchers tend to use their empirical findings to encourage expanded use of such practices by firms which, in turn, will ostensibly yield positive economic returns.

What is overlooked in this regard, however, is that most firms have more than one workforce segment or, in other words, more than the core. Another workforce segment can be labelled 'peripheral' and it includes part-time, temporary, and rented/leased employees as well as employees on fixed duration contracts. This workforce is typically not managed through high involvement HR practices and is not viewed by a firm's management as an asset on which expenditures will yield a positive economic return. Rather, the peripheral workforce segment is managed primarily for labour (or payroll) expense control, and the HR practices that are used to do so are characterized by low involvement rather than by high involvement (Lewin, 2003, 2001). In particular, and as shown in Table 2.1, compared to core employees, peripheral employees have little or no employment security, are not selected carefully, typically work individually rather than in teams (and are monitored closely), are paid a fixed wage (price) rather than having their pay contingent on organizational performance, receive little or no training, and business information is rarely shared with them by management. In addition and also compared to core employees, peripheral employees have few promotion opportunities, and employers do not manage peripheral employees' performance so as to identify candidates for promotion to higher level jobs.

Table 2.1 Extent of high involvement HRM practice usage among core (C) and peripheral (P) employees, 1998 (mean values on a 1 = low, 5 = high scale)

Variable	Companies		Business units		Manufacturing plants		Sales and service field offices		All	
	C*	P*	C*	P*	C*	P*	C*	P*	C*	P*
Employment continuity	3.4	1.5	3.2	1.4	3.0	1.6	3.3	1.3	3.3	1.5
Selective hiring	4.3	1.7	4.4	1.8	4.2	1.8	4.1	1.4	4.3	1.6
Training/Development	3.9	1.4	4.0	1.5	3.8	1.3	4.2	1.6	4.0	1.4
Teams/Participation	4.2	1.3	4.3	1.4	4.0	1.6	3.8	1.3	4.1	1.4
Performance management	4.5	1.6	4.4	1.5	4.1	1.8	4.2	1.6	4.3	1.6
Promotion opportunity	3.9	1.2	4.2	1.4	3.6	1.2	3.8	1.3	3.9	1.3
Variable pay	4.6	1.4	4.5	1.3	4.2	1.3	4.5	1.7	4.5	1.4
Business information sharing	4.0	1.5	4.2	1.6	4.5	1.5	3.8	1.4	4.1	1.5
All practices	4.1	1.5	4.2	1.5	3.9	1.5	4.0	1.4	4.1	1.5
N	289	289	313	313	457	457	249	249	1308	1308

*All differences between means within pairs of columns significant at p = <.01.
Source: Lewin, 2001, 275–292.

This example of selection bias in HPHR research is increasingly important because in the US and in other developed nations, the ratio of peripheral employees to core employees has grown markedly during the past quarter century or so (Lewin, 2008a). This means, in turn, that relatively more employees are managed through low involvement HR practices and relatively fewer employees are managed through high involvement HR practices. Further, this shifting ratio does not include employees in jobs that have been outsourced by firms to domestic or foreign (i.e. offshore) contractors, or jobs (and the employees holding those jobs) that have been moved from firms to the suppliers (i.e. vendors) of those firms. It is highly likely that these contractors and suppliers make even greater use of low involvement HR practices to manage their workforces for labour expense control and less use of high involvement HR practices to manage their workforce as assets. These developments are also and for the most part disregarded in HPHR research.

Limitations of contemporary HPHR research: misspecification

The second limitation of contemporary HPHR research can best be described as 'misspecification'. To illustrate this limitation, consider the following equation that is characteristic of the HPHR research literature that focuses on firm performance:

$$ROI = (HIHRI_1, IND_2, SZ_3, SR_4, CI_5, R\&D_6 + e)$$

where,

ROI = Return on investment (to a firm)
HPHRI = An index of high involvement HR practices
IND = Industry
SZ = Firm size
SR = Systematic risk
CI = Capital intensity
R&D = Research and development expenditures
e = an error term

In this equation, ROI is used to measure firm (business) performance and is therefore the dependent variable, HIHRI is an index that the extent to which a firm uses high involvement HR practices and is therefore the main independent variable, and IND, SZ, SR, CI, and R&D are control variables. In a typical HPHR study, regression analysis of data drawn from a sample of firms (typically, several hundred firms) is used to estimate this equation, thereby yielding regression coefficients on each of the independent and control variables and an overall coefficient of multiple determination (i.e. R^2). In this research, large, positive, statistically significant coefficients on the HIHRI variable have been reported frequently (e.g. Huselid, 1995; Huselid, Jackson & Schuler, 1997). These and related findings constitute the main evidence supporting the conclusion that high involvement HR practices contribute positively to business performance.

The misspecification limitation on this evidence, however, stems fundamentally from what is not included in the aforementioned equation rather than from what is included in it. To grasp this point, it is necessary to consider functional specialties other than HR that may contribute to business performance; these specialties include marketing, operations, and finance (Crainer & Dearlove, 2001). In marketing, for example, advertising (or brand identification) practices and customer relationship management (CRM) practices are widely thought to affect business performance. In operations, supply chain management practices and quality improvement practices (such as six-sigma) are frequently claimed to enhance business performance. In finance, certain investment management practices and debt-to-equity ratio management practices are often advocated to enhance business performance. While the extent to which any sets of marketing, operations, and/or finance practices actually affect business performance must (as with HR practices) be determined empirically, the exclusion of such practices from the estimating equations that predominate in the HPHR literature constitutes a clear case of misspecification with potentially important consequences (Kaufman, 2010a). This is because if independent (or control) variables representing a firm's marketing, operations, and finance practices, respectively, were included in these equations and were then estimated using data drawn from large samples of firms, the results would very likely reduce the size and significance of the regression coefficients on the HR practice variables – and might even change the signs on these variables from positive to negative. Speculation aside, it is clear from this analysis that HPHR research needs to go well beyond the narrow framing of the relationship between HR practices and business performance that has characterized it to date.

Limitations of contemporary HPHR research: duration and churn

The third limitation of HPHR research can be described as 'duration and churn'. To grasp this limitation, consider that the bulk of HPHR research consists of cross-sectional studies in which one-time and occasionally one interval (i.e. two time) surveys are used to generate the types of quantitative data and indices that are subsequently used to estimate the effects of high involvement HR practices on business performance. This is understandable because whereas the financial performance of publicly traded firms is regularly reported to government agencies and to shareholders and is therefore available to researchers from a variety of data sources and databases, the HRM practices of these firms (and, of course, privately held firms) are not regularly or even irregularly reported or tracked. Indeed, information about such practices is often considered by firms to be proprietary information and is therefore only rarely made public. Consequently, and with the exception of certain data on firms' (especially manufacturing firms') employee hiring and turnover rates, work-related injuries and illnesses, and the incidence of and work time lost due to strikes, which in the US are obtained through monthly surveys administered to a sample of employers by the US Department of Labor and which have counterparts in some other nations, data on firms' HRM practices that are of most interest to researchers must be obtained by the researchers themselves. This is a formidable task and means that in most instances researchers have to settle for one-time cross-sectional surveys or in a few instances one-interval repeat surveys in order to obtain the requisite data.[6]

As a result, the HPHR literature largely features cross-sectional studies that paint a picture of firms' then current HRM practices and that provide point-in-time estimates of the relationships between those practices and firms' financial performance. Even those relatively few HPHR studies that incorporate one (or occasionally two) interval repeat surveys of firms' HRM practices and that analyze data about such practices in relation to changes in firms' financial performance do so over relatively short time periods, typically two and three years (Gibbons & Woock, 2007). As such, there is very little in the way of long-term longitudinal (i.e. time-series) research in the contemporary HPHR literature.[7] In other words, this literature has lots of photographs and an occasional short video, but not a full length movie showing the sustained and changing relationships between HRM practices and firms' financial performance.

This limitation, which characterizes numerous other areas of research, is important especially to HPHR research because of what might best be termed the developmental nature of high involvement HRM practices. To illustrate, it is often claimed that the adoption and diffusion of high involvement HRM practices by a firm requires a substantial organizational change effort in which new norms, values, beliefs, and expectations must be introduced and then internalized by organizational members – employees (Becker & Huselid, 2006, 2009). This basically amounts to establishing or attempting to establish a new organization culture, and specialists in organization culture consistently advise that such cultural change cannot be achieved quickly (O'Reilly & Tushman, 2004). For such a change to be successful, old norms, values, beliefs, and expectations must be unfrozen and dissipated; new norms, values, beliefs, and expectations must be introduced; and the new norms, values, beliefs, and expectations must be diligently pursued, supported, and monitored by management in order for them to take hold widely and deeply among organization members – employees (Schein, 1997, Lewin, 1947).

Such change is the province of organizational behaviour specialists, not of human resource management specialists, yet the insights provided by organizational change researchers are important for understanding the time-bound nature of most HPHR research and the implications of that research for HRM practice. In this regard, consider the main conclusions reached by Pfeffer and Veiga (1999) in explaining why most firms do not, in fact, practice high involvement type HRM. These authors claim that despite the evidence attesting to the business performance-enhancing effects of high involvement HRM practices, half of all businesses will not accept (believe) such evidence, half of the remaining half adopt only one 'best' high involvement HRM practice which is therefore unlikely to have any noticeable (i.e. significant) effect on business performance, and half of that remaining half adopt the full set of high involvement HRM practices but then dilute or abandon them because they did not 'produce' business performance results quickly enough (i.e. in the short term). Hence, only about one-eighth of all businesses adopt and sustain high involvement HRM practices for sufficiently long periods to have positive effects on business performance.

There is reason to think that these authors' conclusions, reached about a decade ago, continue to hold true. Consider that the average tenure of employment of high ranking business executives – Chief Executive Officers (CEOs), Chief Operating Officers (COOs), Chief Financial Officers (CFOs), Chief Marketing Officers (CMOs), and, yes,

Chief Human Resource Officers (CHROs) – has declined, in some cases markedly (SHRM, 2010). Accompanying this decline and most likely contributing to it is the increased demand by financial analysts and investors for short-term financial returns. This short-term perspective is very much at odds with longer-term oriented high involvement HRM practices. Furthermore, when turnover occurs at the top of a business enterprise, new leaders emerge and typically adopt new strategies which result in new or substantially altered practices, including in the area of HRM. This 'churn' phenomenon is ignored by most contemporary HPHR researchers,[8] yet it is clearly germane to key issues and questions regarding the type of HRM practised by a firm, especially the balance between core and peripheral employees and, therefore, the balance between high involvement and low involvement HRM practices. To the extent that new business leaders are more short-term oriented than their predecessors, the use of high involvement HRM practices is likely to decline, and, correspondingly, the use of low involvement HRM practices is likely to increase.

Limitations of contemporary HPHR research: unpaid customer labour

If HPHR research has, for the most part, ignored peripheral employment and the low involvement HRM practices that are applied by businesses to peripheral employees, it has completely ignored the phenomenon of what can best be termed 'unpaid customer labor'. This phrase refers to work performed by customers of businesses that was previously performed by paid employees (core and/or peripheral employees), and constitutes the fourth limitation of HPHR research considered here.

In the wake of the commercialization of the World Wide Web during the mid-1990s and the development by virtually all businesses of their web sites during the late 1990s and early 2000s, it appears that more and more tasks once performed by employees have come to be performed by customers. These tasks include on-line tracking of packages shipped for delivery by express/overnight delivery companies; on-line purchases of airline flight tickets, specification of (and paying extra for) seating preferences, and downloading and printing of boarding passes; electronic checking-out from hotels, ordering of in-room meals, and (most recently) checking into hotels; on-line booking of restaurant reservations; on-line instructed repair of electronic equipment and home appliances; on-line financial transactions, including bill-paying, direct deposits, and stock trading; on-line 'management' of retirement benefits; and, more broadly, on-line purchases of a wide array of goods and services.

These examples of unpaid customer labour are directly germane to the aforementioned distinction between core employees managed as assets and peripheral employees managed for labour expense control. By extending this distinction, unpaid customer labour can be seen as representing the ultimate in labour expense control; in effect, customers are increasingly performing free labour (even as they value the flexibility of conducting 'business' on-line). And if businesses have been slow or reluctant to adopt and sustain the high involvement HRM practices that the HPHR literature commends to them, they have been anything but slow in pursuing and supporting the use of unpaid customer labour. Therefore, in future, HRM researchers will have to substantially expand their horizons by systematically documenting and analyzing businesses' use of unpaid customer labour and the effects of such use on businesses' financial performance.[9]

Implications of HPHR research for the employment relationship

The high involvement HRM practices that constitute the central focus of HPHR research virtually require that employee values and goals be consistent with organizational – management – values and goals. This is perhaps most clearly reflected in the frequent use of the phrase 'high commitment work systems' in the HPHR literature (Whitener, 2001; Wood & de Menezes, 1998; Walton, 1985). This phrase begets certain questions, such as 'whose commitment to what?' The answer to this question typically turns out to be employee commitment to the values and goals of the organization which, in turn, suggests that employees will be selectively hired for the match of their values to those of the firm, and will be committed to working in teams and to having a proportion of their pay at risk. This individual-organizational goal congruence, in turn, implies that employee-employer conflict will be minimal if not entirely absent from business enterprises.

If this implication seems extreme, consider the research of industrial relations and human resource management scholars which finds that the presence of a grievance procedure (together with other human resource management practices) is positively associated with businesses' ROI, market value, productivity, and product quality (Huselid, 1995), whereas actual employee use of a grievance procedure is negatively associated with such outcomes (Katz, Kochan & Weber, 1985; Katz,

Kochan & Gobeille, 1983). In other words and from an organizational/ business perspective, the 'best' grievance procedure is one that is not used at all. Or consider related research which finds that employees of non-union businesses that maintain grievance-like procedures suffer enhanced employment relationship deterioration (in terms of job performance evaluation, promotion, work attendance and turnover) after they actually use these procedures compared to employees who do not use the procedures (Lewin, 1999, 1987a). These findings suggest that HPHR research and practice is for the most part antithetical to employee exercise of voice in the employment relationship – unless that voice is exercised in support of dominant organizational values and goals. Succinctly stated, HPHR appears to mitigate conflict in the employment relationship and may even seek to excise it altogether. Therefore, employees who do experience conflict in their relationships with employers are decreasingly likely to pursue the resolution of those conflicts through internal mechanisms, such as grievance procedures, and are increasingly likely to purse the resolution of those conflicts through external mechanisms – i.e. the courts, arbitration, and ad hoc tribunals.

The failure of employees to pursue either internal or external redress of employment relationship conflict, however, does not mean that such conflict does not exist. Rather it means that aggrieved employees either suffer in silence, or, if they have marketable skills, seek employment elsewhere (Lewin, 1999). This dynamic, which is as old as the employment relationship itself, has also apparently escaped the attention of contemporary HPHR research. In sum, HPHR research does not offer a new paradigm for the management of people in organizations or for the employment relationship more broadly, not only because of the aforementioned limitations on HPHR research, but because, for the most part, this research ignores conflict in the employment relationship.[10]

Notes

1. For a summary of this research, see Gibbons & Woock (2007). That HRM practices are said to 'contribute to' business performance implies causality, however, the HPHR literature consists largely of statistical associations between HRM practice measures and business performance measures. The issue of causality in this regard is addressed directly in Wright, Gardner, Moynihan & Allen (2005). Further, the HPHR literature has morphed into/been supplanted by what has become known as 'evidence-based' HRM. See, as examples, Gibbons & Woock (2009, 2008) and Lewin & Casoinic (2009).

2. Correspondingly, much of the HPHR literature strongly emphasizes the 'strategic' uses of human resources, with high-involvement type human resource management practices in particular being frequently characterized as strategic. Indeed, the phrase 'strategic human resource management' (SHRM) is widespread in this literature (Becker & Huselid, 2009, 2006; Wright & Snell, 1998; Huselid, Jackson & Schuler, 1997; Delery & Doty, 1996; Cappelli and Singh, 1992; Kochan, Katz & McKersie, 1986). The present paper does not attempt to assess the strategic underpinnings of high involvement or other types of human resource management practice but, instead, identifies and analyzes certain limitations and assumptions of HPHR research. For critical assessments of SHRM theory (and evidence), see Kaufman (2010a, 2010b, 2001) Wall & Wood (2005), Guest (2001); Lepak & Snell (1999); Kleiner, Block, Roomkin & Salsburg (1987); Lewin (1987b).

3. In commenting on a draft of this paper my colleague, Prof. Bruce Kaufman, has suggested that this focus is too narrow a reading of 20th-century industrial relations research. He argues in particular that industrial relations research conducted prior to the 1930s, when union density was quite low, focussed on firms' human resource management (HRM) practices and attempted (largely through case studies) to identify HRM practices that led to high firm performance. While I appreciate this point, I have chosen to concentrate on the types of qualitative and quantitative industrial relations research conducted largely during the middle half of the 20th century that sought to assess the effects of unionization on the firm. In my judgement, it was this research that laid the analytical foundation for subsequent quantitative studies of the effects of HRM practices on firm performance.

4. An additional factor contributing to the rise of quantitative assessments of the effects of HRM practices on business performance was an emerging popular literature on management which often claimed that 'the management of people (employees)' was *the* differentiator between very high performing firms and other firms. See, for example, Peters & Waterman (1982).

5. For other, related assessments see (Kaufman, 2010a; Frost, 2008; Blasi & Kruse, 2006; Cappelli & Neumark, 2001; Guest, 2001; and Ichniowski, Kochan, Levine, Olson & Strauss, 1996).

6. The validity of responses to surveys that are administered by HPHR researchers is called into question by Gardner & Wright (2010), who identify several factors that may contribute to response bias in this regard.

7. Something of an exception in this regard is the UK's Workplace Industrial Relations Survey, which is administered every two years to a sample of British establishments (Wood & de Menezes, 1998). However, as its name implies, this survey does not elicit data on firm-level HRM practices.

8. An exception in this regard is Baron & Hannan (2002), who studied the effects of changes in founders' 'HR and organizational blueprints' in a sample of approximately 200 Silicon Valley, CA-based start up firms. They found that changes in those blueprints (which were typically made by professional manager successors to the founders) were significantly negatively associated with several measures of organizational performance. These researchers, however, did not construct indices of HRM practices.

9. Whether and to what extent businesses' can 'manage' customers in their role as free providers of labour, including through formal customer relationship management programmes and practices, is an open question, one that could potentially be addressed by marketing researchers.
10. For more on this conclusion, see Kaufman, 2010c; Godard, 2010; Frost, 2008; Lewin, 2008b; Delaney & Godard, 2001; and Godard & Delaney, 2000.

References

Appelbaum, E., Bailey, T., Berg, P., & Kalleberg, A. (2000). *Manufacturing advantage: why high performance work systems pay off.* Washington: Economic Policy Institute.

Arthur, J. (1992). The link between business strategy and industrial relations systems in American mini-mills. *Industrial and Labor Relations Review*, 45, 488–506.

Baron, J., & Hannan, M. T. (2002). Organizational blueprints for success in high-tech start ups. *California Management Review*, 44, 8–34.

Batt, R. (1999). Work organization, technology, and performance in customer service and sales. *Industrial and Labor Relations* Review, 52, 539–564.

Becker, B, & Huselid, M. (2009). *The differentiated workforce: transforming talent into strategic impact.* Boston: Harvard University Press.

Becker, B., & Huselid, M. (2006). Strategic human resource management: where do we go from here? *Journal of Management*, 32, 898–925.

Blasi, J., & Kruse, D. (2006). U.S. high performance work practices at century's end. *Industrial Relations*, 45, 457–478.

Boxall, P., & Macky, K. (2009). Research and theory on high performance work systems: progressing the high-involvement stream. *Human Resource Management Journal*, 19, 3–23.

Cappelli, P., & Neumark, D. (2001). Do 'high-performance' work practices improve establishment-level outcomes? *Industrial and Labor Relations Review*, 54, 737–775.

Cappelli, P. & Singh, H. (1992). Integrating Strategic Human Resources and Strategic Management. In D. Lewin, P. D. Sherer & O. S. Mitchell (eds), *Research frontiers in industrial relations and human resources*, 165–192. Madison, WI: Industrial Relations Research Association.

Chamberlain, N. W. (1948). *The union challenge to management control.* New York: Harper & Brothers.

Crainer, S., & Dearlove, D. (2001). *Financial times handbook of management.* London: Prentice Hall/Pearson Education.

Delaney, J., & Godard, J. (2001). An industrial relations perspective on the high-performance workplace. *Human Resource Management Review*, 11, 395–430.

Delaney, J. T., Lewin, D., & Ichniowski, C. (1989). *Human resource policies and practices in American firms.* Washington: Bureau of Labor-Management Relations and Cooperative Programs, U.S. Department of Labor, BLMR #137.

Delery, J., & Doty, D. H. (1996). Modes of theorizing in strategic human resource management: tests of universalistic, contingency, and configurational performance predictions. *Academy of Management Journal*, 39, 802–835.

Dunlop. J. T. (1998). Industrial relations theory. In D. Lewin & B. E. Kaufman (Eds.), *Advances in industrial and labor relations*, 8, 15–24. Greenwich, CT: JAI Press.

Dunlop, J. T. (1958). *Industrial Relations Systems*. New York: Holt.

Dunlop, J. T., & Weil, D. (1996). Diffusion and performance of modular production in the U.S. apparel industry. *Industrial Relations*, 35, 334–355.

Freeman, R. B. & Medoff, J. L. (1984). *What do unions do?* New York: Basic Books.

Friedman, M. & Friedman, R. (1962). *Capitalism and freedom*. Chicago: University of Chicago Press.

Frost, A. (2008). The high-performance work systems literature in industrial relations. In P. Blyton, N. Bacon, J. Fiorito & E. Herry (eds), *The Sage Handbook of Industrial Relations*, 420–433. London: Sage.

Gardner, T., & Wright, P. M. (2010). Believable or biased? Overestimating the impact of HR practices on firm performance. Ithaca, NY: Cornell University ILR School Center for Advanced Human Resource Studies, Research Link No. 7, April.

Gibbons, J., & Woock, C. (2009). *Evidence-based human resources: a Practitioner's guide*. Research Report R-1427-09-RR. New York: The Conference Board.

Gibbons, J., & Woock, C. (2008). *Evidence-based HR in action: case studies*. Research Report 1427-08-CS. New York: The Conference Board.

Gibbons, J. & Woock, C. (2007). *Evidence-based human resources: a primer and summary of current literature*. Research Report E-0015-07-RR. New York: The Conference Board.

Godard, J. (2010). What is best for workers: the implications of workplace and human resource management practices revisited. *Industrial Relations*, 49, 466–488.

Godard, J., & Delaney, J. T. (2000). Reflections on the 'high performance' paradigm's implications for industrial relations as a field. *Industrial and Labor Relations Review*, 53, 482–502.

Guest, D. 2001. Human resource management: when research confronts theory. *International Journal of Human Resource Management*, 12, 1092–1106.

Hartman, P. (1969). *Collective bargaining and productivity: the longshore mechanization agreement*. Berkeley: University of California Press.

Hirsch, B. T. (2007). What do unions do for economic performance? In J. T. Bennett & B. E. Kaufman, (Eds.), *What do unions do? A twenty-year perspective*, 193–237. New Brunswick, NJ: Transaction Publishers.

Huselid, M. A. (1995). The impact of human resource management practices on turnover, productivity, and corporate financial performance. *Academy of Management Journal*, 38, 635–672.

Huselid, M. A., Jackson, S. E., & Schuler, R. S. (1997). Technical and strategic human resource management effectiveness as determinants of firm performance. *Academy of Management Journal*, 40, 171–188.

Ichniowski, C., Shaw, K., & Prennushi, G. (1997). The effects of human resource management practices on productivity: a study of steel finishing lines. *American Economic Review*, 87, 291–313.

Ichniowski, C., Kochan, T. A., Levine, D., Olson, C., & Strauss, G. (1996). What works at work: overview and assessment. *Industrial Relations*, 35, 299–333.

Katz, H. C., Kochan, T. A, & Weber, M. R. (1985). Assessing the effects of indus-trial relations and quality of work life efforts on organizational effectiveness. *Academy of Management Journal*, 28, 509–527.

Katz, H. C., Kochan, T. A., & Gobeille, K. R. (1983). Industrial relations perfor-mance, economic performance, and QWL programs: an interplant analysis. *Industrial and Labor Relations Review*, 37, 3–17.

Kaufman, B. E. (2010a). SHRM theory in the post-huselid era: why it is funda-mentally misspecified. *Industrial Relations*, 49, 286–313.

Kaufman, B. E. (2010b). *Hired hands or human resources? Case studies of HRM policies and practices in early American industry*. Ithaca, NY: Cornell University Press.

Kaufman, B. E. (2010c). The Theoretical foundation of industrial relations and its implications for labor economics and human resource management. *Industrial and Labor Relations Review* (forthcoming).

Kaufman, B. E. (2001). The theory and practice of strategic hrm and participa-tive management: antecedents in early industrial relations. *Human Resource Management Review*, 11, 505–533.

Kleiner, M., Block, R., Roomkin, M., & Salsburg, S. (eds) (1987). *Human resources and the performance of the firm*. Madison, WI: Industrial Relations Research Association.

Kochan, T. A., Katz, H. C., & McKersie, R. B. (1986). *The transformation of American industrial relations*. New York: Basic Books.

Lee, M. B. & Johnson, N. B. (1998). Business environment, high-involvement management, and firm performance in Korea. In D. Lewin and B.E. Kaufman (eds), *Advances in Industrial and Labor Relations*, 8, 67–87. Greenwich: JAI Press.

Lepak, D., & Snell, S. (1999). The human resource architecture: toward a theory of human capital allocation and development. *Academy of Management Review*, 24, 31–48.

Lewin, D. (2008a). Human resources management in the 21st century. In C. Wankel (ed.), *21st century management: a reference handbook*, vol. 2., 56–64. Thousand Oaks, CA: Sage.

Lewin, D. (2008b). Resolving conflict. In P. Blyton, N. Bacon, J. Fiorito & E. Heery (eds), *The Sage handbook of industrial relations*, 447–467. London: Sage.

Lewin. D. (2003). Human resource management and business performance: lessons for the 21st century. In M. Effron, R. Gandossy and M. Goldsmith (eds), *Human resources in the 21st century*, 91–98. Hoboken, NJ: Wiley.

Lewin, D. (2001). Low involvement work systems and business performance. In *Proceedings of the 53rd Annual Meeting of the Industrial Relations Research Association*, 275–292. Champaign, IL. IRRA.

Lewin, D. (1999). Theoretical and empirical research on the grievance pro-cedure and arbitration: A critical review. In A. E. Eaton & J. H. Keefe (eds), *Employment dispute resolution and worker rights in the changing workplace*, 137–186. Champaign, IL: Industrial Relations Research Association.

Lewin, D. (1987a). Conflict resolution in the nonunion firm: a theoretical and empirical analysis. *Journal of Conflict Resolution*, 31, 465–502.

Lewin, D. (1987b). Industrial relations as a strategic variable. In M. Kleiner, R. Block, M. Roomkin and S. Salsburg (eds), *Human resources and the performance of the firm*, 1–42. Madison, WI: Industrial Relations Research Association.

Lewin, D., & Casoinic, D. (2009). *Evidence-based human resource management: a review of its major prototypes and guiding principles.* Paper presented to the 69th Annual Meeting, Academy of Management, Chicago.

Lewin, K. (1947). Frontiers in group dynamics. *Human Relations,* 1, 5–41.

MacDuffie, J. P. (1995). Human resource bundles and manufacturing performance: organizational logic and flexible production systems in the world auto industry. *Industrial and Labor Relations Review,* 48, 197–221.

Mitchell, D. J. B., Lewin, D., & Lawler, E. E., III. (1990). Alternative pay systems, firm performance, and productivity. In A.S. Blinder (ed.), *Paying for productivity,* 15–83. Washington: The Brookings Institution.

Morishima, M. (1991). Information sharing and firm performance in Japan. *Industrial Relations,* 30, 37–61.

O'Reilly, C. A., & Tushman, M. L. (2004). The ambidextrous organization. *Harvard Business Review,* 82, 74–81.

Peters, T. J., & Waterman, R. H., Jr. (1982). *In search of excellence: lessons from America's best-run companies.* New York: Harper & Row.

Pfeffer, J. (1998). *The human equation.* Boston: Harvard Business School Press.

Pfeffer, J. (1994). *Competitive advantage through people.* Boston: Harvard Business School Press.

Pfeffer, J., & Veiga, J. F. (1999). Putting People first for organizational success. *Academy of Management Executive,* 13, 37–48.

Rees, A. (1977). *The economics of trade unions* (revised edn). Chicago: University of Chicago Press.

Rynes, S., Gilul, T., & Brown, K. (2007). The very separate worlds of academic and practitioner periodicals in human resource management: implications for evidence-based management. *Academy of Management Journal,* 50, 987–1008.

Schein, E. 1997. *Organizational Culture and Leadership* (3rd edn). San Francisco: Jossey-Bass.

Society for Human Resource Management (SHRM). (2010, April 5). *Leadership Retention Literature Review.* Retrieved from http://www.shrm.org/SearchCenter/Pages/results.aspx

Wall, T., & Wood, S. (2005). The romance of human resource management and business performance, and the case for big science. *Human Relations,* 58, 429–461.

Walton, R. E. (1985). From control to commitment in the workplace. *Harvard Business Review,* 63, 57–74.

Whitener. E. M. (2001). Do high commitment human resources practices affect employee commitment? *Journal of Management,* 27, 515–535.

Wood, S. J., & de Menezes, L. (1998). High commitment management in the U.K.: evidence from the Workplace Industrial Relations Survey, and Employers' Manpower and Skills Practices Survey. *Human Relations,* 51, 485–506.

Wright, P. M., & Snell, S. A. (1998). Toward a unifying framework for exploring fit and flexibility in strategic human resource management. *Academy of Management Review,* 23, 756–772.

Wright, P. M., Gardner, T. M., Moynihan, L. M., & Allen, M. R. (2005). The relationship between HR practices and firm performance: examining causal order. *Personnel Psychology,* 58, 409–446.

3
Gender, Equality, Diversity, and a New Industrial Relations Paradigm?

Gill Kirton

Introduction

Industrial relations (IR), as both a field of scholarship and an area of policy and practice, has the potential to improve working lives.[1] Yet despite the fact that gender, equality and diversity touch the lives of all working people globally, these issues tend to be marginal within IR research, policy and practice. This chapter supports the call for IR to integrate these issues into the agenda, but also argues for them to be seen as a core and necessary area. To achieve this, is a 'new' IR paradigm needed? What might an IR paradigm that takes full account of gender, equality and diversity both in research and in policy and practice look like? What might count as IR? What specific issues need to be central, rather than marginal to the research, policy and bargaining agenda? Within a more inclusive IR paradigm, what do we understand about contemporary employer and trade union action on gender, equality and diversity?

Gender, equality, diversity and the dominant industrial relations paradigm

What place do gender, equality and diversity have in the dominant IR paradigm? It goes without saying that women's employment participation has increased exponentially in the post-war period, especially in the past three decades or so with the growth of the service sector. Women now comprise nearly half of the workforces of industrialized countries and so too has their importance as a source of trade union members grown. In a historical turnaround, women's trade union membership in many countries is now at least in equal proportion to that of men. In the

UK women comprise 52 per cent of trade union members, in the USA the female share is 48 per cent and in Australia the figure is 44%. These changes dislodge the stereotype of the male 'breadwinner' dominating the workforce and of the male, blue-collar worker dominating the trade unions. In another significant shift in the IR landscape, women are now also playing key roles in the institutions of industrial relations; that is, in employers' organizations, government and trade unions. With regard to employers' organizations, for example, the Confederation of British Industry had its first female president (Helen Alexander) from 2009 to 2011 (current president is male); the Business Council of Australia currently has a female chief executive (Jennifer Westacott). In the union movement, Australia currently has a female president (Ged Kearney) of its peak union body, the Australian Council of Trade Unions (ACTU); the UK has a female Deputy General Secretary (Frances O'Grady) of its peak union body, the Trades Union Congress (TUC); the USA has a female Secretary-Treasurer (Liz Schuler) and an African-American female Executive Vice President (Arlene Holt Baker) of its major peak union body, the American Federation of Labor and Congress of Industrial Organizations (AFL-CIO). Arguably, these changes place women (alongside men) at the centre of IR globally.

However, as a field of scholarship, IR is often seen as old fashioned, and the label IR is still generally associated with male-dominated heavy industry, blue-collar trade unions and male leaders in industry, government and unions. In an era of decline in manufacturing and depressed union membership (especially in traditional areas) in most industrialized countries, this image has implications for the perceived centrality and relevance of IR to the social sciences, and, theoretically speaking, it might even miss the point about contemporary employment relationships. For example, the traditional systems approach to IR is criticized for failing to see the links that have always existed for all workers between community, family and work (Jones, 2002). But for this chapter's discussion, a narrow definition and focus also have specific consequences for women and gender within IR. For at least 15 years feminist authors around the globe have been bemoaning the invisibility and marginality of women and gender issues within the IR literature. In the early 1990s IR as a field of study was characterized as a 'malestream' and accused of being, if not oblivious to the presence of women, unaware that their presence makes much difference (Forrest, 1993). Part of the problem seems to lie in the fairly rigid and narrow way many scholars understand what counts as IR. Definitions of IR sometimes reflect masculine issues, priorities and privilege (Wajcman, 2000; Hansen, 2002; Danieli, 2006). There have been various calls to redefine the territory to be more inclusive not only of gender, but also of other bases of 'difference' (Hansen, 2002; Greene, 2003; Holgate, Hebson & McBride, 2006). Without doubt there is now a growing body of work within IR that looks at gender, race/ethnicity, sexuality, disability, age and intersecting equalities issues. In addition, those who attend IR conferences would probably agree that impression-istically the field is less male dominated than it was a couple of decades ago, although it remains white dominated. It is also argued that some IR academics have begun to acknowledge the need to address gender issues even though they might continue to resist treating gender as a *central* issue (Danieli, 2006). But what have these changes meant for the body of IR knowledge and literature overall? A 'straw poll' type look at the editions of the years 2005 to 2009 of four major international IR journals indicates that gender, equality and diversity issues remain on the margins of the field. Over the period, the UK-based *British Journal of Industrial Relations* had seven articles obviously about gender, equal-ity and diversity; the Australia-based *Journal of Industrial Relations* had nine. The UK-based *Industrial Relations Journal* fared better with 21 art-icles, including those in a special issue devoted to gender and equality. The USA-based *Industrial Relations* had 23. Given that these four jour-nals, combined, published around 650 articles in the five-year period, the gender, equality and diversity share was around nine per cent. This perhaps represents some improvement on earlier years – over the longer period between 1973 and 2004 only four per cent of all articles in the *British Journal of Industrial Relations* and the *Industrial Relations Journal* were gender related (Holgate et al., 2006). Of course there are various interpretations of this state of affairs, including the possibility that some academics who might loosely associate themselves with the IR field, have turned their backs on the mainstream IR journals and are publish-ing their work on employment and the employment relationship else-where. One obvious home for work that might previously have counted as IR might be the HRM journals, of which there are many. Whatever the reasons – and they are in all likelihood many and complex – it is problematic that in the 21st century with all the changes in the IR landscape, all the advances in feminist and gender theorizing and in theories of race/ethnicity, sexuality and age, gender, equality and diver-sity remain on the margins of mainstream IR scholarship. This is not just a matter of principle or simply a complaint from feminist authors researching in these areas, rather there are also serious consequences for the body of knowledge available to scholars, students and practitioners, and there are implications for the future of the IR field.

A new industrial relations paradigm, or a reinterpretation of an old one?

So, is a new IR paradigm needed, or might it be more a question of reinterpreting an old one? IR is of necessity a constantly evolving and dynamic field of study that must, if it is to have any value beyond the academy, be responsive to changing contexts. For example, the 1950s–1960s focus on the institutions of collective bargaining, in the UK and some other countries, appropriate as it was at the time, was challenged by developments that gathered pace through the 1970s and 1980s including the growth of non-unionized employment (Edwards, 1995). IR research has kept pace with some of these developments, but not with others. As stated above, part of the critique by feminist authors of the dominant IR paradigm has been its relatively narrow definition and focus that allowed gender-blind or gender-neutral analysis to become the norm. Traditional definitions of IR include 'the study of the rules governing employment' (Clegg, 1979); 'how individuals and groups, the organizations representing their interests and wider institutional forces determine decisions affecting employment relationships' (Farnham & Pimlott, 1995, p. 11); 'the creation of an economic surplus, the co-existence of conflict and cooperation, the indeterminate nature of the exchange relationship, and the asymmetry of power' (Blyton & Turnbull, 1994, p. 31). These definitions are actually quite broad; they potentially capture a range of topics including the non-traditional gender, equality and diversity.

Starting with Clegg's definition, 'rules' can be both formal and informal and are socially constructed in ways that can privilege the interests of one group over another or deny voice to some groups, but give it to others. Thus, exploring the 'rules' that govern the employment relationship could (and should) expose gendered and racialized power asymmetries among IR actors. Moving to Farnham and Pimlott's, and Blyton and Turnbull's definitions, the working lives of individuals and groups are without doubt affected differentially (on the basis of gender, race, ethnicity, sexuality, etc) by employers' strategies and actions and by wider institutional and societal forces. To illustrate with a few examples, at the time of writing, there was, for instance, much talk in the media and in government about the disproportionate impact of the global economic recession on women and black and minority ethnic workers. On 13 October 2009, *The Guardian* reported that in the UK one in five black men were unemployed as the recession 'bites' (Stewart & Hopkins, 2009). Similarly, in the USA, it was argued that the recession was exacerbating long-term trends in black men's employment (Cawthorne, 2009). Early in 2009 the International Labour Organization (ILO) warned that the economic crisis could generate up to 22 million more unemployed women in 2009 worldwide, jeopardizing equality gains at work and at home (ILO, 2009). It must be acknowledged that the 'rules' of employment, the impact of institutional forces, interests, conflict and cooperation and asymmetries of power in the labour market and at the workplace – the mainstay of the IR field – all potentially contain gendered and racialized dimensions that need to be confronted if IR is to contribute to improving working lives. Thus, even traditional definitions of IR do not necessarily have to close off discussions about gender, equality and diversity. The fact that they might have done so in the past and might continue to do so in the contemporary era is really a question of researchers' interpretations of the world around them and of their ideological/political orientations informing what they think is important.

So, how can we ensure that gender, equality and diversity are at the forefront of IR? Kaufman (2008) argues that the IR field has had two distinct paradigms – an original paradigm (founded in the early 1920s) centered on the employment relationship, and a modern paradigm (replacing the original paradigm by the early 1960s) centered on unions and labour-management relations. In practice many IR scholars, for pragmatic, intellectual and ideological reasons, adopted the former as a broad principle (reflected in the definitions above), but followed the latter in research and teaching until fairly recently at least. Thus, despite the potential within common definitions for a broader agenda, the IR literature in many industrialized countries has focused predominantly on unionized employment, and within that on strikes, conflict, pay and basic terms and conditions (Kaufman, 2008). One consequence has been that gender, equality and diversity issues have been under-researched. Even during the long period of union membership decline in the 1980s and 1990s, the predominant focus was on the possibilities and strategies for union renewal, rather than on the evolving and increasing non-union labour-management relations. Further, it is largely feminist authors who have made sure that women have been visible within the renewal debate (Kirton & Healy, 1999; Briskin, 2002; Cobble, Bielski & Michal, 2002; Colgan & Ledwith 2002), but that is not to say that women have been completely ignored by 'mainstream' IR authors (e.g. Heery & Kelly, 1988).

Although women's union density now (almost) matches that of men's in many industrialized countries – meaning that in theory if unions are the focus, then women should now be highly visible within the discussion – their strength in numbers is a relatively recent phenomenon. During the earlier decades of higher union membership when women were far less likely than men were to work in unionized sectors or to be union members, downplaying gender difference and ignoring women's work and their contribution to the labour movement became a taken-for-granted convention. Despite women's greater significance as workers and union members, the IR field is still struggling to integrate gender, equality and diversity, but hanging on to past conventions merely perpetuates gender- and difference-blind analysis that leaves the field somewhat impoverished (Hansen, 2002; Danieli, 2006). However, it might well be that what is needed is a reinterpretation of the 'old' IR paradigm – with a broader agenda that specifically and for now at least self-consciously includes and confronts gender, equality and diversity – rather than a new one. In this vein, Anne-Marie Greene and I (Greene & Kirton, 2009) deliberately positioned our book on diversity management (DM) within the IR literature (rather than within the human resource management (HRM) literature where much of the discussion on DM takes place). The book deals with both unionized and non-unionized employment contexts and with multiple actors and stakeholders and their perspectives, including employees, trade unions, line managers and diversity practitioners. Our aim, even though we use the label '*diversity management*', is to claim IR as the space where contemporary policy and practice on gender, equality and diversity in the employment relationship are analysed and discussed. We believe that this approach has the added value of keeping trade unions and the collective employment relationship in the picture when in an era of (unitarist) HRM it might be easy to exclude them from DM research as irrelevant (see Kirton & Greene, 2006). Indeed, Kaufman (2008, p. 315) argues that integrating HRM into the IR field is 'a welcome and overdue development' that might help revitalize the field – we might add DM to this. The latter is elaborated further below.

Gender, equality, diversity and trade union and employer action

Are gender, equality and diversity central to IR actors? With regard to unions, there can be no doubt that in many countries they are experiencing the bargaining context as hostile – even with possibly more union-friendly governments at the time of writing in the UK

(Labour), USA (Democrat) and Australia (Labour) than at various points in the recent past – and that this is bound to impact on the potential for equality and diversity bargaining. In 2001 it was argued that although equality bargaining in the UK had taken place in a 'cold climate' from 1979 until 1997 under a Conservative government, the election of a Labour government in 1997 had held out opportunities for the promotion of equality, the promotion of joint engagement and with these an opportunity for joint engagement for equality (Colling & Dickens, 2001). While improvements in equality legislation have since been made within a spirit of joint engagement, the evidence on the extent to which equality bargaining at workplace level is happening in the UK is mixed. On the positive side, evidence from the 2004 UK *Workplace Employee Relations Survey* (WERS) suggests that unions positively influence the availability of some equality initiatives and that unionized workplaces are more likely to have equality policies. However, less positively, this does not necessarily mean that the unions are directly involved in policy making or that they are bargaining for equality; in fact WERS 2004 indicates that management normally negotiates about equality matters in only a tiny minority of workplaces (five per cent) with recognized unions. Even less positively, in the majority (72 per cent) of UK workplaces managers neither *negotiated*, nor *consulted*, nor *informed* union representatives about equality issues (Walsh, 2007). The latter situation is certainly something that resonates with my case study research (with Anne-Marie Greene) in a large private sector firm in the UK where management did not involve the recognized unions in equality and diversity policy development or implementation. The fairly new equality and diversity policy was reportedly presented to the unions as 'here's something we made earlier'.[2] The absence of union involvement was partly explained by the fact that management wanted to get on and 'do it their own way', and also because the unions (according to management informants) had not pressed to be involved in any case. From the union perspective, in a highly unstable, uncertain environment, the workplace representatives' time and efforts were spent on 'firefighting' to defend basic terms and conditions and on individual case work rather than attempting to proactively incorporate equality and diversity into the bargaining agenda (Greene & Kirton, 2009, pp. 107–108). In some countries, however, equality legislation institutionalizes worker participation so that the exclusion of recognized unions from equality policy making is less likely to occur. In Australia, for example, there is a requirement for workers to be consulted and included on employment equity committees (Blackett & Sheppard, 2003).

Evidence gathered more recently by the UK unions paints a different picture from that depicted by WERS 2004 and claims that unions have broadened the bargaining agenda so that they do now play an active role in promoting equality and diversity at work. The Trades Union Congress carries out biennial equality audits where unions complete a questionnaire giving details of their action on equality and diversity issues. All the major unions (with more than 10,000) members responded to the 2009 audit, so it provides a fairly comprehensive picture of the state of equality bargaining in the UK. Table 3.1 shows the areas where the UK unions have current guidance/policy and areas where they have achieved negotiated success since 2005. It is unclear whether greater levels of success in some areas compared with others is because these are the areas that unions have *chosen* to prioritize or whether they reflect the issues to which employers are more receptive. The area where unions had achieved greatest negotiating success was working parents and carers (see Table 3.1), demonstrating that UK unions are bargaining on issues that might formerly have been deemed 'social issues' seen as outside of the scope of collective bargaining, rather than on industrial and economic ones (Blackett & Sheppard, 2003). Unions reported

Table 3.1 UK union action on equality and diversity

Topic	% unions with current guidance/ policy	% unions with negotiated success since 2005
General equalities	65	16
Flexible working/work-life balance	65	44
Women's pay and employment	63	30
Harassment and bullying	61	33
Working parents and carers	58	51
Black and minority ethnic workers	58	35
Lesbian, gay and bisexual workers	56	33
Disability	54	35
Age	49	37
Religion and belief	42	23
Migrant workers	35	23
Transgender workers	35	16

Source: TUC, 2009.

having negotiated agreements providing enhanced maternity/paternity support, leave and pay, enhanced adoption leave and pay, childcare support, enhanced ante-natal support, time off for fertility treatment. Flexible working and work-life balance was the second area of greatest bargaining success. While bargaining that enhances legal rights is always to be applauded, it is hardly surprising to see that employers seem most receptive to work-life balance issues when we consider that so many are dependent on women's labour. Some of the lowest negotiating success rates were on migrant workers, religion and belief and transgender workers. However, even in these potentially more thorny areas, negotiating successes were reported by some unions. For example, the major UK union Unite has concluded successful negotiations with a number of firms in the food industry employing large numbers of migrant workers. Future priorities for equality bargaining mentioned by a large proportion of unions responding to the TUC survey included parental rights, race equality and fighting the far right and disability equality.

Clearly the economic context of bargaining matters a great deal in terms of what it is possible to achieve via bargaining. As to whether it has been more or less difficult over the past couple of years to get employers to address equality issues, UK unions responding to the TUC survey reported mixed experiences. The unions reporting greater difficulty (in both public and private sectors) highlighted the current context of recession that had brought with it financial constraints, cutbacks in services and jobs, organizational restructuring, all of which meant that these unions found many employers to be less willing to tackle equality and diversity issues. The unions reporting less difficulty (again in both public and private sectors) cited the more positive legal climate as having strengthened the equality bargaining climate (TUC, 2009). But it is also argued that the potential to advance equality through collective bargaining may be limited not just by the economic context, but also because of the traditionally restricted scope of bargaining agendas (Colling & Dickens, 1989; Blackett & Sheppard, 2003). This is something for which we can hold the unions accountable, at least to some extent. It is only fairly recently that unions have begun to see collective bargaining as concerned with all aspects of working life for all working people, rather than with just the traditional focus on pay and the basic terms and conditions of the dominant group – usually white males. So the broader agenda encompassing equality and diversity issues that we see reflected in the TUC report referred to above, is a relatively recent one. That said, simply blaming the 'male, pale and stale' union leaders for ignoring gender, equality and diversity would be too simplistic; it is also necessary to confront the fact that there are potentially very real conflicts between majority and minority interests. Although in theory equality bargaining does not have to be a zero-sum game, in practice employers do not have infinite resources to accede to all union demands and equality might not be the highest priority if it is seen to be a minority interest potentially dividing rather than uniting workers. The fact that unions are less likely to be able to mobilize support for action and for sanctions on equality and diversity issues has to be recognized (Palmer, 2003). Further, the Australian experience suggests that unless agreements are carefully equality-proofed, workplace bargaining can disadvantage women workers, compared with more centralized arrangements for setting pay (Teicher and Spearitt 1996).

What might equality and diversity bargaining include? Blackett and Sheppard (2003, p. 437) identify 'creative remedial measures and strategies' as a key aspect of the pursuit of substantive equality through collective bargaining. They state that collective agreements should contain general non-discrimination clauses and a specific clause prohibiting harassment. While this principle is important, as Blackett and Sheppard readily acknowledge, it merely perpetuates an individual, complaints-driven approach to tackling inequalities. Many countries already have in place anti-discrimination legislation that (in theory at least) provides this protection and opportunities for individuals to gain redress. The more challenging question in such cases is what can or should collective bargaining add over and above the protections offered by the legislation? Bargaining can be used more usefully and creatively to identify problems of discrimination and patterns of inequality more proactively and systematically in order to make up for the inadequacies of equalities legislation as well as to build on its strengths. This would include bargaining for initiatives to accommodate group-based differences – again we can find evidence of unions taking this on board (in the UK context, examples are found in the TUC (2009) report). Linking this to the workplace context, both employers and unions should start with an assessment of existing problems of inequality and discrimination – in other words the local workplace context needs to be subjected to close analysis using all available monitoring data (Blackett & Sheppard 2003). On the basis of self-declared bargaining activity, the UK unions have also made considerable progress here (TUC 2009). Some of the most obvious and pressing substantive bargaining issues to place at the centre of the agenda include pay gaps and undervaluation, employment segregation, flexible working arrangements and work-life balance (Baird & Williamson. 2009; Greene & Kirton, 2009). It is of course easy to say that these issues *should* be a high priority for the bargaining agenda, but it is quite evident that this is not always the case, even though the unions' rhetorical commitment to equality is now clear.

Another issue to think about when seeking to explain low levels of equality and diversity bargaining activity, is *how* do unions identify bargaining priorities? The TUC equality report referred to above (TUC, 2009) states that UK unions have a range of methods for identifying equalities priorities including conference or executive committee decisions, recommendations from union equality bodies, discussions among officials, and surveys or discussions with affected groups of members. This means that the agenda can arise from a combination of bottom-up membership demands and the top-down decisions of union officers. This is important. A multi-faceted approach to developing the bargaining agenda should go some way in ensuring the inclusion of groups that are under-represented in union decision-making structures and in negotiating teams, including women and black and minority ethnic members. This is something that has been repeatedly demanded in the context of many countries and, for a long time, something that has been seen as a means of overcoming the barriers in representing minority interests (Blackett & Sheppard, 2003). In the UK context, Heery (2006) finds that member location and officer characteristics influence the degree of union involvement in equality bargaining. Officers with members in public administration (central and local government) are most likely to be involved in equality bargaining, also those representing members in health and education and the privatized utilities. Women officers are marginally more likely than their male colleagues to report involvement in equality bargaining; a personal interest in and commitment to equality (regardless of gender) is also important. The degree to which the wider union supports equality bargaining (by way of training, policy, guidance etc) is also found to be significant. A key finding of Heery is that specialist equality committees and officers are significant influences on the degree of union involvement in equality bargaining. In Canada, similar conclusions were arrived at in Hart's (2002) study, where the unions that were the most effective in pay equity bargaining were those where negotiators had developed formal links with internal equality structures and where women's networking was significant (Hart, 2002). Interestingly, only a small percentage of officers in Heery's (2006) study report that their action on equality arises from encouragement by employers; in other words, equality bargaining is generally initiated by the union side.

However, this does not necessarily mean that employers have no interest in developing equality and diversity policy. As suggested above, it might rather indicate that employers are not willing to *bargain* or even consult with unions on equality issues. 'Diversity management' (DM) has swept around the world and is now the favoured management paradigm that has frequently replaced the traditional equality paradigm that underpinned organizational equality and equity policies in many countries (Humphries & Grice, 1995; Webb, 1997; Jones, Pringle & Shepherd, 2000). There are some negative implications for unions from this paradigm shift – in some countries, DM, like HRM, is something that is introduced into unionized as well as non-unionized contexts (Australia and the UK are examples). In the same way that they were hostile (initially) to HRM, some unions have also seen DM as, if not threatening, then perhaps irrelevant. My research with Anne-Marie Greene has found that UK unions have an uneasy relationship with DM because it emphasizes the business case and individual difference, and it is positioned as a top-down, management-led policy approach that seemingly has no need for union involvement (Kirton & Greene, 2006). However, in an era of HRM and with DM arguably being the HRM (labour control) approach to equality management (Humphries & Grice, 1995; Miller, 1996), it is important that unions attempt to bring DM into the realm of bargaining (or at least consultation) to prevent policy initiatives from simply serving business needs. It is important that unions do not fall into the same trap that some argue befell them when HRM emerged in the late 1980s/early 1990s as the new people management paradigm. Storey (1995, p. 121) found that in some firms when HRM was first introduced, the unions were 'invited to the party' (to discuss new policies and initiatives), but some declined the invitation (Storey, 1995) – something they arguably lived to regret as various individualistic management practices that undermined bargaining, were introduced unilaterally. It is important that unions do not end up being complicit in their marginalization from equality and diversity policy developments. Further, it is argued that the success of DM depends (partly) on its relation with the prevailing employment system (Hunter, 2003). On an optimistic note, our research in the UK found that despite being uncomfortable with management discourses of diversity, unions were prepared and able to work critically with DM towards the objective of improving their members' working lives (Kirton & Greene,

2006). Similarly, in Australia there seems to have been 'qualified' union support for diversity initiatives (Teicher & Spearitt, 1996).

With regard to scholarship on DM, part of the problem from an IR perspective lies in the fact that many authors writing on DM (even where the research context is unionized) tend not to engage with the question of union involvement in policy development and implementation or even the difference (if any) union presence makes.[3] Some might argue that this is because unionization is so low that the unions *do not* make any difference at workplace level. However, we have to remember that rates of unionization are highly variable among sectors and across industries, with the public sector being more highly unionized in most industrialized countries. In our case study of a UK public sector organization, Anne-Marie Greene and I found that unions were consulted about equality and diversity policy developments and that there were examples of where union inputs have led to policy changes (Greene & Kirton, 2009). The type of research that ignores the presence of unions tends to be located in the HRM journals, so although integrating HRM into the field of IR might be welcomed there is also an HRM literature that exists outside of anything that might resemble IR. By this I am referring to HRM articles and studies that focus on and emphasize the importance of management policies and practices and their consequences for organizational performance. Where the impact on employees is sometimes considered, it is likely to be in relation to performance and business issues, and employees are likely to be constructed as passive recipients of management policies. Within this orientation tackling equality and diversity is a management project, and things will improve for 'minority' groups once more, and better management policies and practices are established (by management). In contrast, where HRM studies have an IR orientation, collective and individual conflict, resistance and contestation are all visible within the questions asked, the methods used and the analysis of findings. As stated earlier, Anne-Marie Greene and I have attempted to position DM within IR by opening up an enquiry into the impact on unions of the shift to a diversity paradigm. We argue that this is important, particularly in countries where unionization is still significant in some industries and in occupations where DM is clearly visible (Greene & Kirton, 2009; Kirton & Greene, 2006). But even in the absence of unions, it is still important to consider how different groups of employees are affected by DM and how they experience and resist this management-led policy approach and whether non-union employee 'voice' mechanisms exist.

Conclusion

Because of changes in the structure of society and organizations, research on gender, equality and diversity has the potential to address significant social issues (Palmer, 2003). Arguing for more space for analysis of these issues within IR research, policy and practice does not have to be seen as a zero-sum game. These issues touch the lives of all working people in one way or another – either directly or indirectly or both. After all, we all have friends, partners, families, etc with whom our daily lives are intertwined and who are directly affected by inequalities, disadvantage and discrimination. Arguably, their deprivations are always our own too. In the 21st century, can we leave employers to get on with the job of 'managing diversity'? Analyses of the business case would suggest not (Noon, 2007; Kirton, 2008). Even in an era of relatively low union membership faced by most industrialized countries, collective bargaining can still do a lot to promote equality and diversity in certain employment contexts. But involving unions in equality and diversity policy making at all institutional and organizational levels serves a broader purpose – that of a broader system of governance and regulation that should go some way in ensuring that the voices of disadvantaged groups are heard and their interests represented (Dickens, 1997; Blackett & Sheppard, 2003). Gender, equality and diversity issues should be central for IR within a new interpretation of the 'old' paradigm. These are not new workplace issues, but they are issues that are under-researched by IR scholars who should really 'own' research on the employment relationship. More research is needed to understand the complexities of the relationship between IR systems, processes and practices and diversity issues. We still need a greater understanding of how employment segregation, disadvantage and discrimination are reproduced, especially as these are all 'shifting sands'. Much of what I have said has drawn on evidence from the UK, but it is clear from the international literature that many of the issues raised resonate with other countries' experiences.

Notes

1. This chapter is informed by my previous work (alone and with others) on gender, equality and diversity, as well as by a review of the literature and other publicly available data/sources.
2. A cultural reference to the British TV programme for children – *Blue Peter* – where a presenter would begin demonstrating how to make a complex toy model on air, but would then quickly bring out a finished version to show

the viewers. 'Here's one we made earlier' has come to mean 'we will show you how we have done it, but this is how the finished product looks' – no room for negotiation.
3. I have chosen not to provide examples as my intention is not to attack researchers' work, but simply to highlight the limitations of the DM research that is outside of an IR paradigm.

References

Baird, M., & Williamson, S. (2009). Women, work and industrial relations in 2008. *Journal of Industrial Relations, 51*(3), 331–346.
Blackett, A., & Sheppard, C. (2003). Collective bargaining and equality: making connections. *International Labour Review, 142*(4), 419–457.
Blyton, P., & Turnbull, P (1994). *The dynamics of employee relations*. Basingstoke: Macmillan.
Briskin, L. (2002). The equity project in Canadian unions: confronting the challenge of restructuring and globalisation. In F. Colgan & S. Ledwith (eds), *Gender, diversity and trade unions* (pp. 28–47). London: Routledge.
Cawthorne, A. (2009). *Weathering the storm: black men in the recession*. Washington: Center for American Progress.
Clegg, H. (1979). *The changing system of industrial relations in Great Britain*. Oxford: Blackwell.
Cobble, D., & Bielski Michal, M. (2002). On the edge of equality? Working women and the US labour movement. In F. Colgan and S. Ledwith (eds), *Gender, diversity and trade unions* (pp. 232–256). London: Routledge.
Colgan, F., & Ledwith, S. (2002). Gender and diversity: reshaping union democracy. *Employee Relations, 24*(2), 167–189.
Colling, T., & Dickens, L. (1989). *Equality bargaining - why not?* Manchester: Equal Opportunities Commission.
Colling, T., & Dickens, L. (2001). Gender equality and trade unions: a new basis for mobilisation? In M. Noon and E. Ogbonna (Eds.), *Equality, diversity and disadvantage in employment* Bassingstoke: Palgrave Macmillan.
Danieli, A. (2006). Gender: the missing link in industrial relations research. *Industrial Relations Journal, 37*(4), 329–343.
Dickens, L. (1997). Gender, race and employment equality in Britain: inadequate strategies and the role of industrial relations actors. *Industrial Relations Journal, 28*(4), 282–289.
Edwards, P. (1995). The employment relationship. In P. Edwards (ed.), *Industrial relations: Theory and practice in Britain* (pp. 3–26). Oxford: Blackwell.
Farnham, D., & Pimlott, J. (1995). *Understanding industrial relations*. London, Cassell.
Forrest, A. (1993). A view from outside the whale: the treatment of women and unions in industrial relations. In L. Briskin & P. McDermott (eds), *Women challenging unions* Toronto: Toronto University Press.
Greene, A. M. (2003). Industrial relations and women. In P. Ackers & A. Wilkinson (eds), *Understanding work and employment: industrial relations in transition* (pp. 305–315). Oxford: Oxford University Press.
Greene, A. M., & Kirton, G. (2009). *Diversity management in the UK: Organizational and stakeholder experiences*. London: Routledge.

Hansen, L. (2002). Rethinking the industrial relations tradition from a gender perspective: an invitation to integration. *Employee Relations, 24*(2), 190–210.

Hart, S. (2002). Unions and pay equity bargaining in Canada. *Relations Industrielles/Industrial Relations, 57*(4), 609–629.

E. Heery (2006). 'Union workers, union work: a profile of paid union officers in the United Kingdom'. British Journal of Industrial Relations, 44(3), 445–471.

Heery, E., & Kelly, J. (1988). Do female representatives make a difference? Women FTOs and trade union work. *Work, Employment and Society, 2*(4), 487–505.

Holgate, J., Hebson, G., & McBride, A. (2006). Why gender and 'difference' matters: a critical appraisal of industrial relations research. *Industrial Relations Journal, 37*(4), 310–328.

Humphries, M., & Grice, S. (1995). Equal employment opportunity and the management of diversity. *Journal of Organizational Change Management, 8*(5), 17–32.

Hunter, L. (2003). Research developments in employment relations and diversity: a British perspective. *Asia Pacific Journal of Human Resources, 41*(1), 88–100.

ILO (2009). *Global employment trends for women.* Geneva: International Labour Organization.

Jones, S. (2002). A woman's place is on the picket line: towards a theory of community industrial relations. *Employee Relations, 24*(2), 151–166.

Jones, D., Pringle, J., & Shepherd, D. (2000). 'Managing diversity' meets Aotearoa/New Zealand. *Personnel Review, 29*(3), 364–380.

Kaufman, B. (2008). Paradigms in industrial relations: original, modern and versions in-between. *British Journal of Industrial Relations, 46*(2), 314–339.

Kirton, G. (2008). Managing multi-culturally in organizations in a diverse society. In S. Clegg and C. Cooper (eds), *Handbook of macro organizational behaviour.* London: Sage.

Kirton, G., & Greene, A. M. (2006). The discourse of diversity in unionised contexts: views from trade union equality officers. *Personnel Review, 35*(4), 431–448.

Kirton, G. & Healy, G. (1999). Transforming union women: the role of women trade union officials in union renewal. *Industrial Relations Journal, 30*(1), 31–45.

Miller, D. (1996). Equality management: towards a materialist approach. *Gender, Work and Organization, 3*(4), 202–214.

Noon, M. (2007). The fatal flaws of diversity and the business case for ethnic minorities. *Work, Employment and Society, 21*(4), 773–784.

Palmer, G. (2003). Diversity management, past, present and future. *Asia Pacific Journal of Human Resources, 41*(1), 13–24.

Stewart, H. & Hopkins, K. (2009, 13 October). One in five black men out of a job figures reveal, and worse to come. *Guardian.* Retrieved from http://www.guardian.co.uk/world/2009/oct/13/black-men-unemployment-figures?INTCMP=SRCH

Storey, J. (1995). *Human resource management: a critical text.* London: Routledge.

Teicher, J., & Spearitt, K. (1996). From equal employment opportunity to diversity management: the Australian experience. *International Journal of Manpower, 17*(4/5), 109–133.

TUC (2009). *TUC equality audit 2009. Progress on bargaining for equality at work.* London: Trades Union Congress.

Wajcman, J. (2000). Feminism facing industrial relations in Britain. *British Journal of Industrial Relations, 38*(2), 183–201.

Walsh, J. (2007). Equality and diversity in British workplaces: the 2004 Workplace Employment Relations Survey. *Industrial Relations Journal, 38*(4), 303–319.

Webb, J. (1997). The politics of equal opportunity. *Gender, Work and Organization* 4(3), 159–169.

4
Employment Relations across Organizational Boundaries

Mick Marchington, Kari Hadjivassiliou,
Rose Martin, and Annette Cox

Introduction

Most academic studies of employment relations still operate within a framework which assumes that the single employer-employee relationship is the norm. This is hardly surprising given traditional definitions of the subject, even by theorists as diametrically opposed as Clegg (1970) and Hyman (1975). Moreover, historically, the majority of workers were employed in this sort of relationship, where employers had direct, line management authority over them with ultimate power to discipline or sack workers who did not comply with their wishes. The idea that one employer (say, a client), in a supply chain or partnership, could shape employment relations at the site of another employer (say, a supplier) is usually not addressed directly in existing theoretical approaches but instead is regarded as part of the context within which employer-employee relationships take place.

Definitions of employment law also rely on the notion of a contract between a single employer and an employee, and it has been assumed that legal rights could be delineated primarily within the boundaries of a single organization (Earnshaw, Rubery & Cooke, 2002). This is because common law rights and duties arise by virtue of the contract of employment and therefore concern only the parties to that contract. Clearly, this varies in detail between countries depending on their systems of employment law (Harvard, Rorive & Sobczak, 2009). This is most apparent when comparing coordinated market economies (CMEs) and liberal market economies (LMEs) because the role of the law in protecting workers is more embedded in the former than in the latter (Shire, Mottweiler, Schonauer, & Valverde, 2009b), but it is also clear that there are significant differences within both CMEs such as

Germany and the Netherlands (Mitlacher, 2006) and LMEs such as the USA via employment-at-will clauses – which require no notice of termination to be given – and the UK and Canada, both of which have well-established systems for regulating dismissal cases (Van Jaarsveld, Kwon & Frost, 2009).

In order to address this deficiency, this chapter focuses specifically on cases where workers are 'employed by one organization whilst to some extent being managed by another'. This scenario creates additional tensions in the discharge of the employment relationship as workers might (a) remain under the direction of their own employer while being located at the site of another, (b) be part of an alliance, working directly alongside staff from another organization, or (c) have their terms and conditions shaped by a client as well as by their own employer. The notion of employment across organizational boundaries has meaning where more than one employer is directly or indirectly involved in shaping an individual's contract irrespective of where they actually work; it can range from relatively direct multi-employer influence in the case of a partnership to more indirect pressure as in a supply chain. In other words, it is more appropriate to conceive of a triangular relationship between the parties (Havard, Rorive & Sobczak, 2009).

The consequences of employment relations being shaped by more than one employer can vary depending on several factors – such as societal norms and policy/legal frameworks, employer goals and relationships across the network, the occupational groups involved in the collaboration, and the role of trade unions. In coordinated market economies (CMEs), for example, institutional frameworks, employment laws, and accepted social norms promote higher levels of worker protection and long-term approaches, while in liberal market economies (LMEs) patterns of employment relations tend to vary depending on contextual circumstances, though they tend to be more short-term in orientation (Edwards, 2010; Grimshaw, Rubery & Almond, 2010). Accordingly, in simple terms, there is likely to be a tendency towards 'high-road' systems of employment relations in some contexts and to 'low-road' systems in others. The former revolves around employment relations policies that regard workers as assets that need to be developed in order to ensure high levels of product quality or customer service, while the latter treats workers as costs that need to be minimized because their contribution to organizational goals is limited (Marchington & Wilkinson, 2008). We return to this point in the concluding section.

The purpose of this chapter, therefore, is to show how current definitions of employment relations are of limited value when analyzing multi-employer networks, and in explaining when the high-road or low-road systems might be applied in practice. While most organizations now outsource services such as cleaning and catering, as well as elements of their IT, HR, administrative, or manufacturing operations, unfortunately much research still seems to assume a dominant role for the relationship between an on-site employer and its workers. This ignores cases where workers' conditions and employment are shaped, influenced, or largely determined by other employers in the network or supply chain. To address this, it is necessary to analyse relations among *employers* as well as between employer and employee.

The multi-employer framework for employment relations

The phenomenon of employment relations across organizational boundaries takes many forms. *Public-private partnerships* (PPPs) – where large tranches of what was previously public sector work is transferred to private sector suppliers – are well-established in a number of countries, typically driven by government rather than by business interests. They often reflect contrasting organizational goals – profit versus social motives – that foster additional tensions for employment relations across a network. *Alliances and partnerships* operate within or among sectors (public and private) on specific contracts over widely differing timescales. While these may appear simple in principle where there is a joint commitment to partnership, they can also be highly complex because only parts of each organization combine together, thus creating even greater potential for contradictions in employment relations. *Agency working* is a third example; this occurs when agencies act as a supplier of either short-term temporary work (e.g. in offices) or more established arrangements such as in schools, hospitals, or call centres. *Supply chain networks and clusters* offer a final example where, despite being employed on a separate site from the client, the latter may be able to exert a major influence over employment relations at the sub-contractor firm. In some cases, multi-employer networks are even more complex as they contain more than one of the forms outlined above. For example, call centres often use workers not just from one or more partner firms but also from several agencies (Rubery, Marchington, Grimshaw, Carroll & Pass, 2009). Moreover, some workers move between different forms of employment over time, say from an agency to a partner employer, or from one contractor to another when a business contract changes hands (Forde, MacKenzie & Robinson, 2009).[1]

Although all multi-employer collaborations are similar in moving beyond simple and traditional ownership structures, they also differ substantially. Some involve workers from different employers working alongside each other at the same workplace whereas others are geographically separated, either within the same country or across national boundaries and therefore subject to varying national business and employment relations systems (Marchington & Timming, 2010). The extent of collaboration between different employers also varies, both in terms of the length of deals (for example, a typical private finance initiative deal in the UK can last 35 years compared with an agency worker being deployed somewhere for one day) and how many staff from each of the respective organizations is involved – again from a single worker through to many thousands. Power is also an issue. In some cases, a large client can effectively dictate terms to a small sub-contractor in relation to, for example, the working hours of truck drivers, the pay levels of manufacturing workers, or the disciplinary standards expected from call centre staff (Marchington, Grimshaw, Rubery & Willmott, 2005).

Therefore, other things being equal, the longer the relationship between organizations, the more it is based on a relatively equal balance of power, and the greater the similarity in objectives between the partners, the more likely that employment relations will be based on a high-road model. By contrast, the greater the disparity in the relationship, the more likely the weaker party will be forced to adopt the low-road model (Rainnie, 1989). Accordingly, workers at sub-contractor firms can suffer a double whammy, not only at the disposal of firms with little bargaining power but also at the edge of specific industries (Friedman, 1986). Workers' rights at the actual point of production become even weaker when chains of outsourcing extend significantly beyond the original client organization, and responsibility for maintaining standards is passed down the line. The implications for unions (and workers) are summed up well by Erickson, Fisk, Milkman, Mitchell & Wong (2002, p. 544): 'Organizing workers in industries where the employer is elusive and where layers of sub-contracting diffuse responsibility across multiple actors is a problem for unions throughout the world.' Of course, employers in strong market positions do not automatically take advantage of workers in this way; as the Fair Trade movement and some ethically motivated employers show, employers still have choices in whether they sub-contract work to other firms, and if so where they choose to locate and with which firms they decide to collaborate.

The remainder of this chapter reviews evidence from four different settings: PPPs, alliances and partnerships, agency working, and supply chains and clusters. Data are analysed from countries operating under different societal regimes, but much is from LMEs such as the UK, the USA, and Australasia. Fortunately, some data are available from CMEs – such as Germany, Austria, the Netherlands, and Sweden – which allows us to widen the net. However, the predominance of studies from LMEs probably reflects the fact that employers are encouraged to move away from so-called standard employment systems in societies where short-term targets and notions of shareholder value are common. We review evidence for both procedural and substantive aspects of employment relations so as to illustrate how multi-employer networks shape workplace activity. While not attempting slavishly to examine every component of employment relations in each section, the majority of the evidence relates to the following: trade union organization and collective bargaining; employee involvement and participation (EIP) and commitment to employers; pay, working time, and employment security; and selection, performance management, and career development.

Public-private partnerships (PPPs)

PPPs arose partly from a requirement to raise money for public projects, but also from Best Value initiatives aiming to maximize value for money. Efficiency and cost savings have been important drivers in many of these contracts. Although efficiencies may be achieved through use of improved technology or systems (Lattemann, Stieglitz, Kupke & Schneider, 2008), there are areas of public service where the emphasis is on workers – as a key resource and cost – and pressure to deliver savings impacts heavily on employment relations.

A comparison of public and private prisons in the UK suggests that private sector employees receive lower pay, work longer hours, and receive fewer holidays and poorer pensions than their public sector counterparts (Taylor & Cooper, 2008). Employment security may also suffer (Hall, 2008). When contracts are protected – as under Transfer of Undertakings (Protection of Employment) (TUPE) legislation in the UK – some degree of temporal consistency in terms and conditions is maintained but the working environment can change. Work intensification has been noted as a frequent outcome of these new organizational arrangements. Although this is not an automatic outcome of PPPs, the evidence suggests that lower morale is often found (Hebson, Grimshaw, & Marchington, 2003), largely due to reductions in staffing levels and even threats to worker safety and health (Taylor & Cooper, 2008).

Client pressures often lead to increased monitoring of partners and individual workers, and in some cases private sector managers have been encouraged to adopt a harder line on performance management. For example, an HR manager employed by one of the private sector contractor firms studied by Grimshaw, Rubery, & Marchington (2010) reported that 'we probably have a lower tolerance than the public sector ... I think we're much more effective at managing these people and making sure that they do what they're employed to do.' PPPs can also erode the 'public sector ethos'. Using case studies of a health sector partnership and the outsourcing of housing benefit claims in local government, Hebson et al. (2003) suggest that workers who are transferred to the private sector retain their wish to do a good job – valuing public interest and continuing to work beyond contract to meet patient and claimant needs – but increased pressure and decreased job security can ultimately lead to lower levels of engagement. On the other hand, Coyle-Shapiro, Morrow and Kessler(2006) found that workers can maintain a high level of commitment simultaneously to both private and public sector organizations. They do add, though, that a fine balance is necessary, with strong alignment between public sector managers and private sector contractors necessary to minimize tensions for workers. Such relationships between employers are likely to be important in order to maintain amicable relationships with the unions as well.

Trade union organization and collective bargaining can also be adversely affected due to the multiplicity of parties involved, and fragmentation is likely to occur as workers splinter into smaller interest groups (Hall, 2008). Private sector contractors, especially when these are small employers, are typically less willing to work with trade unions perhaps because they are less accustomed to dealing with them (Hall, 2008). There have been some gains for workers in PPPs, however; for example, UK unions have argued successfully for 'Retention of Employment' for those working at some healthcare PPPs, who are now allowed to remain as employees of the National Health Service while being seconded to private sector firms. Agreements have also been negotiated to keep pension schemes consistent with the rights afforded to other public sector employees (Hall, 2008). Indeed, some agreements are now in place to limit the adverse effects of PPPs on employment relations. For example, a recent ILO Convention, ratified by 60 countries, aims to prevent companies from bidding for public contracts by cutting labour costs, although in practice this may not be implemented fully (Hall, 2008). At the national level, some countries have adopted protective employment legislation – such as the TUPE Regulations in the UK, which has provided some degree of temporal consistency for transferred workers' terms and conditions. Of course any workers recruited following the transfer typically receive lower rates of pay, thus leading to a 'two-tier workforce'. Attempts to prevent this have been seen in the UK, with the Two-Tier Code (Grimshaw & Roper, 2007), and in Hungary, Slovakia, and Latvia through procurement laws (Hall, 2008).

Alliances and partnerships

Alliances and partnerships can vary widely in terms of format and intensity. It is important, therefore, to differentiate between (a) long-term, strategic alliances/partnerships between organizations that employ high-skilled, professional workers and (b) business relationships relying on the employment of lower skilled staff for activities such as sales, customer service, and technical assistance – as in call centres for example. The former is typically more integrative/relational whereas the latter is more contractual/transactional in nature. In both cases, however, the boundaries between and hierarchies within organizations become blurred, employment relations more fragmented, and the identities of employer, employee, and organization destabilized (Marchington, Grimshaw, Rubery, & Willmott, 2005; Rainnie, Barrett, Burgess, & Connell, 2008).

In more collaborative alliances, questions about employee identity, loyalty, and commitment are complicated since they involve people working in different locations and coming from different occupational groups. George and Chattopadhyay (2005) found that IT contract workers in the USA experienced dual and simultaneous identification with both the parent and the client organization in which they were based for assignments. On the other hand, Grimshaw and Miozzo's (2009) study of IT outsourcing in four countries (UK, Germany, Argentina, and Brazil) reported considerable employment insecurity for these workers both before, during, and after business contracts were established; many were sacked before the transfer in attempts to cut costs while some of the more 'expensive' managers were made redundant within 12 months of the contract starting. Marchington, Carroll, Grimshaw, Pass and Rubery's (2009) study of a UK health and social care partnership examined integrated teams comprising nurses and social workers, both of which are characterized by strong but distinct professional identities. As a result, these two groups of workers were allowed choice as to which organization should be their employer. Consequently, despite working side by side, these professionals were subject to different employment conditions, including levels of pay and working hours, and 'among employee' consistency was not achieved within teams. On the other hand, because the organizations involved shared some key attributes – notably a public sector ethos and a shared commitment to patient care – some degree of shared identification was realized with the aims of the partnership.

Collective bargaining and employee participation have particular salience in cross-boundary working, since these tend to reside with existing employers rather than with the alliance or partnership. In general, it is more difficult to instil a sense of common purpose and 'real shared interests' among workers straddling organizations that have diverse employment conditions (Saundry, Antcliff & Stuart, 2006). Although it is much easier to develop informal or direct communications systems, it is inappropriate to introduce integrated collective bargaining and joint consultation arrangements when terms and conditions are determined by two separate employers. Yet most of the employers studied by Marchington et al. (2009) had attempted to maintain communications and contact with professional staff working for lengthy periods at the site of a different employer. In the IT case, regular meetings were held and project managers ensured that time was allocated to speak over the phone with staff working at client organizations, while in the health and social care partnership different types of EIP techniques – team briefings, newsletters, joint forum – were used depending on local circumstances. In the sports network, meetings and training sessions were set up for part-time and temporary workers supplied from elsewhere, including volunteers, while in another part of this network, the private sector supplier made no attempt to communicate with its managers on long-term secondment, relying instead on the client's managers to develop informal systems. In short, despite some positive outcomes for employment relations in these alliances, there is also evidence of harsher and/or under-developed employment practices.

Many of the more transactional alliances are in call centres, especially in outsourced units, and several studies have explored the impact such organizational arrangements can have on employment relations (Walsh & Deery, 2006; Van Jaarsveld, Kwon, & Frost, 2009). It is clear from Batt, Holman, & Holtgrewe (2010) global survey across 17 countries that outsourced call centres offered lower pay, used more part-time and temporary staff, opted for much greater work standardization and performance monitoring, and were less likely to engage in collective bargaining. Walsh & Deery (2006) found that staff working for an outsourced airline call centre received 7%–8% less pay, had fewer benefits and none of the travel perks enjoyed by the staff working at the in-house call centre operated by the same airline. Staff in the former also faced greater work intensification through higher and more tightly monitored performance targets than their counterparts in the in-house call centre. Specifically, they handled about one-third more calls per day, were given less 'downtime' between calls, and were not able to access career development opportunities. Not surprisingly, workers at the outsourced call centre were less satisfied with their pay, and they exhibited lower levels of organizational commitment and a higher intention to quit.

Several studies have highlighted how companies in CMEs (e.g. Sweden, France, Germany) are increasingly turning to transactional alliances which in the past were typically associated with LMEs (e.g. US, Canada, UK, Ireland) and to less regulated labour markets in order to circumvent strict employment regulations in CMEs. Shire, Schonauer, Valverde & Mottweiler (2009a), examining data from call centres in six EU countries, found a wide range of variation *within* CMEs and LMEs rather than clear differences between the two. A further complication in call centres is that in many cases, it is not just a simple matter of one client and one provider. Rather, a much more fragmented web of sub-contractor firms and agencies exists, each of which employs staff on different conditions depending on the segments of business they cater to and the type/level of service the client is seeking to offer its customers.

Havard et al.'s (2009) analysis of relations between an industrial cleaning company and its clients in France and Belgium found that client pressures dominated employment relations. The asymmetric nature of the business relationship shaped employment relations to such an extent that performance expectations went way beyond the strict bounds of the employment contract. Supervisors at the client firm frequently asked cleaning staff permanently based at the client's premises, who wore its logo and uniform, to carry out tasks not specified in the commercial contract. The client was also involved in selection and performance assessment and, together with the supplier, determination of work schedules. Interestingly, cleaning staff progressively developed a stronger sense of loyalty to the client, even asking its employee representatives (as opposed to their own) to handle grievances. Similarly, Kinnie, Purcell, & Adams (2008) found that clients with large contracts exerted considerable direct influence over employment relations, such as offering higher wages than the sub-contractor in order to attract better candidates.

Agencies and agency workers

Pay and working conditions for agency workers are, on average, less favourable than for staff on standard contracts in comparable jobs. Surveys suggest that this applies in a range of countries even when controlling for a number of personal and job effects (Forde & Slater, 2005; Nienhüser & Matiaske, 2006). There is, however, variation across sectors and skill levels. While the pattern of disadvantage may hold for the bulk of low-skilled temporary agency workers, higher-skilled workers may be able to benefit from working through an agency (Forde & Slater, 2005). For example, UK nurses have been able to command higher rates of pay through agency work than through standard forms of employment (Purcell, Purcell & Tailby, 2004), and one survey suggests that specialist nurses in particular have a pecuniary motivation to join agencies (de Ruyter, 2007).

Temporary agency work tends to be inherently less secure than work on open-ended contracts because, in the event of a downturn, failing to renew the contracts of agency workers is a relatively easy way to cut costs. Terms and conditions can be significantly less advantageous than in standard employment contracts – especially in de-regulated markets such as Australia where lower pay may be accompanied by no provision for holidays, sickness, or severance pay. Lack of protection may lead to other pressures, such as the perceived need to work continuously to avoid going to the 'back of the queue' for jobs (Burgess, Connell, &Rasmussen, 2005). Where there is greater regulation, agency workers are afforded some protection – for example, in Germany and the Netherlands, there are principles of equal pay and of equal treatment so that agency workers must have conditions equal to those employed in similar jobs under other contract forms. The triangular relationship – between worker, temporary staffing agency, and client – may also be clarified by law to protect the worker, as the agency is deemed to be the employer (Mitlacher, 2006), thus avoiding situations where no one takes responsibility for the worker's rights. The 2008 EU Directive 2008/104/DC on temporary agency work[2] is likely to have an impact, especially on LMEs such as the UK, giving agency workers similar rights to comparable in-house workers in relation to pay and other benefits; however, it is not yet clear how this will affect temporary agency workers in practice.

Temporary agency workers are often seen as a threat to the employment contracts of in-house staff, and this meant that unions have, historically, been ambivalent to them. However, there has been a shift in recent years in several countries from a strategy of opposition to contingent labour to one of engagement, to raise standards for contingent workers and to prevent them from undercutting the traditional membership base (Mackenzie, 2010; Shire et al., 2009b). Indeed, some trade unions have made active attempts to engage with temporary work agencies. In the UK, for example, the Transport and General Workers Union (now part of Unite) negotiated agreements with two large agencies – Manpower and Adecco. However, such attempts have had only limited success in achieving real improvements for agency workers – partly because agencies' competitive positions still depend heavily on cost minimization but also due to fears of union disruption to client services (Heery, 2004).

Agency workers also face problems in raising grievances and ensuring they are part of the EIP arrangements at the place they work, as well as at their own employer (the agency). As Grimshaw, Earnshaw, & Hebson (2003) noted, supply teachers found difficulty trying to persuade trade union representatives to progress their concerns, especially as their worries were often different from those facing in-house teachers on permanent contracts. At the same time, it was also hard to develop allegiances with other agency staff, to some extent because they were competing for the best jobs but also due to working at diverse locations and rarely having the chance to meet up. To some extent, agency workers are invisible to all concerned. A similar problem arises in relation to EIP in any organization, as the issues which are communicated to in-house staff often have little meaning for someone who might be on site for days or at most weeks at a time. It is difficult in view of the 'employment triangle' and the attendant dual (and even competing) sources of identity and commitment to ensure that agency workers receive an integrated and consistent organizational message (Marchington et al., 2009). Moreover, despite the presence of Information and Consultation of Employees' Regulations in the UK, there is no provision for consultation across organizational boundaries.

Supply chain networks and clusters

Supply chain relationships are now a well-established form of interaction between organizations, both in manufacturing (for example, vehicles) and in services (for example, food retailing). In general, power relations between customers and suppliers tend to be unequal, with the former – especially large multi-national corporations – able to dominate the relationship and shape employment relations at supplier firms. The precise impact on suppliers depends on their position and value in the supply chain (Scarborough, 2000; Marchington & Vincent, 2004). It has been argued that supply chains, along with corporate codes of conduct and stricter procurement standards, provide a diffusion mechanism capable of producing significant changes in employment relations at supplier firms (Hunter, Beaumont, & Sinclair, 1996; OECD, 2002 and 2008). This effect can either be direct or indirect (Hunter et al., 1996; Koulikoff-Souviron & Harrison, 2007), and it can drive suppliers towards higher- and/or lower-road employment systems.

Direct client influences on employment relations at supplier firms include audits, corporate codes of conduct, approved supplier lists, and even supplier development programmes to ensure that the supplier's employment relations policies – for example, in relation to EIP, pay and working conditions, and health and safety – are mutually compatible. Winfield & Hay (1997) describe how Toyota's supplier development programme aims to push its suppliers to align their HRM policies with that of Toyota. Suppliers are encouraged to promote team working, develop new approaches to training, enhance employee commitment and involvement by, *inter alia*, improving communications through less reliance on top-down briefings by supervisors.

Similarly Nike, in response to negative publicity about its global supplier network, introduced a Code of Conduct in 1992 requiring its suppliers to conform to basic labour, environmental, and health and safety standards (Locke, Quin, & Brause, 2007). The Code stipulates, *inter alia*, that employees working for its suppliers worldwide should enjoy freedom of association, be paid the country's minimum or industry's prevailing wage (whichever is higher), and so on. The main elements of Nike's process of supplier auditing includes an in-depth management and working conditions audit (M-Audit); this includes recruitment practices, treatment of employees, employee-management communications, and pay and working conditions. Research on the effect of Nike's supplier requirements has yielded mixed results, however, and although suppliers performed above the average in relation to the M-Audit – meaning that working conditions in the factories were improving – performance varied considerably across countries and regions. Indeed, the use of corporate codes of conduct has become a well-used mechanism for influencing employment relations in global corporations. The Ethical Investment Research Service (EIRIS) noted that, of the 147 firms on its database[3] which head a supply chain in sectors 'of concern' with regard to working conditions, only about 20 per cent had a code of conduct on supplier working conditions (OECD, 2002).

Indirect pressure along the supply chain is a more common form of customer influence. It is manifested through increased customer demands on suppliers for improved performance, enhanced levels of service and quality, and cost reduction which, in turn, put the onus on suppliers to overhaul internal work organization, production processes, and working practices. For example, Beaumont, Hunter, & Sinclair (1996) and Scarborough (2000) found that elements of employment relations at supplier firms – such as training/upgrading of skills, workforce performance, employee communications, and team working – were affected as a result of customer pressure. While indirect effects can be benign, for example, by enhancing employee communications, they can also be disruptive and create tensions. For example, Scarborough (2000) describes how new working practices linked to the introduction of cell manufacturing disrupted a supplier's internal pay structure by creating divisions on the shop floor, and for some workers greater levels of work intensification and stress.

The above examples are drawn mainly from manufacturing and involve relatively stable buyer-supplier relationships, as well as skilled labour. However, a major expansion in outsourcing and sub-contracting has taken place across the service sector, involving a complex web of sub-contractors, which targets both low- and high-skilled labour. In the case of the former, Dube and Kaplan (2010) demonstrate how outsourced janitors and security guards in the USA were paid less and had access to fewer benefits than their in-house counterparts. The wage penalty for janitors ranged between 4 per cent and 7 per cent and for guards between 8 per cent and 24 per cent. Significantly, industries that have historically paid higher wage premiums were also more likely to outsource service jobs. Union membership was also an important factor, with the outsourced workers receiving a smaller union wage premium than their in-house counterparts, even if the outsourced labour was unionized.

Several attempts have been made to address the employment relations problems created by having multiple sub-contractors and the related diffusion of responsibility across employers. Attempts to achieve more effective representation for outsourced/sub-contracted workers have included official union campaigns, such as 'Justice for Janitors' and 'Living Wage', as well as community organizing in the USA (Erickson, Fisk, Milkman, Mitchell, & Wong, 2002; Osterman, 2006). In the Justice for Janitors campaign, launched in Los Angeles in 1988 by the Service Employees International Union (SEIU), the aim was both to reverse the then growing trend towards de-unionization of janitors and to improve the terms and conditions of low-skilled, low-paid, and vulnerable migrant workers by targeting the building owners and managers (the users of janitors' services) rather than the cleaning companies (the actual employer of the janitors). By focusing on building owners and managers, the campaign managed to circumvent the elusive employer, as well as garner support from residents. Moreover, by focusing negotiations on the two main cleaning services contractors in the city, the SEIU managed to achieve across-the-board improvements to the terms and conditions of low-wage, migrant workers.

For high-skilled workers, MacKenzie (2010) examines how the Communications Workers Union (CWU) in Ireland managed to secure union recognition rights at Telserv – the main subcontractor to Eircom – and expand its coverage to outsourced labour, including engineers. An 'Atypical Working Scheme' was jointly developed with the CWU as an alternative to Eircom's redundancy programme; this secured three years' work at a major subcontractor, while maintaining Eircom's terms and conditions, including union membership.

Conclusion

This short review of employment relations across organizational boundaries has shown that multi-employer networks operate in many countries and sectors across the globe. To date, they have been the subject of relatively little analysis, and, if they are considered, it is often the case that all forms of multi-employer collaboration are assumed to take a similar form. However, as we have seen, employment relations systems in these situations can vary substantially, and it is not always the case that workers at supplier firms come off worse. They often do, of course, but it is important to identify the factors which are associated with attempts to achieve either high- or low-road employment relations. So much depends on the country in which the partnership or network is located, the purpose of collaboration, the nature of the relationship among employers, the types of workers involved, and whether unions are present across the network. Table 4.1 summarizes the principal factors which help to explain whether a high-road or low-road employment system is likely to occur.

The purpose of this table is not to set out some determining factors which specify precisely how employment relations will be characterized in any individual network, but to outline the types of forces that need to be taken into account in any particular situation. So, for example, while we might expect – other things being equal – that

Table 4.1 Factors shaping employment relations across different multi-employer networks

Factor shaping employment relations	Tendency towards high-road employment relations system	Tendency towards low-road employment relations system
Societal norms and policy/legal framework	Coordinated market economies	Liberal market economies
	Strong legislative base providing worker protection	Weak legislative base providing worker protection
	Long-term stakeholder perspective dominant	Short-term shareholder value perspective dominant
Main reasons for collaboration	Product/service quality or innovation key to success	Cost reduction and shifting of risk critical for success
	Access to technical expertise key reason for collaboration	Desire to outsource work so as to focus on core capabilities
Nature of relationship between employers	Organizations relatively equal in size and access to resources	Organizations vary considerably in size and access to resources
	Vary in size but client seeks improved quality from supplier	Vary in size but client wants nothing more than reduced costs from supplier
Length of collaboration between employers	Long-term trust relations at centre of collaboration	Short-term, arms-length relations envisaged for collaboration
	Prior evidence of trust and working together successfully	Not worked together previously and trust not yet developed
Occupational groups and workers involved in collaboration	High-skill professional workers	Low-skill manual/call centre workers
	Requirement for workers to use their discretion	Workers expected to follow instructions
	Shortage of these workers on the external labour market	Plentiful supply of these workers on the external labour market
Role of trade unions and social partners within network	Workers involved belong to and wish to remain in a union	Workers involved may or may not belong to a union
	Management support continued role for unions	Management opposes continued role for unions

high-road employment systems are more likely to be found in CMEs than in LMEs, we have already noted that differences can also occur between individual LMEs or CMEs. Similarly, while the nature of the relationship among employers across the network gives us clues as to which form of employment system might emerge, individual employers might decide that they want to break with existing norms and do something different. The whole point of Table 4.1 is that it offers pointers for researchers and practitioners who are interested in examining/developing employment relations systems across organizational boundaries.

In addition, a major question also arises about how *responsibility* for employment relations is distributed across organizational boundaries in any multi-employer network. At one extreme, where two or more parties have instigated a long-term partnership, or a PPP, it is possible that both parties will work together to try and iron out tensions caused by the new organizational form. Where the relationship is shorter-term and/or based on cost savings and competing employer goals, greater degrees of complexity are likely to appear because a key element of the contract might be to pass risk to the supplier firm. Moreover, line managers might be charged with trying to achieve on-going performance improvements that result in work intensification. In some cases, responsibility is shared *de facto* among employers, for example, in the case of agency workers where issues concerning pay and conditions are dealt with by the agency while matters of work organization are overseen by the on-site employer. If there is more than one supplier of labour, each of which has different procedures or employs managers who lack knowledge or expertise of the client's procedures, then the potential for contradictions and feelings of unfairness becomes starker and more problematic (Rubery et al., 2009). Finally, at the other extreme, the supplier retains, in law at least, full responsibility for employment relations decisions, but in practice powerful clients put pressure – directly or indirectly – on the supplier to make changes if the business contract is to continue.

Multi-employer networks, in their variety of forms, are now an important feature of the employment relations landscape, and worthy of theoretical attention which addresses the triangular nature of the relationships which exist in this context. Models assuming a traditional authority relationship between an employer and its employees do not have the sophistication to cope with the increased complexity brought about when a partner employer can influence and shape the terms and conditions of workers employed by another employer in the network. As we intimated earlier in the chapter, if employment relations research is to advance, especially on a global scale, it needs to focus more explicitly on relations between employers, as well as on the employer-employee relationship.

Notes

1. We have chosen not to include joint ventures in this review partly for space reasons but more importantly because the creation of a new legal entity removes the likelihood of employment relations being determined by more than one employer. Joint ventures have more in common with mergers and acquisitions in this respect than they do with situations where more than one employer has direct and indirect influence over the employment relationship. However, this is not meant to downplay the considerable tensions that can arise during transition, and in some cases for some years after, under such forms of collaboration.
2. http://eur-lex.europa.eu/LexUriServ/LexUriServ.do?uri=OJ:L:2008:327:000 9:0014:EN:PDF
3. It should be noted that the EIRIS analysis is of a sample of 147 firms, about 40 per cent of which were UK companies. Other countries represented on the database include Japan, France, Greece, Australia, Canada, Belgium, and Italy (see OECD, 2002, p. 5). Sectors 'of concern' included retail, clothes and sporting goods manufacturing and tobacco. Suppliers may well be outside the EU.

References

Batt, R., Holman, D., & Holtgrewe, U. (2010). The globalization of service work: comparative institutional perspectives on call centres, *Industrial and Labor Relations Review, 62*(4). 453–488.

Beaumont, P., Hunter, L., & Sinclair, D. (1996). Customer-supplier relations and the diffusion of employee relations changes. *Employee Relations, 18*(1). 9–19.

Burgess, J., Connell, J., & Rasmussen, E. (2005). Temporary agency work and precarious employment: a review of the current situation in Australia and New Zealand. *Management Revue, 16*(3), 351–369.

Clegg, H. (1970). *The system of industrial relations in Great Britain.* Oxford: Blackwell.

Coyle-Shapiro, J., Morrow, P., & Kessler, I. (2006). Serving two organizations: exploring the employment relationship of contracted employees. *Human Resource Management, 45*(4), 561–583.

de Ruyter, A. (2007). Should I stay or should I go? Agency nursing work in the UK. *International Journal of Human Resource Management, 18*(9), 1666–1682.

Dube, A., & Kaplan, E. (2010). Does outsourcing reduce wages in the low-wage service occupations? Evidence from janitors and guards. *Industrial and Labour Relations Review, 63*(2), 287–306.

Earnshaw, J., Rubery, J., and Cooke, F.L. (2002). *Who is the employer?* London: Institute of Employment Rights.

Edwards, T. (2010). The transfer of employment practices across borders. In Pinnington, A. & Harzing, A-W. (eds), *International human resource management* (3rd edn). London: Sage Publications.

Erickson, C., Fisk, C., Milkman, R., Mitchell, J., and Wong, K. (2002). Justice for janitors in Los Angeles: lessons from three rounds of negotiations. *British Journal of Industrial Relations, 40*(3), 543–567.

Forde, C., & Slater, G. (2005). Agency working in Britain: character, consequences and regulation. *British Journal of Industrial Relations, 43*(2), 249–271.

Forde, C., MacKenzie, R., & Robinson, A. (2009). Built on shifting sands: changes in employers' use of contingent labour in the UK construction industry. *Journal of Industrial Relations, 51*(5), 653–667.

Friedman, A. (1986). Developing the managerial strategies approach to the labour process. *Capital and Class, 28*, 97–124.

George, E., and Chattopadhyay, P. (2005). One foot in each camp: the dual identification of contract workers. *Administrative Science Quarterly, 50*, 68–99.

Grimshaw, D., Earnshaw, J., & Hebson, G. (2003). Private sector provision of supply teachers: a case of legal swings and professional roundabouts. *Journal of Education Policy, 18*(3), 267–288.

Grimshaw, D. and Roper, I. (2007). Partnership: blurring organizational boundaries and the employment relationship in public service delivery. In P. Dibben, P. James, I. Roper & G. Wood (eds), *Modernizing work in public services: redefining roles and relationships in Britain's changing workplace*, London: Palgrave Macmillan.

Grimshaw, D., & Miozzo, M. (2009). New HRM practices in knowledge-intensive business services firms: the case of outsourcing with staff transfer. *Human Relations, 62*(10), 1521–1550.

Grimshaw, D., Rubery, J., & Almond, P. (2010a). Multinational companies and the host country environment. In A. Pinnington & A-W. Harzing (eds), *International human resource management* (3rd edn). London: Sage Publications.

Grimshaw, D., Rubery, J., & Marchington, M. (2010b). Managing people across hospital networks in the UK: multiple employers and the shaping of HRM. *Human Resource Management Journal, 20*(4), 407–423.

Hall, D. (2008). *Public-private partnerships (PPPs): summary paper*. London: Public Services International Research Unit.

Havard, C., Rorive, B., & Sobczak, A. (2009). Client, employer, and employee: mapping a complex triangulation. *European Journal of Industrial Relations, 15*(3), 257–276.

Hebson, G., Grimshaw, D., & Marchington, M. (2003). PPPs and the changing public sector ethos: case-study evidence from the health and local authority sectors. *Work, Employment & Society, 17*(3), 481–501.

Heery, E. (2004). The trade union response to agency labor in Britain. *Industrial Relations Journal, 35*(5), 434–450.

Hunter, L., Beaumont, P., & Sinclair, D. (1996). A partnership route to human resource management. *Journal of Management Studies, 33*(2), 235–257.

Hyman, R. (1975). *Industrial relations: A marxist introduction*. London: Macmillan.

Kinnie, N., Purcell, J., & Adams, M. (2008). Explaining employees' experience of work in outsourced call centres: the influence of clients, owners and temporary work agencie. *Journal of Industrial Relations, 50*(2), 209–227.

Koulikoff-Souviron, M., & Harrison, A. (2007). The pervasive human resource picture in interdependent supply relationships. *International Journal of Operations and Production Management, 27*(1), 8–17.

Lattemann, C., Stieglitz, S., Kupke, S., & Schneider, A-M. (2008). Impact of PPPs on broadband diffusion in Europe. *Transforming Government: People, Process and Policy, 3*(4), 355–374.

Locke, M., Quin, F., & Brause, A. (2007). Does monitoring improve labour standards? Lessons from Nike. *Industrial and Labour Relations Review, 61*(1), 3–31.

MacKenzie, R. (2010). Why do contingent workers join a Trade Union? Evidence from the Irish telecommunications sector. *European Journal of Industrial Relations, 16*(2), 152–168.

Marchington, M., & Vincent, S. (2004). Analyzing the influence of institutional, organizational and interpersonal forces in shaping inter-organizational relations. *Journal of Management Studies, 41*(6), 1029–1056.

Marchington, M. and Wilkinson, A. (2008) *Human resource management at work*, 4th edn. London: Chartered Institute of Personnel and Development.

Marchington, M., Grimshaw, D., Rubery, J., & Willmott, H. (eds). (2005). *Fragmenting work: blurring organizational boundaries and disordering hierarchies.* Oxford: Oxford University Press.

Marchington, M., Carroll, M., Grimshaw, D., Pass, S., & Rubery, J. (2009). *Managing people in networked organizations.* London: CIPD.

Marchington, M., & Timming, A. (2010). Participation across organizational boundaries. In A. Wilkinson, P. Gollan, M. Marchington & D. Lewin (eds), *The Oxford handbook of participation in organizations.* Oxford: Oxford University Press.

Mitlacher, L, (2006). The organization of human resource management in temporary work agencies – towards a comprehensive research agenda on temporary agency work in Germany, the Netherlands, and the USA. *Human Resource Management Review, 16*, 67–81.

Mitlacher, L. (2007). The role of temporary agency work in different industrial relations systems – a comparison between Germany and the USA. *British Journal of Industrial Relations, 45*(3), 581–606.

Nienhüser, W., & Matiaske, W. (2006). Effects of the 'principle of non-discrimination' on temporary agency work: compensation and working conditions of temporary agency workers in 15 European countries. *Industrial Relations Journal, 37*(1), 64–77.

OECD (2002). *Managing working conditions in the supply chain – a fact-finding study of corporate practices.* Paris: Organization for Economic Co-operation and Development: Roundtable on Corporate Responsibility.

OECD (2008). Do Multinationals promote better pay and working conditions? In *OECD Employment Outlook 2008.* Paris: Organization for Economic Co-operation and Development.

Osterman, P. (2006). Community organizing and employee representation. *British Journal of Industrial Relations, 44*(4), 629–649.

Purcell, J., Purcell, K., & Tailby, S. (2004). Temporary work agencies: here today, gone tomorrow? *British Journal of Industrial Relations, 42* (4), 705–725.

Rainnie, A. (1989). *Employment relations in small firms.* London: Routledge.

Rainnie, A., Barrett, R., Burgess, J., & Connell, J. (2008). Introduction: call centres, the networked economy and the value chain. *Journal of Industrial Relations, 50*(2), 195–208.

Rubery, J., Marchington, M., Grimshaw, D., Carroll, M., & Pass, S. (2009). Employed under different rules: the Complexities of working across organizational boundarie. *Cambridge Journal of Regions, Economy and Society, 2*(2), 413–428.

Saundry, R., Antcliff, V., & Stuart, M. (2006). 'It's more than who you know' – networks and trade unions in the audio-visual industries. *Human Resource Management Journal, 16*(4), 376–392.

Scarborough, H. (2000). The HR implications of supply chain relationships. *Human Resource Management Journal, 10*(1), 5–17.

Shire, K., Schonauer, A., Valverde, N., & Mottweiler, H. (2009a). Collective bargaining and temporary contracts in call centre employment in Austria, Germany and Spain. *European Journal of Industrial Relations, 15*(4), 437–456.

Shire, K., Mottweiler, H., Schonauer, A., & Valverde, N. (2009b). Temporary work in coordinated market economies: evidence from front line service workers. *Industrial and Labour Relations Review, 62*(4), 602–617.

Taylor, P., & Cooper, C. (2008). 'It was absolute hell': inside the private prison. *Capital & Class, 96*, 3–30.

Van Jaarsveld, D., Kwon, H., & Frost, A. (2009). The effects of institutional and organizational characteristics on workforce flexibility: evidence from call centres in three liberal market economies. *Industrial and Labour Relations Review, 62*(4), 573–601.

Walsh, J. and Deery, S. (2006). Refashioning organizational boundaries: outsourcing customer service work. *Journal of Management Studies, 43*(3), 557–582.

Winfield, I., & Hay, A. (1997). Toyota's supply chain: changing employee relations. *Employee Relations, 19*(5), 457–465.

5
Franchise Firms: Changing Employment Relations?

Ashlea Kellner, Keith Townsend, and Adrian Wilkinson

Introduction

Modern franchises can be traced back to the turn of the 20th century when franchising began to emerge as the distribution model of choice in the automotive industry. Henry Ford lacked the required capital to establish company-owned chains to sell vehicles and so focussed his efforts on developing a network of dealers to both market and sell his product (Justis & Judd, 2003). This approach was so successful that it was replicated by other automotive businesses and is still a popular distribution model in the automotive industry. However, modern franchising began to develop more significantly in the mid 1950s, when Ray Croc and Colonel Harlan Sanders opened their iconic American franchises, McDonald's and Kentucky Fried Chicken respectively. Into the 1960s a plethora of businesses followed suit, operating franchise systems that sold products and services as varied as clothing retail, lawn mowing, and convenience stores (Justis & Judd, 2003). Franchising is currently the world's fastest growing form of retailing (Dant, 2008). Franchises are complex forms of organization and hold important implications for the future of employment relations (ER). Some of these implications are explored in this chapter.

Are franchises a developing form of organization?

Franchising has been described over time from differing perspectives as a marketing concept, an inter-organizational relationship, and a distinct organizational form (Spinelli & Birley, 1996; Stanworth & Curran, 1999; Stephenson & House, 1971). When considered as an organizational form, one party (the franchisor) grants the other party (the franchisee) the right to market or distribute their product or service using a market-tested business formula, trading under the company name (Elango & Fried, 1997; Felstead, 1991; Hing, 1995; Shane & Hoy, 1996). This relationship is bound by a long-term contract, a number of restrictions and controls, and the payment of royalties and fees to the franchise company (Felstead, 1993; Spinelli & Birley, 1996).

The term 'franchise firm' refers to the entire organization adopting the franchising model. The 'franchisor' is the centralized organization responsible for developing and managing the business concept. The franchisor offers the opportunity to 'franchisees' to enter into an agreement to operate 'franchise units', which are the stores or shops where the product or service is offered. Franchisees may own only one unit, whereby they are termed 'single-unit franchisees', or they may own more than one unit, making them 'multi-unit franchisees'.

Over time, two distinct approaches to franchising have developed, product franchising, and more recently, business format franchising. Product franchising, also known as first generation franchising, was the model of franchising originally adopted in the automotive industry and is still common in industries such as petrol service stations and soft drink bottlers (Felstead, 1993). In this model, the franchise relationship is outlined by a contract granting the franchisee the right to sell the franchisor's product or service in exchange for the payment of an ongoing fee. In product franchise firms, the franchisor is typically the manufacturer or producer seeking outlets for the sale of goods, or a product component manufacturer seeking a company who can complete and distribute the finished product (Felstead, 1993). In these arrangements, the franchisor may provide a basic level of preliminary business support, in areas such as advertising, location selection, and initial training, but generally, the franchisee operates independently, and ongoing support is not provided. The limited ongoing franchisor support is in contrast to the business format approach to franchising.

Business format franchising is far more comprehensive than the product approach as the franchisee purchases not only the right to sell a product or service, but a full system for business operation (Grant, 1985; Justis & Judd, 2003). This system encompasses a mix of services provided by the franchisor, devised to control, monitor, and support the franchisees' performance in the operation of the franchise unit (Baucus, Baucus, & Human, 1993). From the initial stage of entering the franchise agreement, the franchisee is generally provided with business support, which may include assistance with financing, site selection, training, set up, and opening of the store (Felstead, 1993). Following this phase, most franchise firms provide ongoing support with activities such as managing finances, marketing and promotions, and business management – often including employment relations.

Because the franchise has developed as a new organizational form, academic interest in the subject has focussed on some key areas of discussion. A review of the literature suggests that there are two key theories that shape much of the research into how and why franchise firms operate. Furthermore, there are a number of popular and current debates around issues such as the structure of franchise firms, factors that influence their success and failure, and the complexity of the franchise relationship.

Franchising: the key theories

There are two core theories that prevail in the majority of investigations into the operation of franchise systems, resource scarcity and agency theory. Resource scarcity theory suggests that firms may choose to adopt the franchise model in early years of operation as they lack the particular resources required for continual growth (Combs, Michael, & Castrogiovanni, 2004; Harmon & Griffiths, 2008; Tracey & Jarvis, 2007). Adopting the franchise approach provides the firm with access to the resources it requires: capital for retail expansion, managerial talent, and local knowledge (Combs, Ketchen, & Hoover, 2004; Grunhagen & Mittelstaedt, 2005; Inma, 2005). Although resource scarcity theory has made significant contributions to understanding the rationale for franchising, agency theory appears to have gained more support as the justifiable contribution to franchising theory (Combs & Castrogiovanni, 1994; Dant, 1996). Agency theory is concerned with the relationship between the principal (the franchisor), who delegates work to the agent and the agent (the franchisee), who performs the work (Eisenhardt, 1989). In the context of franchising, agency theory suggests that both parties' interests are divergent and that the franchisor must monitor the franchisees' behaviour or provide incentives to ensure their co-operation (Castrogiovanni, Combs, & Justis, 2006; Eisenhardt, 1989; Phan, Butler, & Lee, 1996).

Both resource scarcity and agency theory have assisted in understanding the concept of franchising and have received wide acceptance in the academic literature. However, there is mounting evidence which suggests that neither can adequately explain the franchising phenomena independently. For example, claims based on resource scarcity theory that large, mature franchise organizations will buy back their profitable units have been refuted in a number of studies (for references to this debate, see Combs & Castrogiovanni, 1994; Inma, 2005; LaFontaine & Kaufmann, 1994; Stanworth & Curran, 1999). Similarly, the theory does not explain why some large companies adopt the franchising model for growth (Kaufmann & Lafontaine, 1994). A challenge to agency theory is the advent of multi-unit franchising, which has seen franchisees employ salaried managers to supervise their additional stores, thereby decreasing managerial effectiveness and increasing reintroducing the costs of monitoring behaviour (Eisenhardt, 1989; Grunhagen & Mittelstaedt, 2005; Harmon & Griffiths, 2008; Inma, 2005; Patrick Kaufmann & Dant, 1996; Lafontaine, 1992). Resource scarcity and agency theories alone may not comprehensively explain all aspects of franchising, and perhaps a combination of theories, or the consideration of other existing theories in the franchise context may be a more appropriate way forward.

Ownership structure and success

The structure of individual unit management is a key area of research, particularly the propensity for organizations to allow franchisees to own multiple units (for instance, see Grunhagen & Mittelstaedt, 2005). Traditionally, throughout the research literature the franchisee was often assumed to play the dual role of franchisee and store manager of a single unit; however, it seems this no longer is the case. Studies have shown that single-unit operations are no longer the norm (see, for instance, Frazer, Weaven, & Wright, 2008; IFA, 2002), with one study as far back as 1996 suggesting that 88 per cent of franchised systems employ franchisees who own multiple units, which cannot all be managed by a single franchisee (Patrick Kaufmann & Dant, 1996). A preliminary study by Weaven and Herington (2007) has indicated that multi-unit systems may have a different approach to ER, displaying lower levels of initial training, staff development, and supervision than franchises with alternate governance structures. It is clear that the structure adopted within franchise firms may have an influence on the ER approach adopted by franchisees.

In addition to business structure, the causes of franchise success and failure are of high importance in the sector. Due to the difficulty in accessing data to assess franchise performance or success, measurement of business failure has been a common theme. However, even this is fraught with problems, such as lack of a central franchise database and inconsistent definition of 'failure' leading to contradictory results (Holmberg & Morgan, 2003). For instance, the variation in reported annual failure rates for franchisors has been reported to be as high as 10.5 per cent (Holmberg & Morgan, 2003), to 7.5 per cent (Shane, 1996) and as low as 4 per cent (Castrogiovanni, Justis, & Julian, 1993). Meanwhile, a small number of studies have investigated the potential causes of franchise failure and success. Studies have suggested that franchise failure can be related to franchisee deviation from prescribed systems (Frazer & Winzar, 2005) or the product mix (Hayashi, 2008), increasing age of the organization (Castrogiovanni et al., 1993) and industry effects such as the high concentration of franchises in the retail industry which is renowned for its high failure rates (Bates, 1995; Holmberg & Morgan, 2003). However, research has not adequately explored the potential relationship between ER support provided to the franchisee and the success or failure of their business. The relationship between franchisee support, particularly in ER activities, and the rate of franchisee success or failure is an interesting dichotomy; high quality support such as training is costly to provide but may be fundamental to achieving the levels of consistency required in a successful franchise organization.

The franchise relationship

In addition to theoretical debates and discussions of franchise business structure and success, another key research theme is the complex relationship between franchisor and franchisee. The franchise relationship can be likened to a marriage or a parent-child relationship. From the franchisees' perspective, they may prefer to describe the relationship as a marriage, an interdependent and equal partnership entered into for the purpose of mutual gain (Frazer & Winzar, 2005). However, to the franchisee it may feel more like a dependent relationship, where their autonomy and independence is constrained. Indeed, the franchise agreement generally limits the franchisees' control over core elements of business, such as product mix, pricing, or introduction of new non-standard products. Little is known about which party has greater responsibility for developing ER approaches, and it is possible that franchisees are afforded a high level of independence in this respect. The role, experience, and perspective of the franchisee is absent from the majority of franchising research, and a number of authors have called for further discussion in this area (Dant, 2008; Grunhagen & Dorsch, 2003; Harmon & Griffiths, 2008; Hing, 1995). There are many areas to investigate ER in franchises, in particular the experiences in managing ER in the context of a franchise firm.

Employment relations in franchise firms

While there is a body of literature that explores the recruitment process of franchisees (see, e.g. Clarkin & Swavely, 2006; Jambulingam & Nevin, 1999), there has been limited attention given to understanding how ER is managed within the franchise unit and between franchisee and franchisor. In a case study of an automotive retail company incorporating four separate franchises, Truss (2004) explores how ER operates in a franchise firm and gives examples from a number of functional activities. Truss explains that each of the four franchises operated recruitment and selection activities (among other ER functions) very inconsistently, despite working for the same company. For example, in each franchise the relationship between the manufacturer and the dealerships varied; while some dealerships exhibited authority over recruitment and selection procedures, others were controlled more by the manufacturer who conducted many of these activities on the dealer's behalf.

Litz and Stewart (2000) conducted an investigation into the relationship between employee training and performance in franchise organizations in comparison to independent organizations. Also, in a brief, preliminary analysis of the relationship between governance structures and the ER approach, Weaven and Herrington (2007) proposed that multi-unit franchises deliver lower levels of initial training than units adopting other structures. Although these studies contribute to the understanding of people management in franchises, they lack the rich, exploratory data required to provide a fundamental understanding of the core issues of training in franchise firms.

Existing research sheds some light on how ER may be operationalized in franchise firms, and suggests a less-than-satisfactory quality of employment for employees of franchise organizations. This view that franchise firms offer poor employment has been supported by researchers who suggest that they are characterized by young and unskilled workers, poor remuneration, low unionization, limited employee benefits, casual contracts, and shift work (Krueger, 1991; Royle, 1995; Schlosser, 2002). Although this appears to be the common perception, there are authors who argue that there is a labour market which relies on this sector to provide opportunities to gain paid employment without prior experience or qualifications, and offer flexible work hours and contracts (Allan, Bamber, Gould, & Timo, 2001; Cappelli & Hamori, 2008). Despite the stereotypical image of a franchise employee as a 17-year-old student flipping burgers in a fast food chain, employment in the franchise sector may be more complex than it seems.

Cappelli and Hamori (2008) challenged this common perception that franchise organizations are bad employers in their analysis of national employer survey data from franchised and non-franchised firms. In their examination of employment variables such as training, education, and remuneration, considerable evidence was found to suggest that employment in franchise organizations was in fact better than in independently owned organizations. Although franchised firms are concentrated in industries such as food and hospitality, where establishments are small and resources are few (Frazer, et al., 2008), franchise organizations adopted more sophisticated management practices and invested more heavily in their staff than independent organizations. Although the data for the survey was collected in 1996, the study was among a sample of 115 franchises across most industries and therefore offers some level of generalizability. This research suggests that employment conditions within franchise organizations are of a reasonable standard, and organizations invest in the role and activities of ER. Due to the significant limitations of the extant research, however, it is difficult to determine the impact of the firm's approach to ER on employment conditions without base knowledge of how it is managed.

Sector, structure, and size in franchising

In order to better understand ER in the context of franchises, we need to look at how franchise firms develop and operate. Franchise systems share common elements with other forms of business relating to their particular sector, structure, and size. This form of organization operates almost exclusively in the service sector, hence ER research in this area will likely offer insights into how people are managed in franchise organizations. Secondly, the structure of franchise systems represents a complex network of relationships surrounding a central head office organization, adding a separate dimension for consideration of the operation of ER. Finally, franchise systems generally comprise of a large business operated by the franchisor and numerous smaller units operated by the franchisee. The size of these businesses provides a final dimension by which to consider how ER is managed. Each of these dimensions offers a theoretical perspective through which to view the questions of how HR is managed in franchise firms.

Sector: managing people in the service sector

It is clear that the franchising concept has been most successfully applied in industries where service is the core component of business

(Baum, Li, & Usher, 2000; Cappelli & Hamori, 2008). In a service organization, there is an inseparability between the customer and the service provider, and this relationship is the cornerstone of the business (Paswan, Pelton, & True, 2005). The employees who deliver this service have a direct impact on customer perceptions of service quality, and therefore the management of human resources in such firms should be a significant consideration (Hallowell, Schlesinger, & Zornitsky, 1996; Schneider, 1994).

There is a long history of research providing a link between customer service outcomes and the systems of human resource management in service firms. A number of studies have identified specific HR activities which can indirectly influence the quality of customer service, with some dating as far back as the 1960s. For instance, in 1968 a research study suggested that there was a statistically significant correlation between employee and customer satisfaction (Friedlander & Pickle, 1968). Further on, in 1979, research showed that where employee role ambiguity and role conflict are low, customers reported that they had received superior service (Parkington & Schneider, 1979). Hallowell et al. (1996) suggest that functional teamwork and employee training were positively linked to customer satisfaction. A study by Paswan et al. (2005) conducted in a similar industry suggest that customers are likely to perceive service as being of a higher quality if they are served by a motivated employee.

Studies such as these provide evidence supporting the link between ER and customers' perceptions or experiences of service. However, implementing customer-focussed HR practices may be difficult due to factors both outside and inside the firm. For example, Boxall (2003: 12) suggests that in mass-service markets such as fast food franchises, competition is fierce and customers are very sensitive to price variations, which in turn has a significant effect on the HR strategy of the franchise. In these markets, firms generally do not pay above the minimum rate, and where possible, substitute labour with technology or self service in order to minimize costs. Furthermore, Schneider (1994: 68) suggests that assessment of HR effectiveness in service-based firms is often based on internally defined standards related to employee productivity rather than to customer-based outcomes. The research findings presented offer mixed perspectives of how HRM may be approached in franchise firms. The organization's support of the customer service-HR relationship may be strong or weak, and their approach may also be affected by a number of internal and external factors.

Structure: managing people in network-structured firms

Franchise systems are typically service-based operations; however they are structured in a less traditional network type arrangement. The franchisor operates inside what may be referred to as a 'permeable organization', a firm with blurred external boundaries that is based in the centre of a network structure of franchisees (Kelliher, Truss, & Hope-Hailey, 2004; Marchington, Grimshaw, Rubery, & Willmot, 2005). By exploring how a network of relationships operates, a better understanding of the conduct and performance of a firm can be gained (Kinnie, Swart, & Purcell, 2005). The network of relationships between the franchisor and franchisees has been identified as significant in the implementation of HR strategy in franchise systems; therefore it is imperative that the HR approach of a franchise organization is considered in the broad context of the entire system (Kelliher et al., 2004; Truss, 2004).

Research suggests that firms operating within networks of stakeholders can have limited freedom in developing and implementing their HR policies and practice, and may be influenced by more dominant members (Kinnie et al., 2005; Swart, Kinnie, & Purcell, 2004). In a franchise system, franchisees are not direct employees but small business owners and are likely to have some level of autonomy in their interpretation and application of company policy, particularly regarding non-operational aspects of business. For example, franchisees may be audited on the quality of their product or service as the customer expects this to be consistent; however their conduct of performance appraisals or employee inductions may carry less weight. This logic suggests that franchisees may be less dependent on the franchisor for direction in HRM in comparison to other operational activities. Furthermore, the concept of dominant members exerting influence in a network may also apply to franchise systems. In the franchise context, the dominant members may be the multi-unit franchisees, who inherently have more power over the single-unit operators.

Size: business size and people management approach

The typical structure of a franchise system consists of the franchisor and support staff operating in a head office location, and franchisee-owned businesses operating under the trading name of the parent company. The head office location would typically represent a large-sized firm, while the franchise units would operate with fewer staff as a small- to medium-sized enterprise. In Australia, for example, the majority of franchise head offices employ more than 200 employees, while franchise units typically have far fewer than 200 staff (ABS, 2008). By viewing the core components of franchise firms from perspective of their size, it enables comparisons to be drawn between them and similar independent organizations.

ER in the franchise head office – perspective of a large organization

The process of HR strategy development in franchise organizations is unknown in the academic literature; however research in other contexts can help to provide some insight. Research suggests that there is a positive relationship between the size of an organization and the likelihood that it will possess a formal business strategy. In a study by Forth, Bewley, & Bryson (2006), 88 per cent of large businesses surveyed possessed a business strategy, and the majority of these covered people management. In comparison, only 41 per cent of SMEs had developed a business strategy, and only around half of those included a section on managing employees. This discrepancy in development of HR strategy is likely due to large firms' access to resources required to staff a ER department, and their ability to hire professionals who are capable of developing strategy (Bayo-Moriones & Cerio, 2001). The franchisor-led head office is typically defined as a large organization, and therefore it is likely that for the most part, an HR department will exist and that the firm will have a developed business strategy with an HR component.

While the strategy and systems of people management may be primarily developed at the head office level, it is implemented at the level of the franchise unit. As previously discussed, franchise units can generally be categorized as SMEs; therefore the manner in which ER is managed in these firms may be influenced by their size. The following section will further define SMEs and briefly outline the literature on how ER is managed in these firms. This discussion will lead us closer to understanding how ER is managed in franchise firms.

HRM in the franchise unit – perspective of a SME

The significant proportion of franchisee-owned units fall into the category of SMEs. SMEs play a vital and increasingly important economic role; hence research interest in these firms has evolved, and understanding is beginning to catch up to the level of large organizations in some fields. However, ER research in this context is still rather undeveloped. This may be due to some common assumptions that research outcomes from large firms have universal relevance, and that small firms are simply embryonic large firms which must learn from their older counterparts and 'grow up' (Cassell, Nadin, Gray, & Clegg, 2002).

The ER literature that has developed in the field of SMEs tends to view these firms from two contradictory perspectives. As Wilkinson (1999) describes, the first perspective is that 'small is beautiful'; smaller firms communicate openly and informally and foster harmonious relationships between management and employees. This perspective was perhaps first represented in the Bolton Committee Report (1971) who suggested that smaller firms provide a better working environment than larger firms, with less conflict and a more motivated and committed workforce. These findings may be attributable to the high proportion of small businesses that are family owned (71 %) which has been noted as one of the most significant factors in influencing the management of people in small business (Wiseman, Roe, & Elliot, 2006).

On the other hand, some research has suggested that employment in SMEs is more of a 'bleak house' scenario (Sisson, 1993). Some authors have suggested that in smaller firms employment conditions are inadequate, health and safety is poor, union representation is low, and workplace conflict abounds (Dundon & Wilkinson, 2009). It is in such firms that the family-style approach often hides an authoritarian manager and employees who are forced to comply and do not dare question the status quo (Ram, 1994).

In reality, people management in these firms is more nuanced and multifaceted than simply an 'either/or' typology. Research into SMEs has produced some more objective findings which suggest that people management activities differ significantly according to organization size. For instance, SMEs are far less likely to have an ER department, employ ER specialists, or have an ER strategy compared to large organizations (Edwards & Ram, 2009). The lack of focus on ER in small firms is likely due in part to resource limitations, which lead to informal routines determining the daily operations of the firm rather than formal strategic plans (Matlay, 1999).

Given the classification of most franchise units as SMEs, ER practices in these firms may be comparable, characterized by traits such as informal external recruitment, limited formal training, and low levels of union membership. However, franchise units are unique in their structure as they are bound by a contract to the franchisor – a large organization – which would likely influence their ER approach. We have found that large organizations are likely to have a developed ER strategy, and this could affect the systems and practice on the shop floor. This raises a number of questions such as whether the franchisor has the same degree of interest in developing ER strategy and systems as would the CEO of a large firm, and the degree to which the franchisors' approach to ER influences the franchisee's practice in stores. Some direction may be found in a Workplace Employee Relations Survey conducted in the UK over ten years ago. This study found that small businesses belonging to larger parent companies (such as franchises) have a higher use of formal ER procedures than independent small businesses (Cully, Woodland, O'Reilly, & Dix, 1998). This suggests that the franchisor is likely to have developed ER systems and strategy and that it is adopted at the franchisee level. However, the limited research and lack of focus on franchising makes it difficult to substantiate such hypotheses (Allan, et al., 2001).

Conclusion

Although franchising has existed in its modern form for just over half a century, it has dominated markets in most of the Western world, growing at a phenomenal rate and significantly impacting international economies. However, the extent of the franchising boom has yet to meet its full potential, with franchising still emerging in new industries and developing markets such as Asia, South America, and Western Europe. As new franchise firms emerge each year across the globe, it is clear that franchising is still in its infancy and is a developing form of organization. Like many other developing organizational forms, our understanding of how they operate is limited, and there are still massive gaps where knowledge and research is required.

This chapter has discussed some of the extant research on the franchise business model from key theories, to firm performance and the franchise relationship. It has detailed the limited studies that have been undertaken in the field of ER and uncovered a clear deficiency in knowledge of how people are managed in franchise firms. In search of alternate theoretical perspectives to assist in understanding ER in franchises, the service sector was taken into consideration. As franchises operate primarily in this sector they are built around customer service, and research suggests that ER should be of great importance in such firms. However, network theory suggests that franchisees may operate quite separately to the franchisor and manage ER with a high degree of autonomy. Finally, a consideration of the size of franchise units and the head office present conflicting views of how ER may be managed; units may operate similarly to SMEs while the franchisor strives to manage

ER in a formal manner typical to a large firm. All theories considered, franchises may, in fact, operate completely differently to what any existing research suggests. A clear picture of the management of ER in franchise firms can be gained only through a commitment to increasing research knowledge in this developing form of organization.

References

ABS (2008). Selected characteristics of Australian business, 2007–08, cat. 8167.0: Australian Bureau of Statistics.

Allan, C., Bamber, G., Gould, A., & Timo, N. (2001). *Good job or bad job? Fast food employment in Australia.* Paper presented at the Employment Relations Stakeholders in the New Economy Conference and Symposium, Singapore.

Bates, T. (1995). Analysis of survival rates among franchise and independent small business startups. *Journal of Small Business Management, 33*(2), 26.

Baucus, D., Baucus, M., & Human, S. (1993). Choosing a franchise: how base fees and royalties relate to the value of the franchise. *Journal of Small Business Management, 31*(2), 91.

Baum, J., Li, S., & Usher, J. (2000). Making the next move: how experiential and vicarious learning shape the location of chains' acquisitions. *Administrative Science Quarterly 45*(4), 766–801.

Bayo-Moriones, J., & Cerio, J. (2001). Size and HRM in the Spanish manufacturing industry. *Employee Relations, 23*(2), 188–202.

Bolton Committee Report. (1971). Report of the Commission of Inquiry on Small Firms, Chaired by JE Bolton, *Cmnd 4811*. London: HMSO.

Boxall, P. (2003). HR strategy and competitive advantage in the service sector. *Human Resource Management Journal, 13*(3), 5–20.

Cappelli, P., & Hamori, M. (2008). Are franchises bad employers? *Industrial and Labor Relations Review, 61*, 147–162.

Cassell, C., Nadin, S., Gray, M., & Clegg, C. (2002). Exploring human resource management practices in small and medium sized enterprises. *Personnel Review, 31*(5/6), 671–692.

Castrogiovanni, G., Combs, J., & Justis, R. (2006). Resource scarcity and agency theory predictions concerning the continued use of franchising in multi-outlet networks. *Journal of Small Business Management, 44*(1), 27.

Castrogiovanni, G., Justis, R., & Julian, S. D. (1993). Franchise failure rates: an assessment of magnitude and influencing factors. *Journal of Small Business Management, 31*(2), 105.

Clarkin, J., & Swavely, S. (2006). The importance of personal characteristics in franchisee selection. *Journal of Retailing and Consumer Services, 13*, 133–142.

Combs, J., & Castrogiovanni, G. (1994). Franchisor strategy: a proposed model and empirical test of franchise versus company ownership. *Journal of Small Business Management, 32*(2), 37.

Combs, J., Ketchen, D., & Hoover, V. (2004). A strategic groups approach to the franchising-performance relationship. *Journal of Business Venturing, 19*(6), 877.

Combs, J., Michael, S. C., & Castrogiovanni, G. (2004). Franchising: a review and avenues to greater theoretical diversity. *Journal of Management, 30*(6), 907–931.

Cully, S., Woodland, S., O'Reilly, A., & Dix, G. (1998). *Britain at work as depicted in the 1998 workplace employee relations survey.* London: Routledge.

Dant, R. (1996). Motivations for franchising: rhetoric versus reality. *International Small Business Journal, 14*(1), 10–32.

Dant, R. (2008). A futuristic research agenda for the field of franchising. *Journal of Small Business Management, 46*(1), 91.

Dundon, T., & Wilkinson, A. (2009). HRM in small and medium sized enterprises. In G. Wood & D. Collings (Eds.), *Human Resource Management: A Critical Introduction.* London: Routledge.

Edwards, P., & Ram, M. (2009). HRM in Small Firms: Respecting and Regulating Informality. In A. Wilkinson, N. Bacon, T. Redman & S. Snell (eds), *The Sage Handbook of Human Resource Management* (pp. 524–540). London: Sage Publications.

Eisenhardt, K. M. (1989). Agency theory: an assessment and review. *Academy of Management Review, 14*(1), 57.

Elango, B., & Fried, V. (1997). Franchising research: a literature review and synthesis. *Journal of Small Business Management, 35*(3), 68.

Felstead, A. (1991). The social organisation of the franchise: a case of 'controlled self-employment'. *Work, Employment and Society, 5*(1), 37–57.

Felstead, A. (1993). *The corporate paradox: power and control in the business franchise.* London: Routledge.

Forth, J., Bewley, H., & Bryson, A. (2006). *Small and medium sized enterprises: findings from the 2004 Workplace Employment Relations Survey.* London: Routledge.

Frazer, L., Weaven, S., & Wright, O. (2008). *Franchising Australia 2008. The Franchise Council of Australia, Asia-Pacific Centre for Franchising Excellence, Griffith University.*

Frazer, L., & Winzar, H. (2005). Exits and expectations: why disappointed franchisees leave. *Journal of Business Research, 58*(11), 1534.

Friedlander, F., & Pickle, H. (1968). Components of effectiveness in small organisations. *Administrative Science Quarterly, 13*, 289–304.

Grant, C. (1985). *Business format franchising: a system for growth.* London: Economist Intelligence Unit.

Grunhagen, M., & Dorsch, M. (2003). Does the franchisor provide value to franchisees? Past, current, and future value assessments of two franchisee types. *Journal of Small Business Management, 41*(4), 366.

Grunhagen, M., & Mittelstaedt, R. (2005). Entrepreneurs or investors: do multi-unit franchisees have different philosophical orientations? *Journal of Small Business Management, 43*(3), 207.

Hallowell, R., Schlesinger, L. A., & Zornitsky, J. (1996). Internal service quality, customer and job satisfaction: linkages and implications for management. *Human Resource Planning, 19*(2), 20.

Harmon, T., & Griffiths, M. (2008). Franchisee perceived relationship value. *Journal of Business & Industrial Marketing, 23*(4), 256.

Hayashi, A. (2008). How to Replicate Success. *MIT Sloan Management Review, 49*(3), 6.

Hing, N. (1995). Franchisee satisfaction: contributors and consequences. *Journal of Small Business Management, 33*(2), 12.

Holmberg, S., & Morgan, K. B. (2003). Franchise turnover and failure: new research and perspectives. *Journal of Business Venturing, 18*(3), 403.

IFA (2002). Multi-unit owners study. Washington, DC: International Franchise Association Educational Foundation.

Inma, C. (2005). Purposeful franchising: re-thinking of the franchising rationale. *Singapore Management Review, 27*(1), 27.

Jambulingam, T., & Nevin, J. (1999). Influence of franchisee selection criteria on outcomes desired by the franchisor. *Journal of Business Venturing, 14*(4), 363.

Justis, R., & Judd, R. (2003). *Franchising*. Ohio: Thomson Custom Publishing.

Kaufmann, P., & Dant, R. (1996). Multi-unit franchising: growth and management issues. *Journal of Business Venturing, 11*(5), 343.

Kaufmann, P., & Lafontaine, F. (1994). Costs of control: the source of economic rents for mcdonald's franchisees. *Journal of Law and Economics, 37*(2), 417–453.

Kelliher, C., Truss, C., & Hope-Hailey, V. (2004). Disappearing between the cracks: HRM in permeable organisations. *Management Revue, 15*(3), 305–323.

Kinnie, N., Swart, J., & Purcell, J. (2005). Influences on the choice of HR system: the network organisation perspective. *International Journal of Human Resource Management, 16*(6), 1004–1028.

Krueger, A. (1991). Ownership, agency, and wages: an examination of franchising in the fast food industry. *Quarterly Journal of Business and Economics, 106*(2), 75–101.

Lafontaine, F. (1992). Agency theory and franchising: some empirical results. *Rand Journal of Economics, 23*(2), 263.

LaFontaine, F., & Kaufmann, P. (1994). The evolution of ownership patterns in franchise systems. *Journal of Retailing, 70*(2), 97–113.

Litz, R., & Stewart, A. (2000). Research note: trade name franchise membership as a human resource management strategy: does buying group training deliver 'true value' for small retailers? *Entrepreneurship Theory and Practice, 25*(1), 125.

Marchington, M., Grimshaw, D., Rubery, J., & Willmot, H. (2005). *Fragmenting Work*. New York: Oxford University Press.

Matlay, H. (1999). Employee relations in small firms. *Employee Relations, 21*(3), 285–295.

Parkington, J., & Schneider, B. (1979). Some correlates of job stress: a boundary role study. *Academy of Management Journal, 22*, 270–281.

Paswan, A., Pelton, L., & True, S. (2005). Perceived managerial sincerity, feedback-seeking orientation and motivation among front-line employees of a service organization. *Journal of Services Marketing, 19*(1), 3–12.

Phan, P., Butler, J., & Lee, S. (1996). Crossing mother: entrepreneur-franchisees' attempts to reduce franchisor influence. *Journal of Business Venturing, 11*(5), 379.

Ram, M. (1994). *Managing to Survive: Working Lives in Small Firms*. Oxford, UK: Blackwell.

Royle, T. (1995). Corporate versus societal culture: a comparative study of McDonald's in Europe. *International Journal of Contemporary Hospitality Management, 7*(2), 52.

Schlosser, E. (2002). *Fast Food Nation*. London: Penguin.

Schneider, B. (1994). HRM – A service perspective: towards a customer-focused HRM. *International Journal of Service Industry Management, 5*(1), 64.

Shane, S. (1996). Hybrid organizational arrangements and their implications for firm growth and survival: a study of new franchisors. *Academy of Management Journal, 39*(1), 216–234.

Shane, S., & Hoy, F. (1996). Franchising: a gateway to co-operative entrepreneurship. *Journal of Business Venturing, 11*, 325–327.

Sisson, K. (1993). In search of HRM. *British Journal of Industrial Relations, 31*(2), 201–210.

Spinelli, S., & Birley, S. (1996). Toward a theory of conflict in the franchise system. *Journal of Business Venturing, 11*(5), 329.

Stanworth, J., & Curran, J. (1999). Colas, burgers, shakes, and shirkers: towards a sociological model of franchising in the market economy. *Journal of Business Venturing, 14*(4), 323.

Stephenson, P. R., & House, R. G. (1971). A perspective on franchising: the design of an effective relationship. *Business Horizons, 14*(4), 35–42.

Swart, J., Kinnie, N., & Purcell, J. (2004). Human resource advantage in the network organisation. *Management Revue, 15*(3), 288–304.

Tracey, P., & Jarvis, O. (2007). Toward a theory of social venture franchising. *Entrepreneurship Theory and Practice, 31*(5), 667.

Truss, C. (2004). Who's in the driving seat? Managing human resources in a franchise firm. *Human Resource Management Journal, 14*(4), 57.

Weaven, S., & Herington, C. (2007). Factors influencing governance choice and human resource management within services franchising networks. *Journal of Management and Organization, 13*(2), 126–144.

Wilkinson, A. (1999). Employment relations in SMEs. *Employee Relations, 21*(3), 206–217.

Wiseman, J., Roe, P., & Elliot, J. (2006). Annual survey of small businesses: UK 2004–2005. *Department of Trade and Industry Research Report.* London.

Part II

New Perspectives on Employment

6
Engaged in What? So What? A Role-Based Perspective for the Future of Employee Engagement

Theresa M. Welbourne

Employee engagement is a topic that has evolved considerably. As it has increased in popularity, the quest to define what it is has continued. For example, Storey, Ulrich, Welbourne & Wright (2009), in their chapter on employee engagement, discuss the various groups that provide definitions of the topic. They start out talking about the definitions proposed by various corporations (e.g. Caterpillar, Dell), then move to the approaches used by consulting firms (e.g. Corporate Leadership Council, Gallup), and next suggest a few definitions provided by academics (e.g. Kahn, 1990; Shaw, 2005). The conclusion, reached by many other authors working in the area, is that engagement describes a process or a set of outcomes versus a clear and agreed upon construct.

At a recent Conference Board meeting on employee engagement (Los Angeles, November, 2010, Senior Communications Program), the audience was asked how their organizations defined employee engagement. At the end of the discussion, one had to ask the question: 'what is it not?' The answers ranged from traditional academic areas of work (e.g. job satisfaction, job involvement, commitment, organization citizenship) to emotional descriptors (e.g. when employees love the company), to statements about well being and fairness (e.g. people bring their 'whole selves' to work), and lastly to company-specific programs (e.g. inspiration, innovation, creativity, caring for the community).

In the exploration of what employee engagement might be, authors also have attempted to break employee engagement up into various parts, such as psychological state engagement, behavioural engagement, and trait engagement (Macey & Schneider, 2008). In some cases, they agree to simply give up with the definitive approach to what employee engagement is and study it because the topic is very popular and does appear to be associated with good outcomes (MacLeod &

Clarke, 2010). In a few rare cases, the topic of employee engagement comes under criticism. For example, a *Forbes* writer (Luisa Kroll) wrote a short piece in September, 2005 that quotes Randall MacDonald of IBM saying 'Soon we'll be talking about marrying all those employees to whom we're engaged.' Ed Frauenheim, a writer for Workforce (2009) wrote an article titled 'A skeptical view of engagement', where he cites professionals who warn about the 'one-size fits all' approaches to employee engagement.

However, it is very difficult to find anything negative in print about employee engagement because it sounds so good. Employee engagement speaks to something most social scientists, employees, and managers truly believe, and that is the fact that when employees go 'above and beyond' and are not just robots doing a simple, repetitive job, then organizations do better. Who can argue with that?

There are volumes of literature and research on employee commitment, empowerment, motivation, organization citizenship research, job satisfaction work, and more that point to the importance of employees in driving performance. This quest is what the fields of organization behaviour, organization development, human resource management, and more are all about.

Thus the point made in this chapter is that employee engagement is an effort worth pursuing. It puts a name on something we know matters to people, society, and business. However, in this chapter the suggestion will be made that employee engagement is not a construct at all. It is a field of study, and it may very well be an industry. Thus instead of focusing any more attention on trying to make employee engagement into a scientific construct, unique from what has been validated and studied using theory and research for many years, this chapter suggests moving beyond the definition and focusing on outcomes. This can be the future of employee engagement. Said another way, consider the 'engaged in what' question.

Could employee engagement be an industry?

The beauty of employee engagement, one could say then, is that it can be everything to everybody. Saks (2006, p. 601) notes that 'most of what has been written about employee engagement can be found in practitioner journals where it has its basis in practice rather than theory and empirical research.' However, with the thousands and thousands of articles, blogs, and magazine pieces on this topic, it is obvious that what the topic lacks in rigour, it makes up for in popularity.

Table 6.1 The words of employee engagement

Authors	Theories or other literature cited when discussing definitions of employee engagement
Macey & Schneider (2008)	Involvement, commitment, attachment, mood, citizenship behaviour, effort, pro-social behaviour, disposition, loyalty, productivity, ownership, job satisfaction, and at some point they point out that it could be 'some combination of the above'
Saks (2006)	Organizational commitment, organizational citizenship, emotional and intellectual commitment, discretionary effort, attention, absorption, antithesis of burnout, energy, involvement, efficacy, cynicism, exhaustion, state of mind, vigour, dedication, absorption
Ferrer (2005)	Job satisfaction, enthusiasm, motivation for work, positive attitude, feeling involved and valued, organization commitment
Report to the UK government by David MacLeod and Nita Clarke (2010)	Commitment, energy, potential, creativity, personal attachment to work, positive attitude, authentic values, trust, fairness, mutual respect, discretionary effort, job satisfaction
The Conference Board report on Employee Engagement (2006)	Cognitive commitment, emotional attachment, connection, discretionary effort, emotional drivers (pride, relationships with manager), rational drivers (pay and benefits), satisfaction. Focus on drivers of engagement, which include trust and integrity, nature of the job, line of sight between individual and company performance, career growth, pride, co-worker and team relationships, employee development, and relationship with one's manager
Kular, Gatenby, Rees, Soane, and Truss (2008)	Role performance, intellectual and emotional commitment, discretionary effort, passion for work, job involvement, flow, organization citizenship behaviours

In a sense, employee engagement has been part of the academic community because the components of employee engagement or what the business leaders, consultants, and interested parties are talking about has been studied in detail by the academic world for many years. Below are examples of what authors writing about employee engagement refer to or reference when they speak of engagement (Table 6.1 is developed to give the reader a sense of the types of theory and bodies of work discussed when employee engagement definitions are attempted; it is not an exhaustive list):

Table 6.1 is not meant to be all inclusive or even to introduce a new definition of employee engagement. It was designed to illustrate how this very broad and all inclusive thing called employee engagement has become. The lack of definition and evidence that employee engagement really is not new has not stopped work in this direcction. The 152-page report on employee engagement prepared by David MacLeod and Nita Clarke (2010) provide some insights into why employee engagement may be better labelled an industry, and why it likely will continue in that form for many years to come. The authors note the following (p. 8):

> Early on in the review, when we spoke to David Guest, Professor of Organizational Psychology and Human Resource Management at King's College London, he pointed out that much of the discussion on engagement tends to get muddled as to whether it is an attitude, a behavior or an outcome or, indeed, all three. He went on to suggest that ... 'the concept of employee engagement needs to be more clearly defined [...] or it needs to be abandoned.' We have decided, however, that there is too much momentum and indeed excellent work being done under the banner of employee engagement to abandon the term.

When discussing the research that provides the compelling business case, the authors then go on to state that (p. 13):

> there is no single study that has provided beyond doubt that engagement explains higher performance, or improving engagement causes improved productivity and performance ... taken together (the cases) offer a very compelling case.

There are some very highly publicized outcomes of employee engagement. Studies from firms such as Gallup (2006) cite data with 23,910 business units, while Towers-Perrin ISR in the same year produced a report with data from 664,000 employees. These studies show that firms in the top scoring quartiles in the employee engagement survey have higher performance than organizations in the lower performing quartile on their surveys. These big statistics are then supplemented with case studies showing primarily how doing an employee survey and then taking action on the data makes the workplace better and then leads to measurable business outcomes.

The firm-level studies have tended to focus on employee survey data. The questions are different from study to study; however, they show relationships between survey scores and measures of firm performance. These studies suggest that employee engagement, regardless of what one agrees to use as a definition, is associated with higher performance. The well published findings have led to growing interest not only in improving employee engagement to lead to higher performance but also in doing employee surveys as the catalyst to the process.

Assumptions about employee engagement survey scores

When scores go up, employees are engaged. When scores go down, employees are disengaged. Having higher scores is better. Being engaged is the preferable state to being disengaged. It seems that the goal of employee engagement is to figure out what it is about employees that drives performance and then once the secret is uncovered, employers can take steps to improve bottom-line performance. To date, a lot of work has focused on employees' surveys, which are dependent on some sort of definition of employee engagement. However, we continue to be in a state where there is lack of consensus about the term employee engagement.

Newman and Harrison (2008) suggest that employee engagement indeed is nothing new. The title of their article starts with 'Been there, bottled that', and they go on to argue that employee engagement should be considered a higher order construct, or an overall mega job attitude (they provide a helpful table that links engagement survey questions to existing constructs). This chapter spells out a point of view that focuses the answer in a different direction. Employee engagement, whatever it is, can be helpful to a company only if it leads to behaviours that the organization needs in order to execute its strategy and to be successful. This suggests that there are likely some types of employee engagement behaviours are not ideal, thus, making the employee engagement process more complex than it would be if we were talking about simply raising scores on a mega construct survey.

Does raising scores on any employee engagement survey question really lead to improved firm performance? Although there are many research reports published on engagement, none have provided conclusive evidence of this link. There are questions of causality, lack of adequate control variables, and the rather irritating problem of not knowing what employee engagement really is that continue to plague interpretations of the findings.

In addition, what if all the disaster cases are unpublished? There are, for example, cases of firms winning the 'most engaged company' award and declaring poor performance very soon after receiving these awards (e.g. see discussion started by Paul Kearns on www. energizeengage.com). In the behavioural sciences, research proceeds from simple to complex, showing that mediator and moderator variables are important in understanding the effects of attitudes on performance. To date, very little work has been done including more complex modelling of the employee engagement research. This means that there may be some conditions under which the employee engagement treatment that is being given does not apply equally to all employees.

From a pure onlooker perspective, given the popularity of employee engagement, one may wonder why the economy has not picked up sooner. The lack of rising revenues alone may give us one reason to ponder the possibility that maybe employee engagement, with its lack of definition, is not the magic answer to improved performance. Maybe there is something more, and the future of employee engagement should be focused on that line of work.

Maybe the quest is off target

Perhaps the answer lies in something other than employee engagement. If we accept that employee engagement is indeed an industry (not just a simple construct), and that the 'idea' of employee engagement is to find the thing about employees that improves firm performance, then we can get past worrying about what employee engagement is and redirect effort. With that goal in mind, there appear to be two things missing from the discussions of employee engagement. They are both related to the target of engagement or the 'engaged in what' question.

1. Engaged in what behaviours? Employees can be engaged in baking cookies all day, but if you are not a bakery that sells lots of cookies,

this particular activity may not drive business success. There seems to be consensus that employee engagement leads to 'above and beyond' behaviours, and in many cases this is defined as organizational citizenship behaviours. However, that's a fairly simple answer to what we are seeing is a complex phenomenon.
2. What do employees get in exchange for being more engaged? To date, the discussions appear to be somewhat one way in nature. Employees need to be engaged rather than disengaged; they need to go above and beyond, and they need to expend discretionary effort, but what do they get in return?

Redirect the conversation to role-based performance

Rather than continue the discussion about being engaged or disengaged, the next section aims to redirect the conversation to the outcomes of employee engagement. However, the focus is on employee behaviour versus firm-level outcomes. In order to further streamline the behaviours studied a role-based perspective is applied. By using roles at work to understand outcomes, researchers and business executives can access a lens that is generalizable across industries, cultures, and people. Examining roles is not new; in fact, many of the employee engagement researchers refer to Kahn (1990) as providing some of the earliest work on employee engagement, and in his early research, Kahn frames engagement using role theory. Although the use of roles in learning about employee engagement is not a recent phenomenon, what is uniquely explored in this chapter is the focus on five work-related roles simultaneously in the study of employee engagement. The reason we focus on more than one role at a time is because to do otherwise limits understanding of the consequences of engagement as it is practiced. It is quite possible that the employee engagement intervention has a positive effect on one role while also creating a negative effect on other role-based behaviours.

For example, let's take an example described in many practitioner articles. In this case, employee engagement leads to 'above and beyond' behaviours, and for the sake of this discussion we specifically define 'above and beyond' as organizational citizenship behaviour (doing things good for the company that are not part of the core job). Does an employee reduce the time devoted to the core job in order to find the hours needed for the 'above and beyond' work? When engagement is defined as volunteering for outside work activities (an example of citizenship), there is a commitment to time that must be considered.

And if the employee is doing the core job work and citizenship behaviours, what about spending time in other roles at work? Does doing citizenship behaviours have a negative impact on innovation? What happens to the employee's time needed for career development and for helping teams? The premise behind the roles lens is that employees have a limited amount of time, and employees and managers need to have clear and regular discussions about how employees should spend their time at work.

Jessica Pryce-Jones (2010) wrote a short piece called 'Protect your energy at work' where she helps the reader understand that there is a limited amount of energy that people have to use at work. The roles terminology provides a way for managers to have conversations with employees about what roles they should be engaged in. If done well, the roles lens will provide guidance for managers who can then help employees balance their time on the right activities, not just more actions.

The roles-based research used for this chapter identifies five roles that are important at work (Welbourne, Johnson & Erez, 1998). Short descriptions of each follow:

1. Core functional job holder role (think of this as the core functional work that is in the job description or associated with one's professional occupation).
2. Entrepreneur or innovator role (improving process, coming up with new ideas, helping others implement innovations).
3. Team member role (participating in teams, working with others in different jobs).
4. Career role (learning, engaging in activities to improve skills and knowledge).
5. Organizational member role (citizenship role or doing things that are good for the company).

What is new and unique about applying the role-based work noted above to the topic of employee engagement is that all five roles are considered simultaneously. When looking at all of the roles at the same time, one can see that interventions can have positive impacts on behaviour in one role while having negative impacts on other roles. Thus tradeoffs are visible, and they are not evident when one role is studied in isolation. Unfortunately, most of the research done to date in the area of employee engagement has focused on one role at the expense of understanding the impact on the whole person or at least on the multiple roles people engage in at work.

Linking engagement with role-based outcomes

Most of the employee engagement research to date has been focused on the predictors of employee engagement, with different definitions of employee engagement being used in almost every study. However, a number of consultant-based studies link employee engagement survey scores to overall firm performance (e.g. studies done by Gallup, Towers Watson, Mercer, and other consultants). These data provide inspiration that employee engagement processes change employee behaviour and then lead to organizational outcomes; however, the specific process by which these human behaviours happen is not studied.

To get a sense of how much work is devoted to defining engagement versus understanding the outcomes, take a few literature reviews as examples. Robertson-Smith and Markwick (2009) prepared a report for the Institute of Employment Studies on employee engagement, and four of their 61 pages are devoted to the outcomes of employee engagement. In this section, they cite firm-level outcomes (e.g. profitability, successful organizational change) and a number of employee-centred results (e.g. retention, loyalty, productivity, advocacy of the organization). None of the studies cited included outcomes that would be in multiple roles and then most research examining individual-level outcomes do not go on to focus on the overall impact of those same employee-centred consequences with firm performance. The studies hint at the outcomes; however, the models and research linking employee engagement to firm performance are incomplete. Another example is a literature review by Kular, Gatenby, Rees, Soane, and Truss (2008) They have a section on the antecedents and consequences of employee engagement (pp. 6–9).

A review of the research shows that most of these limited studies focus on two of the roles in the role-based performance work. The main area of work seems to be addressing the core job role and the organizational member role (e.g. citizenship behaviour).

For example, Saks (2006) examined predictors of job satisfaction and intention to quit, both of which we would classify under the core job role. The Saks research also encompassed organizational commitment and citizenship behaviours, which represent the organization member role. Rich, Lepine, and Crawford (2010) published a study that examined engagement's effects on task performance (core job role) and citizenship behaviour (organization member role). Harter, Schmidt, and Hayes (2002) conducted a meta analysis of employee satisfaction and engagement and produced results for two job-related dependent variables, productivity, and turnover. Sonnentag (2003) examined the relationship between recovery and engagement and then engagement and behaviours that come under the career or learner role. Carmeli, Waldman, and Rupp (2009) study vigour (a measure of engagement of energy) and core job-related outcomes (ratings of job performance).

In terms of roles other than the core job role and the organizational member role, there is less research and mention of the consequences of engagement on these outcomes. One reads references to practices such as Google's popular model of giving employees 20 per cent of their time for innovation; however, no one (that we know) has studied the impact of engagement at Google simultaneously on core job, innovation, team, career, and organizational member-based behaviours. Systematic study of all five roles is non-existent at this point in time.

Employee engagement literature and role-based performance

The contribution of the role-based work points to one other important concern. Can organizations increase job and organization role-based performance, for example, and not affect other aspects of work? Can leaders expect employees to do more of the non-core job roles and still keep doing more of the core job role? For example, think about your own work. How easy is it to continue to come to your place of work and deliver on the core-job aspects while at the same time be a good citizen and do things for the company that are not part of your core job? And on top of these duties, can you spend time on innovative ideas, helping other teams, advancing your own knowledge and career, and taking on a few non-work related roles (e.g. husband, wife, father, church leader, community member, etc.)?

Are today's organizations asking employees to be super people who go above and beyond in everything? The notion is not sound. However, the employee engagement literature has not dealt with 'engaged in what'; therefore, to date, the positive of employee engagement is featured without looking, as much, at the potential negative consequences.

The core job alone may be resulting in burnout and exhaustion

One of the other key contributions of the role-based work has been to diagnose the amount of time it takes to do just the core job role. We are finding in many of our research sites that the mere mention of employee engagement gets middle managers up in arms. They are being asked to do more than one core job due to layoffs, and then adding the task of engaging their employees is one more burden.

If organizations really want citizenship behaviours, innovation, and other non-core job role behaviours, then they have to figure out how to support employees engaging in those behaviours. This work is needed, but it is not being done in most organizations. What we are calling for is deliberate attention to what employees should be engaged in so that policies, systems, leaders, managers, and reward systems can align the rest of the organization around the role-based behaviours.

What's missing is an examination of all role-based behaviours simultaneously and links to strategy

By limiting conversations to just one or two roles at a time, as has been done in most of the employee engagement literature, performance is not ideally linked to business strategy. It's highly inappropriate to assume that all businesses at all times benefit from 'above and beyond' organizational citizenship behaviours or that firms always benefit from innovation. There may be times when employees should focus simply on their core job and not worry about the 'above and beyond'. In fact, there are cases when employees get so enamoured with the citizenship behaviours that this activity takes time away from the job and causes negative performance outcomes for themselves and their peers.

Business strategies demand different types of roles; various departments require unique weightings of role-based work, and lastly, seasonality, task demands, and impact what roles employees should be engaged in to drive success.

Lessons learned from role-based research:

- The non-core job roles drive competitive advantage and long-term firm performance.
- Engaging in non-core job roles takes time away from the core job.
- In many firms, regardless of what is being communicated, pay increases and promotions are based only on the core job role.

- Using the language of the roles helps managers and employees focus on what's important to drive business strategy because the roles are more concrete than concepts like 'above and beyond' behaviours.
- Role-based discussions need to occur regularly because things change, and the importance of roles are altered seasonally and as business needs are altered.
- Employees want to engage in the non-core job roles, but not everyone really wants to do all of them equally.
- The non-core job roles help build strong and positive relational capital within and outside the firm (e.g. when working on teams, you get to know more people; when developing innovations, employees cross over to other departments to learn).
- The non-core job roles create challenge for employees (challenge builds positive and strong relational capital).

Core and non-core roles and firm performance

Firm-specific competitive advantage is not gained through employees doing only the core job (Barney, 1990). If employees spend time in only the core job, then a competitor can easily replicate what they are doing and move the work to a country where people can be trained to do the same activities for less money.

A firm's long-term competitive advantage is built with the non-core job roles. The activities that bring firm-specific competitive advantage are innovating and supporting new idea development and deployment (innovator role); teams working together in unique ways, creating synergy that is not easily copied (team member roles); employees supporting the company in ways that bring in more business, being fans of the firm, and spreading the word about new products (organizational member role); and continually learning so that they can improve their performance and the work of others (career or learner role). This is because non-core job roles cannot be easily copied. The key to driving success, then, is knowing which non-core job roles are important for what groups of employees at what time – in order to drive business strategy and goals.

What does the employee get when they are engaged in new roles?

Reading through the mass of models, definitions, and studies on employee engagement, one is struck by the lack of equity in the concept.

The talk is all about employees; however, the only one appearing to get anything out of the newfound interest in employees doing more is the employer. There is no explicit contract associated with the 'above and beyond' work that employees are being asked to do. Perhaps this is why we continue to see statistics from national polls showing lower job satisfaction and employee engagement levels.

This lack of connection between rewards and non-core job role behaviour may be due to the fact that employers don't know what they are really getting when they start an employee engagement program. If the definition is unclear, and outcomes are not specified, then employers are going to be hesitant to set up any type of new employment relationship based on employees being more engaged.

However, given that the origins of the role-based model have its roots in identity theory, role theory, and the compensation literature, then perhaps the roles-based model can be useful in thinking through the 'so what' question that is also part of employee engagement. If employees engage, then 'so what' or what do they receive in return? At the organizational level, performance management systems need to change so that employees who take time away from the core job to spend on important non-core job roles are not punished. Rewards for success in non-core job roles need to be developed, implemented, and communicated. Unfortunately, in many organizations, employees are expected to become 'engaged' and spend more time and energy in the non-core roles at the expense of their own job performance and with no recognition or rewards.

One-more role: the non-work role

Lastly, let's not forget that there is life beyond work. This is a topic becoming more important in the employee engagement research as studies find employees, trying to do perhaps all roles and more, are experiencing burnout, health problems, disengagement, and what Macey, Schneider, Barbera, and Young (2009) call the dark side of engagement. They state: 'too much of an engagement culture can also have bad consequences, including burnout, disengagement, and other negative and psychological behavioral outcomes.' (p. 137) This caution is echoed by Jim Loehr and Tony Schwartz (2003), where they discuss ways to manage and replenish energy at work.

From an organization's perspective, it is very difficult to know what non-work roles people are engaged in and how they are affecting their energy levels at work. Therefore, organizations must strive to do what they can at work. What this chapter is calling for is a move to deliberate discussions on what employers need and want employees to be engaged in at work, what sacrifices, if any, employees are expected to make and then to help employees manage their work and non-work roles in a way that does not lead to burnout and total disengagement from the organization.

There's an old saying: 'you manage what you measure.' One would think that the tremendous influx of employee engagement and the survey frenzy that has come with it would be good for employees. However, with all the positive talk about engagement, the research is inconclusive. It is very difficult to make adequate conclusions when the key construct in question may not even be a construct, when the performance part of the equation is in doubt, and when perhaps the combination of lack of definition and unfocused performance discussions put employees sadly in the middle.

Conclusion

This chapter began by stating that employee engagement is an industry, not a construct. The evidence seems to point to employee engagement evolving into a term that represents overall people management at work. This is not necessarily a negative outcome of the employee engagement work; however, it has the potential to lead to much confusion in the minds of everyone working on employee engagement initiatives.

The suggestion to focus on 'engaged in what' with the roles-based work as a solution to start building models and clarifying the work offers a solution for moving forward or for the future of employee engagement. The roles proposed were validated and have been used in several studies; therefore, they present a reasonable start towards a more complete model. In my research, I have linked competencies to the roles and developed 360 tools using the roles. They are robust and easy to apply within businesses.

However, the five roles introduced in this chapter may not be the complete solution for every organization. There may be roles that are critical and that are not included in this list. For some firms, they may prefer to go directly to their business strategy to answer the 'engaged in what' question. Other organizations may want to focus on competencies. Regardless of what solution is best, the aim of this chapter is to challenge the current state of the work in the employee engagement industry to move forward.

References

Carmeli, A., Ben-Hador, B,, Waldman, D. A., & Rupp, D. E. (2009). How leaders cultivate social capital and nurture employee vigor: implications for job performance. *Journal of Applied Psychology, 94*(6), 1553–1561.

Conference Board, The. (2010). *Senior corporate communications management conference.* November 3–5, 2010. Davidson Conference Center on the Campus of USC, Los Angeles, CA.

Ferrer, J. (2005). Employee engagement: is it organizational commitment renamed? (Victoria University, School of Management, Working Paper Series). Melbourne: Victoria University.

Frauenheim, E. (2009). 'A skeptical view of engagement'. *Workforce Management Online* December.

Gibbons, J. M. (2006). *Employee engagement: a review of current research and its implications.* (Conference Board Report Number: E-0010–06-RR). New York: The Conference Board.

Harter, J. K., Schmidt, F. L., & Hayes, T. A. (2002). Business-unit-level relationship between employee satisfaction, employee engagement, and business outcomes: a meta-analysis. *Journal of Applied Psychology, 87*(2), 268–279.

Kahn, W. A. (1990). Psychological conditions of personal engagement and disengagement at work. *Academy of Management Journal, 33*(4), 692–724.

Kroll, K. (2005, September 15). No employee left behind. *Forbes Online.* Retrieved December 15, 2010, from http://www.forbes.com/forbes/2005/1003/060. html

Kular, S., Gatenby, M., Rees, C., Soane, E., & Truss, K. (2008). *Employee engagement: a literature review.* Kingston Hill: Kingston University.

Loehr, J. & Schwartz, T. (2003). *The power of full engagement: managing energy, not time, is the key to high performance and personal renewal,* New York: The Free Press.

Macey, W. H., & Schneider, B. (2008). The meaning of employee engagement. *Industrial and Organizational Psychology, 1*(1), 3–30.

Macey, W. H., Schneider, B., Barbera, K. M., & Young, S. A. (2009). *Employee engagement: tools for analysis, practice, and competitive advantage.* Rolling Meadows, IL: Wiley-Blackwell.

MacLeod, D., & Clarke, N. (2010). *Engaging for success: enhancing performance through employee engagement.* Surrey: Department for Business Innovation and Skills.

Newman, D. A., & Harrison, D. A. (2008). Been there, bottled that: are state and behavioral work engagement new and useful construct 'wines'? *Industrial and Organizational Psychology, 1*(1), 31–35.

Pryce-Jones, J. (2010, June 11). Protect your energy at work. *Psychology Today.* Retrieved from http://www.psychologytoday.com/blog/happiness-work/201006/protect-your-energy-work

Rich, B. L., Lepine, J. A., & Crawford, E. R. (2010). Job engagement: antecedents and effects on job performance. *Academy of Management Journal, 53*(3), 617–635.

Robertson-Smith, G., & Markwick, C. (2009) *Employee engagement: a review of current thinking.* (IES White Paper). Brighton, UK: Institute for Employment Studies.

Saks, A. M. (2006). Antecedents and consequences of employee engagement. *Journal of Managerial Psychology, 21*(7), 600–619.

Shaw, K. (2005). *Employee engagement: how to build a high performance workforce,* Chicago: Melcrum Publishing Limited.

Sonnentag, S. (2003). Recovery, work engagement, and procactive behavior: a new look at the interface between nonwork and work. *Journal of Applied Psychology, 88*(3), 518–528.

Storey, J., Ulrich, D., Welbourne, T. M., & Wright, P. M. (2009). Employee engagement. In J. Storey, P. Wright, & D. Ulrich (eds) *The Routledge Companion to Strategic Human Resource Management* (pp. 299–315). New York: Routledge.

Welbourne, T. M., Johnson, D., & Erez, A. (1998). The role-based performance scale: validity analysis of a theory-based measure. *Academy of Management Journal, 41(1),* 50–55.

7
Developing a Contemporary Approach to Conceptualizing Employee Actions

Keith Townsend and James Richards

Introduction

Work and employment have changed dramatically in recent decades, and it is reasonable to assume that dramatic changes will continue into the future. As the way people work changes, so must the conceptual lenses with which we examine the workplace and associated issues. Our interest in this chapter lies primarily in understanding what workers do outside the formal, consensual, and expected actions in the workplace. This chapter argues that a range of disciplines develop sound and reasonable explanations of action choices made by labour (individually, collaboratively, or collectively). Typically, critical scholars have examined resistance with consent (each with a variety of different names) as two distinct and separate avenues for employees to act in the workplace. However, it is only when the totality of action alternatives are arranged, that the collage of employee behaviour is complete. According to Edwards, Collinson, and Della Rocca (1995, p. 294) employees are likely to engage in 'mutually embedded practice(s) of consent, devotion and resistance'.

When we consider all employee actions in conjunction with an analytical eye to the future of employment relations, then we have some interesting questions worth revisiting. Importantly, however the labour process changes and develops, how the individual responds in certain contexts continues to develop accordingly and, to some extent, reflects opportunities presented to employees by broader social, political, and technological trends. Indeed, there is perhaps no better example of such changes creating new avenues for expression than rapid development of new Internet-based technologies and how new spaces created by new communication technologies allow employees to self-organize across workplaces without direct trade union involvement (e.g. Carter, Clegg, Hoggan, & Kornberger, 2003; Schoneboom, 2007; Richards, 2008).

Research on what workers do, and furthermore, why they do it, and what the outcomes of their actions are, comes from a myriad of disciplines utilizing as many theoretical approaches. We aim to draw together some of the threads of this extant literature to develop a new conceptual framework for understanding employee actions into the future. We can no longer examine employee actions through frameworks developed in post-World War II industrial sociology, industrial relations of the Fordist and post-Fordist eras, nor organizational psychology of the 1980s and 1990s. No longer is the manufacturing plant the primary place of employment in industrialized nations; historically low union density and coverage means that unions are no longer providing the outlet for employees as they were fifty years ago, and twin failings at the heart of much of the organizational psychology research – unitarist assumptions and failure to adequately consider context – limits the practicality of that discipline.

The research agenda of the past

The following section will consider the different perspectives provided by some of the key schools studying employees at work. This review is not intended to be exhaustive, but merely a consideration of some of the more substantial literature within each field.

The rise of industrial sociology

Following World War II, researchers such as Dalton (1948), Roy (1952, 1954), Baldamus (1961), Blauner (1964), Cunnison (1966), Gouldner (1954, 1965), Woodward (1965), Lupton (1963), Goldthorpe, Lockwood, Bechhofer, and Platt (1968), and Beynon (1973) provided excellent insights into the world of work at that point in time – a time when the low- or semi-skilled, factory worker was the subject of choice. This research examined primarily the manner in which employees sought some control over the wage-effort bargain. Throughout this body of work it is clear that employees have the ability to work hard for their own benefit, restricting output or under-working when the employee deems that course of action appropriate, as well as strictly conforming to managerial dictums when that course of action suits the employee. Importantly, employees at this time were not in formal teams. However, many of these employees developed (independent from management) informal groups that often held a greater control over the workforce than did managers. This informal group, as Taylor (1911a, 1911b) witnessed, had the ability to control worker output to a standard minimum level. However, Taylor failed to recognize that group norms can also be established at a high level of output, but only when the employees benefit from such increased levels of output.

Burawoy (1979) provided a substantial addition to this field by giving consideration to why employees work as hard as they do. He concluded that employees are somewhat trapped inside a game in which they have been invited to take part in, yet are not allowed to play a part in the formulation of the fundamental rules of the production 'game'. By limiting output in some instances and 'breaking my back to make out ... risking life and limb for that extra piece' in other instances, employees would have some control over the subjective alienation that they felt (Burawoy, 1979, p. xi). What this body of research provides is an excellent depth of information analysing actions related to levels of output. Again, context is important for the employee and for groups of employees. When there is benefit to the group, workers will work very hard. When there are benefits to the individual in working hard, the individual may be controlled by strong group norms.

This body of work, which is part of a further and wider expansion of industrial sociological research (e.g. Nichols & Armstrong, 1976; Friedman, 1977; Edwards & Scullion, 1982), provides a sociological concentration on employees engaging in actions that have an immediate and mid-term benefit for the workers, primarily through resisting managerial control. Certainly, employees can engage in activities that support managerial controls, or alternatively actions that will be viewed positively by management and have positive outcomes for the organization as a whole. Such actions may indeed have deleterious results for the workforce. Burawoy provided an important addition to the control/resistance framework offered by Braverman's reconsideration of the labour process. Researchers from this background were now using a control/resistance/consent model of employee actions.

Workplace 'fiddles' were extensively researched by Mars (see for examples: 1973, 1974, 1994) suggesting that employees who fiddled the system were not irrational employees unable to make their way in society. Rather these actions were 'rational' responses of employees to controls inherent to their occupations. Indeed, Mars claims that between 70 and 90 per cent of employees engage in fiddles and such activities. Taking a different view of similar actions, workplace 'crimes' were further explored by Ditton in the mid 1970s (see for examples: 1976, 1977, 1979). Importantly, Ditton also reaches the conclusion that employees are responding rationally to the situation in which they find themselves, often as a direct response to being 'misled' by management (1977, p. 17). Further, two distinct variables control the extent of pilfering and stealing. The 'scope' or size of the employees reach within their everyday duties to perform fiddles, and 'opportunity' or the factors that allow an employee to engage in such activities with sufficient assistance or without being caught (Ditton, 1977, p. 81–84). In more recent times the work of Mars and Ditton has been developed in the context of tightly controlled and monitored total quality management regimes (e.g. Analoui & Kakabadse, 1989; Webb & Palmer, 1998; Knights & McCabe, 2000; Anteby, 2003). It is also evident that researchers from the field of industrial relations have been uncovering and conceptualizing a range of employee behaviour that goes beyond activities associated with strikes and collective bargaining (Hyman, 1981). For instance, against the backdrop of growing strike activity, studies revealed incidences of "unorganised conflict" (Bean, 1975), covert forms of "getting by" and "getting back" at management (Nichols & Armstrong, 1976), and the role sabotage plays in employer-trade union relations (Zabala,1989). We would suggest that scope and opportunity remain two important factors in our understanding of employee actions, however, this fails to adequately address two critical factors to be discussed later – 'intent' and 'outcome'.

The rise of organizational behaviour

The field of organizational behaviour has made many significant contributions to the understanding of employee actions in the workplace. Certainly, the renowned Hawthorne experiments undertaken in the 1930s (Mayo, 1933, 1949; Roethlisberger & Dickson, 1939) and the Tavistock Institute's contributions in the 1950s (Trist, Higgin, Murray & Pollock, 1963; Emery & Trist, 1965) have provided the basis for the development of the 'human relations' approach to work. The human relations approach emphasizes the importance of the creative involvement of the employees for the management of the labour process (Dohse, Jurgens & Malsch, 1985; Purser, 2000). This approach tends to look at an employee's performance in two dimensions – the in-role performance and extra-role performance (Bergeron, 2007).

The Hawthorne and Tavistock programmes played a significant role in the development of a research stream focussing on team-based organization within organizations (Beyerlein, 2000). What has developed from the seminal works of team-based research is a lineage spanning a number of fields and showing us a number of things.

First, a team structure has the ability to combine social and technical aspects of work in an attempt to reach benefits of increased productivity for the organizations and an increased degree of job satisfaction for the employee (Jurgens, 1991; Katzenbach & Smith, 1993; Kenney & Florida, 1988; Mueller, 1994; Trist, Higgin, Murray & Pollock, 1963).

The second aspect that we have learnt about teams is that employees can be confronted with a degree of peer-induced, coercive control when placed within a team structure (Barker, 1993; Baldry, Bain, & Taylor, 1998; Willmott, 1993; Sewell, 1998; Townsend, 2005;). Third, not all teams are created equal. That is to say that there are distinct differences between the impacts a high autonomy team will have on employees compared to a team structure that provides little or no autonomy (Bacon & Blyton, 2000; Mueller, 1994). With these considerations noted, the literature clearly indicates that team structures allow opportunities for employees to engage in activities that can be both positive and negative for the productivity levels of organizations and just as importantly, both positive and negative outcomes for themselves and their colleagues (Findlay, McKinlay, Marks & Thompson, 2000a, 2000b; Knights & McCabe, 2000, 2003).

Organizational behaviour has also emerged as a key contributor to our understanding of non-standard employee behaviour. For instance, important contributions have been made in this field in terms of studying drug and alcohol misuse at work (Mangione & Quinn, 1975), romancing during work time (Quinn, 1977), and staff stealing from customers (Anderton & Keily, 1988; Hollinger & Clark, 1983; Hawkins, 1984). Despite the interest in such forms of employee behaviour, in more recent years there has been a rapid growth of research on what has been coined 'organisational citizenship behaviours' (OCBs) (Podsakoff, Mackenzie, Paine, & Bacharach, 2000). One of the seminal works on the topics describes OCB as

individual behaviour that is discretionary, not directly or explicitly recognised by the formal reward system ... the behaviour is not an enforceable requirement of the role of the job description ... the behaviour is a matter of personal choice, such that its omission is not generally understood as punishable (Organ, 1988, p. 4).

Podsakoff et al. (2000) have reviewed the mass of literature that has spawned in the area of OCB and organize the different forms of behaviours into seven common themes that have very positively constructed labels: 1) helping behaviour, 2) sportsmanship, 3) organizational loyalty,

4) organizational compliance, 5) individual initiative, 6) civic virtue, and 7) self development. However, the study of OCB has typically failed to adequately consider the other possibilities of employee actions. As we know, there are a range of employee actions that have a direct, negative impact on the profitability of the organization. Such actions include sabotage, theft, and soldiering to name a few.

Organizational behaviourists have, in the last decade or so, begun to develop the way that they consider some actions that prove problematic for managers in the workplace. Within this discipline, such actions in the workplace are referred to as 'counter-productive behaviours' (CPBs) (see for examples: Bies & Tripp, 2005). Numerous researchers have investigated particular behaviours, while others have attempted to incorporate a range of behaviours for more integrative theoretical developments. CPBs have been defined to include actions such as rule-breaking and day-dreaming while on the job, through to theft and sabotage (Ones, Viswesvaran, & Schmidt, 1993). Collins and Griffin (1998) make the point that despite the various nuances, all the definitions are characterized by a disregard for societal and organizational rules and values. There is an implied assumption that the employee has intent to perform damage and also has control over the outcome of their particular actions. This leaves little room for unintended consequences of behaviours that might not begin with the intention of being counter productive.

Furthermore, the unitarist assumption that presupposes that what is good for the organization is good for the employee remains problematic. Certainly, a successful organization means jobs for people. However, the employment relationship is a complex web of legal rules, institutional practices and policies, and informal actions. Given this complexity as a starting assumption within the radical research agenda, it is reasonable to acknowledge that some of this complex web will result in oppositional outcomes for the employee and the employer. By failing to acknowledge the important structural and institutional aspects of the employment relationship this perspective remains incomplete.

Hence, the implicit assumption in much of the CPB research that the management of the organization is 'doing the right thing' and it is the employees' response that is the 'counter-productive behaviour' is a fundamental flaw. The currently accepted view of counter-productive behaviours is far too broad and all encompassing. Some actions may indeed be 'counter-productive' from the perspective of the organization, yet reflecting the sociological research of decades before, these actions allow an important means of maintaining situational power on the part of the employee (Chen & Spector, 1992, cited in Miles, Borham, Spector and Fox, 2002). Some suggest that using the label 'counter-productive' is, in itself, counter productive (Townsend & McDonald, 2008).

Recent critical developments

The failure of the organizational behaviourists to adequately analyse *all* perspectives of behaviour was one motivating factor for the publication of *Organizational Misbehaviour* (Ackroyd & Thompson, 1999). The authors describe misbehaviour as a 'failure to work very hard or conscientiously, through not working at all, deliberate output restriction, practical joking, pilferage, sabotage and sexual misconduct' (Ackroyd & Thompson, 1999, pp. 1–2). In essence, these behaviours constitute any actions that are outside the formal and consensual rules of the workplace that will have a negative affect on the organization's productivity levels. This research maintains academic rigour while providing an excellent and amusing antithesis to the plethora of organizational behaviour texts. Watson (2003, p. 230) provides a longer and more detailed definition:

> Activities occurring within the workplace that (a) according to official structure, culture and rules of the organisation, 'should not happen', and (b) contain an element of challenge to the dominant modes of operating or to dominant interest in the organisation.

The inclusiveness of both the Watson and the Ackroyd and Thompson work reflects some authors considering the issues of sabotage in the workplace. Dubois (1997) and Sprouse (1992), for example, take the approach that everything that an employee does that does not contribute to the organization's aim of capital accumulation is to be considered sabotage. While an interesting proposition, this is a difficult perspective to reconcile when considering the range of behaviours that are therefore included. Just as the all-encompassing approach of CPB is not helpful it is stretching the notion of sabotage a little to consider the person who has returned to work five minutes late after a lunch break to be a saboteur. Nevertheless, a range of authors have provided examples of employees at all levels of the organization covertly disrupting the production process when the processes interfered with the employee's individual or collective best interests. For instance, deliberate employee absence or lateness (Palmer, 1996), irresponsible team working (Vallas, 2003; Townsend, 2003; Richards & Marks, 2007), defiance in call centres (Bain & Taylor, 2000; Mulholland, 2004), and, humour are used to subvert management plans in work meetings or more general work settings (Holmes & Marra, 2002; Taylor & Bain, 2003; Marra, 2007).

Discussion

The review of some seminal pieces of literature that consider employees' actions in the workplace demonstrates that the world of work can be viewed, and indeed researched from many perspectives. Different perspectives tend to start with different ideological assumptions, ask different questions (often through different methods), and not surprisingly, find different answers. Within all the different answers we have quite an understanding of isolated aspects of employee actions in the workplace, particularly, employee actions that are a response to management strategies and styles. For example, many employees appreciate and embrace the opportunity to engage in TQM processes while other employees resist such managerial controls (Wilkinson, Godfrey & Marchington, 1997). The process of teams and team working can have very different impacts on different people within workplaces (Knights & McCabe, 2000; McCabe, 2000; Wigfield, 2001; Townsend, 2004a). Clearly, different regimes impact employees differently.

But more than different regimes impacting upon different employees, employees can engage in a range of actions in the same organizational context. What makes one employee a 'good soldier' (Organ, 1988), another employee one with a knack for 'goldbricking' (Roy, 1952), and another a thief (Ditton, 1976) or saboteur (Dubois, 1997)? In fact, these *different* employees can be one and the same person. Employees are confronted with a range of situations and contexts throughout their working lives. Different workplaces have various expectations of employees and managers. Different employees can have diverse expectations of what are acceptable actions and what are unacceptable actions.

Technology has had a dramatic impact on employees in the last thirty years. In 1998, Zuboff suggested that hardly a sector of the economy has not been penetrated by some form of computerized technology. One would think that the time passed since this publication has allowed for total penetration of some form of computerized technology. There is a range of literature from different fields over many years that refer to the ability of management taking greater control over employee actions through the use of technology (Braverman, 1974; Edwards,

1979; Noble, 1986; Sewell & Wilkinson, 1992a, 1992b; Shaiken, 1984; Webster &Robins, 1993; Zuboff, 1988). However, there is equally as much evidence presented, including some from the aforementioned authors, which argues that employees maintain the ability to resist the controls of management, even while considering the technological controls and surveillance (Bain & Taylor 2000; Barnes, 2004; Edwards & Scullion, 1982; Edwards, 1979; Taylor & Bain, 1999; Thompson, 2003; Townsend, 2005; van den Broek, 1997, 2002). Clearly, there can be no simple answer to the question of what employees do in the workplace: employees work hard, employees resist managerial controls, employees work for the benefit of themselves and their colleagues, employees work for the benefit of their employer.

Technologies have become personalized in the past decade and appear to be on a significant trajectory of becoming substantially more central to an individual's work and non-work existence. The internet has become a tool for many workplaces to engage in commercial activities, and provides many employees with access to the world from their workspace. Generally, such new developments have been examined in a negative context. For example, many organization behaviour studies have been aimed at examining 'new' forms of employee behaviour that includes cyber slacking (Block, 2001), cyber loafing (Lim, 2002), internet abuse on work time (Griffiths, 2003), personal Web usage in the workplace (Mahatanankoon, Anandarajan, & Igbaria 2004), and internet misuse (Lara, Tacoronte, Ding & Ting, 2006). Further, industrial sociological researchers have argued the case that employees blogging about work, colleagues and employers is a form of resistance to the labour process (Schoneboom, 2007; Richards, 2008). Yet for some, new technological developments that allow significant changes in how employees communicate with each other are viewed in quite a different light. Indeed, recent research suggests that employees are just as likely to express "passion" for their work when encouraged to use new internet communication technologies by employers (Kaiser, Muller-Seietz, Lopes, & e Cunha, 2007; Efimova, 2009).

Formal rules and expectations differ between workplaces and industries, worksite culture and managerial approaches can differ greatly between organizational departments or divisions, and as such, context is a critical component of any analysis. Regardless of the context, an employee can 'get the job done', working within the formal and consensual framework of rules. Alternatively, they can approach their work in a fashion that assists the organization to have higher levels of productive output. Another alternative allows employees to bend or break the rules, and engage in activities that lower productivity levels within the organization. But most significantly, that 'intent' does not always equate with 'outcome'. That is to say, there can often be a difference between the intent behind an employee's actions, and the final result of that action. As the meta-theoretical approach of critical realism offers, humans operate in 'open' systems constantly exposed to influence and change at any moment.

Another important point to acknowledge is that any employee on any given day can engage in a number of activities that have conflicting impacts on the organization, their co-workers, and even themselves. For example, the same employee who works long hours of unpaid overtime may also be pilfering stock during those late nights alone in the office. An employee may be taking long lunch breaks everyday, however this employee may also be the type of lateral thinker who solves problems in the production chain and passes this information on to managers. The employee who works through lunch everyday might also be spending hours of work time responding to personal e-mails, mobile phone calls and messages, catching up with 'Facebook' friends, or 'tweeting' their every thought. Equally as important as recognizing employees have a range of action options available to them, is the fact that employees can engage in such decisions individually, collaboratively (with their work team or informal group), or collectively (through their union).

That is to say, the best individual employee may simply be too individualistic to be a successful "team player" and cause friction within the work group lowering overall productivity measures. Alternatively, a work team may provide excellent feedback to management in quality circle meetings; however two or more team members may work collaboratively to sabotage the production chain or to maintain knowledge over production short cuts. The employee who is the union delegate may spend a number of hours per week on union related issues and hence, not directly assist production and therefore productivity, yet have a strong influence over the workforce to circumvent wildcat strikes. This complex and conflictual nature of employee action choices are summarized in Table 7.1.

Far from solving the mysteries of employee actions in the workplace and how employees contribute to productivity levels and their own existence, this typology indeed raises more questions. For example, it is acknowledged that employees engage in actions that float throughout the nine sectors of this schema. For example, a workplace with a strong culture of union avoidance may perceive union meetings negatively.

Table 7.1 A typology of employee action alternatives

	Conflict	Consent	Engagement
Individualistic	Wage/effort bargain; Pilfering, theft; sabotage of goods; practical jokes	Performing tasks adequately	Unpaid overtime (more work); Faster work; Using own tools/ equipment
Collaborative	Collude to keep information from managers;	Team and group work	Quality circles (giving up tricks) Sharing time saving and productivity gaining information
Collective	Strikes; Work bans	Union meetings; Joint Consultative Committees (JCCs)	Employee Involvement Programmes

The manager who wants their employees to 'take that extra step' may certainly perceive a worker *only* performing tasks adequately as not doing enough, and hence *negatively* impacting the productivity of an organization. How does a manager or an organization measure the productivity benefits of that employee to the organization? How does an employee determine the degree to which extrinsic and intrinsic rewards adequately compensate the subjective, alienating factors of the workplace before engaging in negatively perceived actions? A third dimension to this typology might consider the *actual* results of an action for employees and the organization.

This is of course, one problem with such a simplistic two-dimensional typology. This typology partially assumes that employees recognize that their actions will have a particular outcome. Also it assumes that a particular action will have the intended outcome with no regard for unintended outcomes. In practice, this is not always the case. Indeed, it is the case that a growing number of theorists (e.g. Galperin 2003; Vardi & Weitz, 2004; Kidwell & Martin, 2005; Langan-Fox, Cooper & Klimoski, 2008; Greenberg, 2010) believe that certain acts which might be considered misbehaviour in some workplaces or industries can be viewed as ethical, proper, and ultimately deliver effective outcomes for organizations. This is particularly salient in the case of whistle-blowing activities.

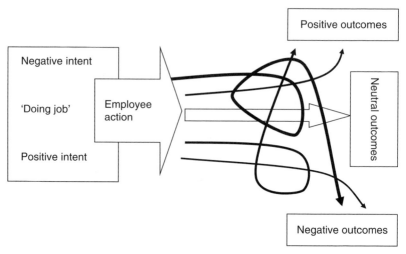

Figure 7.1   Complex outcomes of action inputs

Figure 7.1 illustrates that despite the best intentions of management and indeed any particular focus of intent by and individual employee of group of employees, the outcome of any particular action might be unintended. We can make many assumptions, yet for many things that occur in the workplace we simply do not know what the outcome will be nor do we fully appreciate how to 'measure' the outcomes.

It would be somewhat an understatement to mention at this point that the employment relationship can be a complicated one. There are so many nuances within each employment relationship that simple conclusions cannot be drawn. Employees do not simply 'hate' their job as though the capitalist constantly stands over them with a big stick. Nor do people simply love their jobs without question and completely adopt the rhetoric of management. There is evidence of people shifting across comparative jobs within the same industry and engaging in a variety of different actions influenced by the management structures of each workplace (Townsend, 2003). There is evidence of employees engaging in different actions within a single workplace (see for examples: Burawoy, 1979; Cunnison, 1966; Ditton, 1977; Roy, 1954). This body of literature also shows the non-work lives of people are also influential in determining the outcomes of employee actions in the workplace. There is evidence of employees using personalized technologies for both positive and negative outcomes for themselves and others in the workplace (e.g. Schoneboom, 2007; Ellis & Richards, 2009; Efimova, 2009).

Almost thirty years after the wave of organizational culture literature began to link a workforce culture to organizational profitability (Peters & Waterman, 1982), there has been a wealth of literature that suggests many employees are cynical, jaded, and even disgusted with management's attempts to manipulate and coerce the employees through cultural interventions including ubiquitous, but meaningless teams (see for examples: Kunda, 1992; Townsend, 2004a; 2004b; van den Broek, 2002; van den Broek, Callaghan & Thompson 2004; Waring, 1998; Welsh & Dehler, 2001). This indicates that the 'soft' HRM approach and associated cultural interventions have not been completely successful. Still, there is substantial research indicating employees preference, albeit mixed at times, for working in successfully developed and implemented team systems (e.g. Knights & McCabe, 2003; Geary & Dobbins, 2001; Bacon & Blyton, 2005; Kersley, Oxenbridge, Dix, Bewley, Bryson & Forth, 2006).

Union density has dropped substantially since the 1980s throughout the world. While once the outlet for disgruntled employees to voice their concerns over managerial decision making and to redress dissatisfaction with wages and conditions, the role of unions has changed at the same time as the decrease in membership. Unions of recent decades are more likely to be engaged in works councils and joint consultative committees and partnerships (e.g. Millward, Byrson & Forth, 2000; Kersley, Oxenbridge, Dix, Bewley, Bryson & Forth, 2006). What is more, the fall in the frequency and length of strikes and lock-outs does not seem to equate with a reduction in employee dissatisfaction with working conditions.

So, we are witnessing collectivity being squeezed out of the employment relationship through government intervention and capital activity (not to mention poor union servicing and organizing and individual employee apathy or disinterest). Yet we are also well aware that employees have a range of action alternatives in the workplace. If the collective action alternatives for resistance and voice are less available and the management's cultural interventions have had limited success, what actions will employees engage in at the workplace? We know too much to think that because unions are marginalized, conflict in the workplace will be absent. It is the suggestion of this chapter that this is a point in time when there needs to be a refocus of attention at the employee, to understand *all* ways in which their workplace actions are affected. Employee actions are complex, extensive, conforming, rebellious, and opportunistic to list just a few possible descriptors. As such, it is argued that the analysis of workplace behaviour must involve multiple lens to view employee actions, rather than maintain the myth that only one view is right and only one 'group' of actions are legitimate in the workplace.

Conclusion

The aim of this chapter was to explore the richness and variety of employee behaviour in the workplace. It began with a review of classical industrial sociological, organizational behaviour and industrial relations literature, before moving on to more contemporary studies that paint quite a different picture than their classical counterparts. What appears clear, however, is that we are no closer to determining an accurate and 'one-size fits all' perspective of the employment relationship and how best to understand the practice of managing employment relations. Indeed, the traditional organization of employees via trade unions may now be a rarity in vast swathes of new industry, yet it does not seem to have been replaced by a new model of managing employment relationships and employment relations that encompasses high levels of conformity with organizational values. As such, and with the help of consulting a wide range of organization studies, there is good reason to believe that individualism has not replaced collectivism, although the collective is increasingly more likely to be a self-organized group than a membership of a trade union. That said, there is evidence that the HRM paradigm that emerged some thirty years ago has had a level of influence on employment relations, yet more research clearly needs to undertaken in terms of identifying and conceptualizing employee engagement behaviour.

Perhaps what is most important to note in our brief review of many decades of organization research and what may well turn out to have a significant bearing on the discipline of employment relations is the emergence of a very new form of communication, i.e. email and the internet, and more recently communication technologies given the broad label of Web 2.0. However, in many ways it would be fair to say that the more that things change the more that they stay the same. As such, we need a full analysis of employee behaviours which impact the organization and employees in positive and negative ways. Just as importantly, we must include two more critical factors in our analysis – the intent and the outcome of particular action. All considered, we believe a key challenge for scholars and students of employment relations is to see the employment relationship in much broader terms than before. If not, we believe debates about the employee-employee relationship will not progress at the pace as has been noted in previous decades.

References

Ackroyd, S., & Thompson, P. (1999). *Organisational misbehaviour*. London: Sage.
Analoui, F., & Kakabadse, A. (1989). Defiance at work. *Employee Relations, 11*(3), 2–62.
Anderton, B., & Keily, J. (1988). Employee theft. *Personnel Review, 17*(5), 37–43.
Anteby, M. (2003). The 'moralities' of poaching: manufacturing personal artefacts on the factory floor. *Ethnography, 4*(2), 217–239.
Bacon, N., & Blyton, P. (2000). High road and low road teamworking: perceptions of management rationales and organizational and human resource outcomes. *Human Relations, 53*(11) 1425–1458.
Bacon, N., & Blyton, P. (2005). Worker responses to teamworking: exploring employee attributions of managerial motives. *International Journal of Human Resource Management, 16*(2), 238–255.
Bain, P., & Taylor, P. (2000). Entrapped by the electronic panopticon? Worker resistance in the call centre. *New Technology, Work and Employment, 15*(1), 2–18.
Baldamus, W. (1961). *Efficiency and effort: an analysis of industrial efficiency*. London: Tavistock Publications.
Baldry, C., Bain, P., & Taylor, P. (1998). 'Bright satanic offices': intensification, control and team Taylorism. In P. Thompson & C. Warhurst (eds), *Workplaces of the future* (pp. 163–183). London, Macmillan.
Barker, J. (1993). Tightening the iron cage: concertive control in self-managing teams. *Administrative Science Quarterly,38*, 408–437.
Barnes, A. (2004). Diaries, dunnies and discipline: resistance and accommodation to monitoring in call centres. *Labour and Industry, 14*(3), 127–137.
Bean, R. (1975). Research note: the relationship between strikes and 'unorganized' conflict in manufacturing industries. *British Journal of Industrial Relations, 8*(1), 98–101.
Bergeron, D., (2007). The potential paradox of organizational citizenship behaviour: good citizens at what cost? *Academy of Management Review, 32*(4), 1079–1095.
Beyerlein, M. (ed.). (2000). *Work teams: past, present and future*. London: Kluwer Academic.
Beynon, H. (1973). *Working for Ford*. Wakefield: Allen Lane and Penguin Education.
Bies, R., & Tripp, T. (2005). Badmouthing the company: bitter employee or concerned corporate citizen. In R. Kidwell & C. Martin (eds), *Managing Organizational Deviance* (pp. 97–108). London: Sage.
Blauner, R. (1964). *Alienation and freedom: the factory worker and his industry*. Chicago: University of Chicago Press.
Block, W. (2001). Cyberslacking business ethics and managerial economics. *Journal of Business Ethics, 33*(3), 225–231.

Braverman, H. (1974). *Labor and monopoly capital: the degradation of work in the twentieth century.* New York: Monthly Review Press.

Burawoy, M. (1979). *Manufacturing consent: changes in the labor process under monopoly capitalism.* Chicago: University of Chicago Press.

Callaghan, G. & Thompson, P. (2002). 'We recruit attitude': the selection and shaping of routine call centre labour. *Journal of Management Studies, 39*(2), 233–254.

Carter, C., Clegg, S., Hoggan, J. & Kornberger, M. (2003). The polyphonic spree: the case of the Liverpool dockers. *Industrial Relations Journal, 34*(4), 290–304.

Chen, P., & Spector, P. (1992). Relationships of work stressors with aggression, withdrawal, theft and substance use: an exploratory study. *Journal of Occupational and Organizational Psychology, 65,* 177–184.

Collins, J., & Griffin, R. (Eds.). (1998). *Dysfunctional behaviour in organisations: violent and deviant behaviours.* Stamford, CT: JAI Press.

Cunnison, S. (1966). *Wages and work allocation: a study of social relations in a garment workshop.* London: Tavistock Publications.

Dalton, M. (1948). The industrial 'rate-buster': a characterization. *Applied Anthropology, 7,* 5–23.

Ditton, J. (1976). Perks, pilferage and the fiddle: the historical structure of invisible wages. *Theory and Society, 4*(1), 39–70.

Ditton, J. (1977). *Part-time crime: an ethnography of fiddling and pilferage.* London: Macmillan.

Ditton, J. (1979). *Controlology: beyond the new criminology.* London: Macmillan.

Dohse, K., Jurgens, U. & Malsch, T. (1985). From 'Fordism' to 'Toyotism'? The social organisation of the labour process in the Japanese automobile industry. *Politics and Society, 14*(2), 115–146.

Dubois, P. (1997). *Sabotage in industry.* Harmondsworth: Penguin.

Edwards, P. & Scullion, H. (1982). *The social organisation of industrial conflict: control and resistance in the workplace.* Oxford: Basil Blackwell.

Edwards, P., Collinson, D., & Della Rocca, G., (1995). Workplace resistance in Western Europe: a preliminary overview and a research agenda. *European Journal of Industrial Relations, 1*: 283–316.

Edwards, R. (1979). *Contested terrain: the transformation of the workplace in the twentieth century.* London: Heinemann.

Efimova, L. (2009). *Passion at work: blogging practices of knowledge workers.* Enschede, The Netherlands: Novay.

Ellis, V. & Richards, J. (2009). Creativity, connecting and correcting: motivations and meanings of work-blogging among public service workers. In S. Bolton & M. Houlihan (Eds.), *Work matters: reflections on contemporary work* (pp. 250–268). London: Palgrave Macmillan.

Emery, F., & Trist, E. (1965). The causal texture of organizational environments. *Human Relations, 18,* 21–32.

Findlay, P., McKinlay, A., Marks, A,. & Thompson, P. (2000a). 'Flexible when it suits them': the use and abuse of teamwork skills. In S. Proctor & F. Mueller (Eds.), *Teamworking* (pp. 222–243). New York: St Martin's Press.

Findlay, P., McKinlay, A., Marks, A., & Thompson, P. (2000b). In search of perfect people: teamwork and team players in the Scottish spirits industry. *Human Relations, 53*(12), 1549–1571.

Friedman, A. (1977). Industry and labour: class struggle and labour at work and monopoly capitalism. London: Macmillan.

Galperin, B. (2003). Can workplace deviance be constructive? In A. Sagie, S. Stashevsky & M. Koslowsky (eds), *Misbehaviour and dysfunctional attitudes in organizations* (pp. 154–170). Basingstoke: Palgrave Macmillan.

Geary, J. & Dobbins, A. (2001). Teamwork: a new dynamic in the pursuit of management control. *Human Resource Management Journal, 11*(1), 3–21.

Goldthorpe, J., Lockwood, D., Bechhofer, F., & Platt, J. (1968). *The affluent worker: industrial attitudes and behaviour.* Cambridge: Cambridge University Press.

Gouldner, A. (1954). *Patterns of industrial bureaucracy: a case study of modern factory administration.* New York: The Free Press of Glencoe.

Greenberg, J. (2010). *Insidious workplace behavior.* London: Psychological Press.

Griffiths, M. (2003). Internet abuse in the workplace: issues and concerns for employers and employment counselors. *Journal of Employment Counseling, 40*(2), 87–96.

Hawkins, R. (1984). Employee theft in the restaurant trade: forms of ripping off waiters at work. *Deviant Behavior, 5,* 47–69.

Hollinger, R. C., & Clark, J. P. (1983). *Theft by employees.* Lexington: Lexington Books.

Holmes, J., & Marra, M. (2002). Over the edge? Subversive humor between colleagues and friends. *Humor, 15*(1), 65–87.

Hyman, R. (1981). *Strikes* (2nd edn). London: Macmillan.

Jurgens, U. (1991). Departures from Taylorism and Fordism: new forms of work in the automobile industry. In B. Jessop, H. Kastendiek, K. Neilson & O. Pederson (eds), *The politics of flexibility: restructuring state and industry in Britain, Germany and Scandinavia* (pp. 233–247). Aldershot: Edward Elgar.

Kaiser, S., Muller-Seietz, G., Lopes, M., & e Cunha, M. (2007). Weblog-technology as a trigger to elicit passion for knowledge. *Organization, 14*(3), 391–412.

Katzenbach, J. & Smith, D. (1993). *The wisdom of teams: creating the high-performance organisation.* Boston: Harvard Business School Press.

Kenney, M. & Florida, R. (1988). Beyond mass production: production and the labor process in Japan. *Politics and Society, 16*(1), 121–158.

Kersley, B., Oxenbridge, S., Dix, G., Bewley, H., Bryson, A., & Forth, J. (2006). *Inside the workplace: findings from the 2004 Workplace Employment Relations Survey.* London: Routledge.

Kidwell, R., & Martin, C. (eds). (2005). *Managing organizational deviance.* London: Sage.

Knights, D., & McCabe, D. (2000). Bewitched, bothered and bewildered: the meaning and experience of teamworking for employees in an automobile company. *Human Relations, 53*(11), 1481–1517.

Knights, D., & McCabe, D. (2003). Governing through teamworking: reconstituting subjectivity in a call centre. *Journal of Management Studies, 40*(7), 1587–1619.

Kunda, G. (1992). *Engineering culture: control and commitment in a high-tech corporation.* Philadelphia: Temple University Press.

Langan-Fox, J., Cooper, C., & Klimoski, R. (eds). (2008). *Research companion to the dysfunctional workplace: management challenges and symptoms.* London: Edward Elgar.

Lara, P., Tacoronte, D., Ding, J., & Ting, J. (2006). Do current anti-cyberloafing disciplinary practices have a replica in research findings? A study of the effects of coercive strategies on workplace internet misuse. *Internet Research, 16*(4), 450–467.

Lim, V. (2002). The IT way of loafing on the job: cyberloafing neutralizing and organizational justice. *Journal of Organizational Behavior, 23*, 675–694.

Lupton, T. (1963). *On the shop floor: two studies of workshop organisation and output.* Oxford: Pergamon Press.

Mahatanankoon, P., Anandarajan, M., & Igbaria, M. (2004). Development of a measure of personal web usage in the workplace. *Cyberpsychology and Behavior, 7*(1), 93–104.

Mangione, T.W. & Quinn, R.P. (1975). Job satisfaction, counterproductive behavior, and drug use at work. *Journal of Applied Psychology, 60*(1), 114–116.

Marra, M. (2007). Humour in workplace meetings. In R. Westwood & C. Rhodes (eds), *Humour, work and organization* (pp. 139–157). London: Routledge.

Mars, G. (1973). Chance, punters, and the fiddle: institutionalised pilferage in a hotel dining room. In M. Warner (ed.), *The Sociology of the Workplace* London: Allen and Unwin.

Mars, G. (1974). Dock pilferage. In P. Rock & M. McIntosh (eds), *Deviance and Control* (pp. 109–128). London: Tavistock.

Mars, G. (1994). *Cheats at work: an anthropology of workplace crime.* Aldershot: Dartmouth.

Mayo, E. (1933). *The human problems of an industrial civilisation.* New York: Arno Press.

Mayo, E. (1949). *The social problems of an industrial civilisation.* London: Routledge and Kegan Paul.

McCabe, D. (2000). The team dream: the meaning and experience of teamworking in an automobile manufacturing company. In S. Proctor & F. Mueller (eds), *Teamworking* (pp. 203–221). New York: St Martin's Press.

Miles, D., Borman, W., Spector, P., & Fox, S. (2002). Building and integrative model of extra role work behaviours: a comparison of counterproductive work behaviour with organizational citizenship behaviour. *International Journal of Selection and Assessment, 10* (1/2), 51–57.

Millward, N. Byrson, A., & Forth, J. (2000). *All change at work? British employment relations 1980–1998, as portrayed by the Workplace Industrial Relations Survey Series.* London: Routledge.

Mueller, F. (1994). Teams between hierarchy and commitment: change strategies and the internal environment. *Journal of Management Studies, 31*(3), 383–403.

Mulholland, K. (2004). Workplace resistance in an Irish call centre. *Work, Employment and Society, 18*(4), 709–724.

Nichols, T., & Armstrong, P. (1976) *Workers divided: a study of shopfloor politics.* Glasgow: Fontana.

Noble, D. (1986). *Forces of production: a social history of industrial automation.* New York: Oxford University Press.

Ones, D., Viswesvaran, C., & Schmidt, F. (1993). Comprehensive meta-analysis of integrity test validities: findings and implications for personnel selection and theories of job performance. *Journal of Applied Psychology Monograph, 78*, 679–703.

Organ, D. (1988). *Organizational citizenship behaviour: the good soldier syndrome.* Lexington: Lexington Books.

Palmer, G. (1996). Reviving resistance: the Japanese factory floor in Britain. *Industrial Relations Journal, 27*(2), 129–142.

Peters, T. & Waterman, R. (1982). *In search of excellence: lessons from America's best run companies.* New York: Harper and Rowe.

Podsakoff, P., Mackenzie, S., Paine, J. & Bacharach, D. (2000). Organizational citizenship behaviours: a critical review of the theoretical and empirical literature and suggestions for future research. *Journal of Management, 26*(3), 513–563.

Purser, R. (2000). The human relations myth unveiled: deconstructing the history and origins of work teams. In M. Beyerlein (ed.), *Work teams: Past present and future* (pp. 59–83). Boston: Kluwer Academic Publishers.

Quinn, R. (1977). Coping with cupid: the formation, impact, and management of romantic relationships in organizations. *Administrative Science Quarterly, 22*(1), 30–45.

Richards, J. (2008). 'Because I need somewhere to vent': the expression of conflict through work blogs. *New Technology, Work and Employment, 23*(1–2), 95–109.

Richards, J., & Marks. A. (2007). Biting the hand that feeds: social identity and resistance in restaurant teams. *International Journal of Business Science and Applied Management, 2*(2), 42–57.

Roethlisberger, F. & Dickson, W. (1939). *Management and the worker: an account of a research program conducted by the Western Electric Company, Hawthorne Works, Chicago.* Cambridge: Harvard University Press.

Roy, D. (1952). Quota restriction and goldbricking in a machine shop. *The American Journal of Sociology, 57*, 427–442.

Roy, D. (1954). Efficiency and 'the fix': informal intergroup relations in a piecework machine shop. *American Journal of Sociology, 60*, 255–266.

Schoneboom, A. (2007). Diary of a working boy: creative resistance among anonymous workbloggers. *Ethnography, 8*(4), 403–423.

Sewell, G. (1998). The discipline of teams: the control of team-based industrial work through electronic and peer surveillance. *Administrative Science Quarterly, 43*, 397–428.

Sewell, G., & Wilkinson, B. (1992a). Empowerment or emasculation? Shopfloor surveillance in a total quality organisation. In P. Blyton & P. Turnbull (eds), *Reassessing Human Resource Management* (pp. 97–115). London: Sage Publications.

Sewell, G., & Wilkinson, B. (1992b). Someone to watch over me: Surveillance, discipline and the just-in-time labour process. *Sociology, 26*, 271–289.

Shaiken, H. (1984). *Work transformed: automation and labor in the computer age.* New York: Holt, Rinehart, and Winston.

Sprouse, M., Ed. (1992). *Sabotage in the American workplace.* San Francisco: Pressure Drop Press.

Taylor, F. (1911a). *The principles of scientific management.* Toronto: General Publishing Company.

Taylor, F. (1911b). *Shop management.* New York: Harper and Brothers Publishers.

Taylor, P., & Bain, P. (1999). An assembly line in the head: work and employee relations in the call centre. *Industrial Relations Journal, 30*(2), 101–117.

Taylor, P., & Bain, P. (2003). 'Subterranean worksick blues': humour as subversion in two call centres. *Organization Studies, 24*(9), 1487–1509.

Thompson, P. (2003). Fantasy island: a labour process critique of the 'age of surveillance'. *Surveillance & Society, 1*(2), 138–151.

Townsend, K. (2003). Leisure at work, who can resist? An investigation into workplace resistance by leisure service employees. *Journal of Industrial Relations, 45*(4), 442–456.

Townsend, K. (2004a). Union avoidance, postponement or de-unionisation? A Greenfield site case study. Proceedings from AIRAANZ Conference, Noosa, Association of Industrial Relations Academics of Australia and New Zealand.

Townsend, K. (2004b). When the LOST found teams: a consideration of teams within the individualised call centre environment. *Labour and Industry, 14*(3), 111–126.

Townsend, K. (2005). Electronic surveillance and cohesive teams: room for resistance in an Australian call centre? *New Technology, Work and Employment, 20*(1), 47–58.

Townsend, K., & McDonald, P. (2008). The influence of recruitment and teams on counter-productive behaviours: an Australian case study. *International Journal of Organizational Behaviour, 13*(2), 41–55.

Trist, E., Higgin, G., Murray, H., & Pollock, A. (1963). *Organizational choice.* London: Tavistock Publications.

Vallas, S. (2003). The adventures of managerial hegemony: teamwork, ideology, and worker resistance. *Social Problems, 50*(2), 204–225.

van den Broek, D. (1997). Human resource management, cultural control and union avoidance: an Australian case study. *The Journal of Industrial Relations, 39*(3), 332–348.

van den Broek, D. (2002). Monitoring and surveillance in call centres: some responses from Australian workers. *Labour and Industry, 12*(3), 43–58.

van den Broek, D., Callaghan, G. & Thompson, P. (2004). Teams without teamwork? Explaining the call centre paradox. *Economic and Industrial Democracy, 25*(2), 197–218.

Vardi, Y. & Weitz, E. (2004). *Misbehavior in organizations: theory, research and management.* Mahwah, NJ: LEA.

Waring, P. (1998). *The paradox of prerogative in participative organisations: the manipulation of corporate culture?* Proceedings of the 12th AIRAANZ Conference, Wellington.

Watson, T. (2003). *Sociology and work* (3rd edn). London: Routledge.

Webb, M. & Palmer, G. (1998). Evading surveillance and making time: an ethnographic view of the Japanese floor in Britain. *British Journal of Industrial Relations, 36*(4), 611–627.

Webster, F. & Robins, K. (1993). 'I'll be watching you': comment on Sewell and Wilkinson. *Sociology, 27*(2), 243–252.

Welsh, A. & Dehler, G., (2001). *Paradigms, praxis and paradox in the analysis of organisation change: the generative nature of control.* Proceedings from Critical Management Studies Conference, Manchester.

Wigfield, A. (2001). *Post-Fordism, gender and work.* Sydney: Ashgate.

Wilkinson, A., Godfrey, G., & Marchington, M. (1997). Bouquets, brickbats and blinkers: total quality management and employee involvement in practice. *Organization Studies, 18*(5), 799–819.

Willmott, H. (1993). Strength is ignorance; Slavery is freedom: managing culture in modern organisations. *Journal of Management Studies, 30*(4), 515–552.

Woodward, J. (1965). *Industrial organisation: theory and practice.* London: Oxford University Press.

Zabala, C.A. (1989). 'Sabotage at General Motors' Van Nuys assembly plant, 1975–83. *Industrial Relations Journal, 20*(1), 16–32.

Zuboff, S. (1988). *In the age of the smart machine: the future of work and power.* New York: Basic Books Inc.

8
Heads, Hearts, and now Bodies: Employee Looks and Lookism at Work

Chris Warhurst, Diane van den Broek,
Dennis Nickson, and Richard Hall

Introduction

Employment relations envelop a set of material practices and a way of looking at those practices. Both are dynamic; what is regarded as a feature of employment relations and how those employment relations are studied changes over time. For example, if employees were once paid 'danger money', now there are health and safety regulations to minimize workplace dangers; and employment discrimination on the basis of sex and race, once common, is now formally proscribed. Similarly, what is now termed 'employment relations' was once studied through the lens of industrial relations, but with the perceived shift from collectivism to individualism in the workplace human resource management has become the vogue lens. At the heart of all of these changes, however, there remains what Nienhüser and Warhurst (2011) term the 'transformation problem' or the conversion of employees' potential to work into actual and efficacious work.

Throughout most of the second half of the twentieth century, and seen through the lens of industrial relations, this transformation need was cast as the 'labour problem' (e.g. Bray, Waring & Cooper, 2009). In the language of human resource management, it has become the 'management of performance' (Guest, 1997). Traversing these approaches, and drawing together study and practices under a veneer of labour process theory, Edwards (1995, p. 45) argues that employment relations focuses attention on 'the organization and control of the employment relationship'. Whether viewed through the lens of industrial relations, human resource management or employment relations, this employment relationship centres on the wage-effort bargain, which essentially involves the exchange of labour by employees for reward by employers.

This employment relationship is complex, not least because what is being exchanged by the employee – labour – is not like other commodities in that it is intangible; it is realized only in its execution. In the language of labour process researchers, this complexity is called the 'indeterminacy of labour'. Employers seek to overcome it not only through a contract but also by asserting the right to direct, monitor, evaluate, and even discipline employees – within reasonable limits of course (Kaufman, 2004). Moreover, the employment relationship also is dynamic. In attempting to deal with the transformation problem, different employer strategies exist over time, location and industry (for discussions see Edwards, 1995 and Nienhüser & Warhurst 2011).

This chapter draws upon this framing to demonstrate how aesthetic labour – in common parlance employee requirements to 'look good' or 'sound right' at work – is now one such employer strategy in a services-dominated economy. This strategy represents not only a new development within employment relations as practice, but also heralds a potential conceptual paradigm shift in its study, one that moves away from the recent focus on the management of employee emotions triggered by Hochschild (1983) onto the management of employee corporeality. It also signals the need to expand conceptual understanding of the performance of work tasks within services as being characteristic of women's work, as Hochschild argued.

After a short discussion of the study of interactive service work, the chapter illustrates the importance of aesthetic labour through the findings of two employer surveys, one in Sydney in Australia, the other in Manchester in the UK. The chapter then examines an attempt to regulate employer demand for aesthetic labour, drawing on analysis of employment discrimination claims on the basis of physical features from the state of Victoria in Australia. Findings from both datasets are then used as a lever to explore the issue of gender and service work in both the study and practice of employment relations. First, however, we start with a short exposition of the shift to services, the feminization of the workforce and how the emotional labour paradigm sought to draw these two developments together in an explanation of how the transformation problem was being addressed in the late twentieth century.

From feeling rules to display work in services

Labour process theory regards the transformation of potential into actual labour as central to capital accumulation and argues that employers have a control imperative arising from the need to reduce the indeterminacy of labour. In other words, employers seek to determine what employees do in the workplace, how they do it and when they do it most obviously. How this control is manifest can vary. Braverman (1974) insisted that Taylorism (or scientific management) was *the* form of control. However subsequent research identified other forms of control – most obviously for example, direct control and responsible autonomy (Friedman, 1977) or simple control, technical control and bureaucratic control (Edwards, 1979). Most of the research revealing these strategies was based upon manufacturing.[1]

In the current economy, it is predominantly service sector employers who have to address the indeterminacy of labour. The service sector provides employment for about three in four waged workers throughout Western Europe, North America and Australasia (McDowell, 2009). The shift to a services-dominated economy means a growing proportion of the workforce are now engaged in face-to-face or voice-to-voice interactions with customers. Research into how employers control employees in interactive services has been dominated in recent years by the seminal work of Hochschild (1983). Hochschild coined the term 'emotional labour' to describe how service organizations seek to shape workers' feelings in order to affect the desired service encounter. Employees are required to be courteous, friendly and helpful to customers for example (see Korczynski, 2002 for an overview of the emotional labour literature; see also Bolton, 2005). Having the right attitude is regarded as a prerequisite of employees appropriately managing their own as well as customers' feelings in this service encounter. To this end, feeling rules prescribe how employees are to interact with customers. Hochschild also signalled the importance of display work in making manifest the required employee emotions within this interaction. Such display work invokes employee corporeality, such as a smile to indicate friendliness.

Hochschild pointed out that women are over-represented in jobs that demand emotional labour and that 'women more than men have put emotional labour on the market' (p. 11). However, she goes further, arguing that 'women are more accomplished managers of feeling' (p. 11) because gender is a 'determinant' (p. 20) of the skill required to manage feelings and that it is women who better understand this management and 'who specialise in emotional labour' (p. 20). The prevalence of women in jobs requiring emotional labour is thus accompanied by an argument that the skills required to enact a good service encounter, such as sociability, communicating and making customers feel good, are inherently feminine (Gatta, Boushey and Appelbaum, 2009). This dominant paradigm thus foregrounds the importance of feeling rules and the feminine 'naturalness' of this work. While useful – and an important step forward in analysis of service work – this conceptualization is blunt; more recent research has sought to shift the emphasis onto the corporeality of service work and how display work is required of both female and male employees.

Although flagged by Hochschild, the corporeality inherent of display work was quickly retired in research of emotional labour, both by Hochschild and subsequent researchers of emotional labour. As first conceived by Warhurst, Nickson, Witz and Cullen (2000), aesthetic labour seeks to retrieve this corporeality. It refers to employees' bodies being organizationally produced or 'made up' to embody the desired aesthetic of the organization and intended to provide for organizational commercial benefit. This aesthetic labour rests on embodied 'dispositions' (Bourdieu, 1984). Such dispositions, in the form of embodied capacities and attributes are, to some extent, possessed by workers at the point of entry into employment. However, and a key point, employers then mobilize, develop, and commodify these embodied dispositions through processes of recruitment, selection, training and management, transforming them into a 'style' of service encounter that appeals to the senses of the customer. As such aesthetic labour is another way of determining the work to be undertaken by employees in interactive services.

This definition makes it clear that interactive service employers seek frontline employees who have or can be made to have a prescribed corporeality, most obviously manifest in these employees' appearance or 'look'. This look can be perceived 'good looks' or the desired 'right look', and different service organizations can have different looks (Pettinger, 2004; Hall & van de Broek, 2011). Employers thus want these employee looks either as part of the corporate image and branding strategies or, more basely, because they are perceived to be attractive to customers and therefore likely to generate new or repeat custom. Ultimately, the use of employee looks is a strategy by employers to secure competitive advantage in what can be highly crowded high streets as economies become service-dominated, with more retail outlets and restaurants for example jostling to attract the attention of customers.

Employer awareness of the utility of employee appearance is not new. As the twentieth century unfolded and interactive customer services became more prevalent, employers became more aware of the utility of employee appearance – enhanced sales – but typically limited intervention to the hiring of employees with appropriate appearance and then leaving these employees to self-determine its mobilization in work. This self-determination, evident for example in Mills' (1951) flirtatious female department store worker, is sanctioned by management but driven by the employee and not organizationally prescribed. Mills cast this use by employees of their appearance as a feature of their 'personality', which included both appearance and attitudes. As Warhurst and Nickson (2009) point out, Mills recognized that his analysis was being undertaken at a time when a customer service orientation was only just emerging; as such it was still under developed and employers had yet to fully grasp the opportunity it afforded by exploiting employee appearance in generating custom. In practice therefore 'personality' became synonymous with attitudes – a practice that continued into later research focused on emotional labour (e.g. Callaghan & Thompson, 2002). However some employers now go beyond the *hiring* of employees who are perceived to be attractive to also *intervening* to work up these employees' looks through training, monitoring and evaluation. In short, such employers are commodifying employee corporeality as a strategy. The bodily display work recognized by Hochschild to characterize the looks inherent to particular styles of service turn employee bodily aesthetic appeal into aesthetic labour; it becomes part of the wage-effort bargain of the employment relationship.

If, with Taylorism and scientific management, employers sought control over what was in workers' heads, and with emotional labour employers seek control of workers' feelings, now, with aesthetic labour, employers have turned to the control of workers' bodies. In this respect, aesthetic labour is beginning to reframe conceptual analysis of interactive service work, foregrounding employer commodification of employee corporeality as a strategy to affect the type of labour that these employers now want. This employer demand also raises the potential for a new form of employment discrimination – 'lookism' – as those employees deemed unable or unwilling to be this type of labour have their job prospects diminished. We now turn to these two issues – employer demand for aesthetic labour and its discriminatory potential – and how they encompass both men and women.

The importance of employee appearance and lookism in the workplace

Drawing on the authors' empirical work, this section illustrates how aesthetic demand impacts the recruitment and selection of men as well as women in interactive service work. The data have been drawn from fashion retail employer surveys undertaken in Sydney and Manchester. Within both studies, the researchers designed and administered a survey questionnaire mailed out to a representative sample of fashion retailers in the cities' central business districts. The questionnaire included questions covering the business and its employees, customers, work clothing and physical appearance policies, employee induction and training, and employee rewards. It included sections on recruitment and selection, skills demand, and whether skills shortages in potential recruits or skills gaps in the current workforce existed (for a discussion of the full findings, see Nickson, Warhurst, Commander, Hurrell, & Cullen, 2011; Hall & van den Broek, 2011). The Sydney employer questionnaire was sent to a representative sample of 717 fashion retailers, with response rate of 30 per cent. The Manchester survey was sent to 500 similar retailers, with a response rate of 35 per cent.[2] The data below focus particularly on the importance employers ascribed to emotional and aesthetic labour, using the proxies of personality (as a proxy for attitudes within the emotional labour literature, as we noted above) and appearance.

As with other recent research by Bunt, McAndrew and Kuechel (2005) and Nickson, Warhurst and Dutton (2005) both Sydney and Manchester employers rated the 'right' personality and appearance as the most important aspects when selecting customer-facing staff (Table 8.1), though there were some differences with regard to the relative importance employers attributed to previous experience and qualifications.

Once inside the organization, employers also sought to further transmute and control employee appearance through appearance standards. Seventy-four per cent of Manchester employers and eighty-eight per cent of Sydney employers rated the appearance of customer-facing staff as either 'very important' or 'essential'. More than four out of five establishments in both Sydney and Manchester had an appearance policy or standards (that is approximately 80 per cent). The most common

Table 8.1   Factors important in employee selection

% 'Important' or 'very important' when selecting front-line staff	Manchester	Sydney
Personality	80	97
Appearance	68	84
Previous experience	41	78
Right qualifications	5	44

aspect covered was personal hygiene and general tidiness, reported by 91 per cent of establishments with an appearance policy. The next most commonly reported aspect, consistent with the results overall, was clothing style (76 per cent of those with a policy). Bodily adornment was also covered widely, with 55 per cent stating that make up and personal grooming was included in the appearance policy, 50 per cent facial and bodily piercing, 49 per cent jewellery, and 44 per cent visible tattoos.

Employers were asked why they had an appearance policy, and in both studies conformity to company brand and image was the key reason (Table 8.2). Ensuring employee conformity to the brand image is an important part of aesthetic labour, as is the use of employers to display the brand through dress codes and clothing policies. Fifty-five per cent of Manchester employers and fifty-eight per cent of Sydney employers stated that clothing policies were used to 'model' current stock, with current stock the most popular source from which staff clothing was drawn. The next most popular source of staff clothing (dedicated company clothing) was reported by less than a third of establishments with a clothing policy.

Employers were asked what types of training were provided for customer-facing staff. The highly aestheticized stores within the Sydney survey sample undertook relatively extensive training across several aspects of aesthetic presentation: training in interpersonal skills, presentation, clothing and dress style, personal grooming, body language, and what to say to customers. Similarly, within Manchester, training in company clothing standards was reported by 71 per cent of employers while 43–44 per cent reported providing training in social/interpersonal skills or self presentation/physical appearance. Those Manchester employers providing training in presentation and physical appearance were asked to delineate this training further into various sub-categories. Sixty-two per cent of all respondents answered this question suggesting that there was an overlap between those providing training in company clothing

Table 8.2   Reasons for appearance policy

% 'Important' or essential	Manchester	Sydney
Conformity to company brand/image	60	76
Local manager's preference	42	46
Customer preference	31	48
Adherence to employment law	19	33

standards and more general self-presentation training. The two most widely cited elements of appearance policy were dress sense and style, and body language, both reported by 46 per cent of employers. In addition, 35 per cent of employers provided training on what employee should say to customers, 25 per cent provided training in make up and personal grooming, and 8 per cent in voice and accent coaching. The fact that dress and style training was one of the two most widely reported aspects of appearance training emphasizes the importance attached to employee appearance in carrying out customer-facing work – that is, not just for employees getting the job but also for doing the job.

Across both surveys aesthetic awareness featured in employee performance appraisal. For example, in Sydney 65 per cent of employers reported that self-presentation and physical appearance were included in performance appraisals. Likewise 60 per cent included adherence to the company clothing standards. Similarly, Manchester employers reported that self presentation and physical appearance (57 per cent) and adherence to company clothing standards (56 per cent) were included in the appraisal process.

The data from the Sydney and Manchester surveys thus highlight how employee appearance is sought, shaped and supervised by employers. Employers in fashion retail routinely recruit and select customer service staff on the basis of their aesthetic attributes – appearance is second only to 'personality' as an important consideration in employee hiring. The surveys also confirm that employers typically use organizational appearance policies in ways that are consistent with the image of their stores. Indeed, it was clear from the surveys that employers continue to ensure their employees appreciate the importance of appearance in frontline service work with training interventions and performance appraisal.

Appearance as a form of employment discrimination

All employers use some form of discrimination to differentiate employees' and those employees' capacity to deliver efficacious labour. At issue with aesthetic labour is the legitimacy of using employee appearance as the discriminator. Ayto (1999, p. 485) defines 'lookism' as 'prejudice or discrimination on the grounds of appearance (i.e., uglies are done down and beautiful people get all the breaks).' Significantly, as Tietje & Cresap (2005, p. 32) acknowledge, 'In our society aesthetic capital, like other kinds of capital, is unequally distributed.' As a consequence, employers have the opportunity to discriminate against some employees perceived to lack the appropriate actual and potential appearance. Complementary research undertaken by the authors and presented in this section of the chapter analyses the extent to which a greater demand for aesthetic labour might lead to a new type of employment discrimination – indeed might be the new frontier of employment discrimination.

While not recognized in other Australian states, the Victorian Equal Opportunity and Human Rights Commission (hereafter referred to as VEOHRC) formally recognizes that discrimination on the basis of physical features occurs and that such discrimination should not be tolerated. Under the Act it is unlawful to treat someone less favourably because of their physical features. The Act defines physical features as height, weight, size, or other bodily characteristics with the implication that people 'do not have control' over these attributes (EOC, 2003). Physical features do not encompass hair, jewellery or dress codes. However, there is considerable ambiguity: it is recognized that the employer may lawfully require staff to dress in an appropriate manner and such decisions are left to management, recognizing that dress codes and appearances can vary depending on organizational positioning. Thus different standards apply to employees working in a bank compared to a construction site or the degree of customer contact required to be made by the employee as part of the job. As a consequence the VEOHRC provides employer guidelines on appearance standards. These guidelines state that it is illegal to discriminate against an employee by treating them less favourably than someone else because of their dress or appearance in relation to hiring, firing, promotion, pay and training, and covering full-time, part-time, casual, probationary and contract workers.

The authors were able to examine the case files over the first ten years of operation of the 'physical features' attribute under the Act. Unfortunately we could only examine in detail the 106 files lodged about alleged discrimination in employment between 1999 and 2005.[3] As this section of the chapter highlights, lookism is emerging as an employment issue that is attracting increasing institutional regulation both in Australia and internationally (for a discussion see Warhurst, van den Broek, Hall and Nickson 2009).

Table 8.3 shows the number of enquiries received each year about physical features. These enquiries are presented as a percentage of the total number of enquiries across all attributes and the relative ranking of enquiries about physical features in comparison to enquires about all other attributes such as age, sex, disability, and political belief etc.

Table 8.3   Enquiries about physical features

Year	No.	Rank
1995–96	93	13th
1996–97	183	11th
1997–98	148	10th
1998–99	136	13th
1999–2000	234	9th
2000–01	244	9th
2001–02	269	9th
2002–03	219	9th
2003–04	169	9th
2004–05	181	7th
Total/Average	**1,876**	**10th**

The data in Table 8.3 reveal that 1876 enquires were made about possible discrimination related to physical appearance over the ten years. Over these years, the number of possible attributes – such as race, disability, physical features etc. – on which enquiries were made has varied though the number has generally been around twenty. Since 1995 physical features represents, on average, the tenth attribute initiating enquiries from employees. However, the relative importance of physical features has risen from ninth at the turn of the century to seventh in the most recently available statistics. In this respect, it is noteworthy that while we have reviewed the case files for 'physical features' in the first ten years of its operation, according to the 2007–08 Annual Report from the VEOHRC, enquiries about discrimination on the basis of physical features has increased by approximately 30 per cent from previous years (2008, p. 23).

As expected, only some of the initial enquiries became formal complaints with the VEOHRC. Complaints related to physical features can be made in a number of areas encompassing, for example, employment, accommodation and education. The total number of such complaints in all areas is shown in the right hand column of Table 8.4. Employment attracts most complaints, making up 639 complaints in employment out of a total of the 1876 enquiries related to physical features. Similarly, although outside the first ten-year-period of analysis, recent annual reports reveal the persistence of complaints related to physical features

Table 8.4   Complaints related to physical features in all areas and employment

Year	Employment physical features cases			Total no. of physical features cases in ALL areas
	F	M	Total	
1995–96	11	4	15	20
1996–97	22	13	35	36
1997–98	21	4	25	32
1998–99	43	13	56	74
1999–2000	81	26	107	128
2000–01	42	28	70	104
2001–02	82	33	115	131
2002–03	42	23	65	81
2003–04	38	25	63	76
2004–05	53	35	88	118
Total	**435**	**204**	**639**	**1,421**

in employment ranging from 72 complaints in 2005, 48 in 2006, and 38 in 2007 (VEOHRC Annual Reports, 2006, 2008, 2009).

Table 8.4 indicates that in its first year of operation very few complaints were registered about physical features in employment. Since then, complaints have risen and, interestingly, although complaints from female employees dominate, there are a significant number of complaints registered by male employees each year. Moreover, while there are fluctuations over the ten years, the gap has narrowed between female and male complaints about discrimination in the workplace related to physical features: for the year 2004–05, complaints were 60:40 in terms of the female–male split.

The legislation explicitly states that an employer 'can create and maintain an image for their organization that best suits their industry and their clients'. It also recognizes how different dress standards apply to different industries, jobs and 'competitive positioning'. For example, a five star hotel will have more rigorous appearance codes than a backpacker inn (VEOHRC, 2010). However, these issues rarely arose in the cases analysed; few companies cited the defence that employees were failing to promote a public image that distinguished them from other companies. The type of workers involved in many of the cases is interesting: security guards, factory workers, forklift and truck drivers, process workers, labourers, manufacturing workers, kitchen hands, asphalters and other less customer-interactive occupations featured alongside the more expected hospitality workers. As such, claims are often made by employees in industries other than interactive services where it might be expected to find employer demand for aesthetic labour. Perhaps less surprising is that most of the VEOHRC claimants tended to be entry level to intermediate positions with very few claimants employed in managerial or professional positions seeking recourse through the VEOHRC in the sample studied.

The data thus throw up some interesting findings. Contrary to expectations, a significant amount of claimants were employed in industries and occupations which might not be expected to require highly aestheticized employees. This finding might reflect two points. First, in those industries and occupations most likely to require aestheticized labour such as retail and hospitality, as the Sydney and Manchester surveys reveal, there is evidence that there is a propensity to 'filter in' appropriate employees during selection. Second, there is some suggestion that the aesthetic qualities demanded by employers are those associated with middle classness (Warhurst & Nickson, 2007). Consequently, it is employees lower in the occupational hierarchy and in less customer-interactive occupations who are just as likely to experience discrimination on the basis of physical features. It may also be that these workers are using the legislation to redress perceived harassment or bullying by managers and co-workers based on physical taunts – an issue that requires further research. As the VEOHRC states, bullying is a major problem both in schools and in workplaces, and it is often linked to a personal characteristic – including gender, sexual orientation, race, religion, disability and physical features. However, in cases in which enquiries are made which relate to issues not covered by the legislation, such as workplace bullying, referrals are made to other associated organizations (EOC, 2005–2006). What the VEOHRC data does highlight is that both women and (increasingly) men allege and file for discrimination on the basis of physical attributes and do so across occupation and industry type, promoting a rethink about gender and employee looks.

Aesthetic labour, services, and gender

Aesthetic labour raises the issue of gender within interactive servcies, more particularly the claimed gendered determinism of the capacity to undertake efficacious service work. There has been a tendency within some research of aesthetic labour to show how it is concerned with creating feminized performativity (Gatta, Boushey and Appelbaum, 2009; Pettinger, 2004, 2005). This research echoes the claim made by Hochschild (1983) that female workers are the more natural providers of emotional labour. However, analysis of the VEOHRC data reveals that both men and women perceive themselves to be discriminated on the basis of their physical appearance. While the Sydney and Manchester surveys were unable to disaggregate the analysis by employee sex, the VEOHRC findings concur with other research on aesthetic labour in the UK by Walls (2008) that reveals that the importance of employee 'styling' equally applies to men working in frontline service jobs. As he notes, the men in his study of fashion retailers would use their aesthetic capital in seeking employment and male workers had to offer 'more than just masculinity, they had to also offer "cool", style and "trendiness"' (p. 110) once in work.

This recognition of how aesthetic labour envelops both women and men is an important analytical step forward in understanding work and employment in interactive services. One explanation for aesthetic labour also involving men, when emotional labour is cited as being a 'specialism' of female workers, might be that interactive service work is now being colonized by male workers, particularly male students needing to underpin their studies with paid employment that is both flexible in terms of working hours and patterns and has low entry and exit barriers (Canny, 2002). With more male employees in interactive service work, both men and women are expected to manage their appearance – and presumably feelings too. In this respect, the emotional labour paradigm erroneously perceived emotional labour as a specialism particular to women because it confused female prevalence with natural inclination within interactive service work – as exemplified most obviously by the flight attendants of Hochschild's study.

It is often forgotten, however, that in the early days of commercial aviation, flights attendants were male, as Mills' (2006) review of the corporate histories of British Airways, Pan Am, and Air Canada notes. It was only in the 1930s that airlines began to introduce female flight attendants and then only slowly. There is no analysis of whether employers demanded what is now termed emotional labour of male flight attendants in the early decades of the twentieth century. There is, however, recent archival research of banking – another favourite research site of emotional labour researchers in the form of call centre work – that does reveal such demands.

In his analysis of the 'curious case of Mr Notman', McKinlay (2009) lifts the lid on a long-forgotten struggle within the Scottish banking industry over the employer's right to control the workplace and non-workplace behaviour of banking clerks. In the 1930s, Mr Notman took his employer to court in a bid to assert his right to marry without employer approval and not be dismissed from his job. In the course of the trial the bank's employee performance appraisal techniques and content were exposed to public scrutiny – and ridicule. Not only was male bank clerks' 'penmanship' assessed – that is, their capacity to write legibly, quickly, and without accounting error, but also their attitudes, both among other staff and with customers. In his overview of employment practices in the industry at that time, McKinlay cites one inter-war commentary: 'we occasionally find men at the counter who are remarkable neither for their courtesy nor their efficiency, whose only strong points are an overwhelming sense of their own importance.' (p. 4) Echoing Hochschild's point that different forms of employee engagement with customers provide different styles of service that help brand organizations, another instructs bank clerks that in exchanges with customers 'there is a wide range between the rough-and-ready at one end of the scale and the stiff-and-stilted at the other; and the middle territory of cordiality tempered by due reserve would be your best choice.' (p. 4) Interestingly, the appraisals also noted the physical appearance of clerks. Similarly, in Australia it has been noted that male banking staff were recruited and promoted in the 19th century on their ability to be numerate; however, aesthetic characteristics of strength and virility were also noted (van den Broek, 2010). These studies indicate that with any remasculinization of interactive services there is a clear need to analyse any gendering of practices underpinning the employment relationship. Indeed, emotional and aesthetic labour is often an outcome of the presence of types of worker – male or female – than any inherent naturalness deemed to be possessed by these different workers.

It should also be noted that intersectionality is occurring here, with gender meeting class in employer strategies to affect the desired service encounter. The feminine and masculine performativity required in doing frontline service work is increasingly middle class as a number of studies of aesthetic labour have revealed (e.g. Leslie, 2002; Walls, 2008; Warhurst & Nickson, 2007). This class issue is not unique to aesthetic labour in services. It is often overlooked that in Hochshild's study of emotional labour, applicants for flight attendant jobs at Pan Am were also 'screened for a certain type of middle-class sociability' (1983, p. 97). This middle-class bias means that young working class men increasingly find themselves disadvantaged and alienated in a service-dominated labour market (McDowell, 2009; Nixon, 2009). Of course the contra situation involves women attempting to break into traditionally masculine areas of employment. For example, research indicates that women, particularly physically attractive women, face bias when attempting to enter employment in industries such as construction (Johnson, Podratz, Dipboye & Gibbons, 2010).

Just as one sex, women have become institutionally excluded from some jobs, the same processes are seemingly developing for the working class and interactive service jobs. In Glasgow, where research into aesthetic labour first occurred (Warhurst, Nickson, Witz and Cullen, 2000), there were expanding retail and hospitality industries, recruitment problems for employers and yet pockets of residual high unemployment in the city not one mile away from the employers who had recruitment difficulties. However, it is not an absolute labour shortage that existed in Glasgow but, from the employers' perspective, a shortage of the right type of workers. The working class were perceived to lack, from the employer's perspective, the appropriate aesthetic (and social) 'skills' that lever their employability and, as a consequence, were being excluded from the city's jobs growth (Nickson, Warhurst, Cullen and Watt, 2003). Aesthetic labour, as with other employer strategies before it, thus creates job opportunities for some workers and closes down opportunities for others. Not only is further research needed that analyses this new form of employment discrimination, but there is also a pressing need for policy responses that address it. More broadly, as the VEOHRC cases indicate, it is not just employees in interactive service work who allege discrimination on the basis of physical features; claims of lookism extend into non-service industries. Indeed, any assumptions that discrimination would be experienced by female employees in interactive services and at the point of hire seem confounded – male workers and workers in non-service industries and already in employment also report it.

Conclusion

This chapter started by pointing out that employment relations as both practice and field of study are concerned essentially with the employment relationship. The transformation problem is at the heart of this employment relationship. We also noted how both the practices and study of employment relations are dynamic. Until recently, the transformation problem in interactive services has been studied typically through the paradigm of emotional labour because employers have sought to control and transmute employee feelings in order to affect the desired service encounter. We have argued that this paradigm is useful but limited because, in focusing only on feelings, it analytically retires awareness and appreciation of employers' recent attempt to also control and transmute employee corporeality for the same reason. As the retail surveys of Sydney and Manchester affirm, employers seek to hire employees with the right appearance and ensure that appearance is mobilized, developed, and commodified through processes of recruitment and selection, training, and performance appraisal. On the basis of such findings, with respect to interactive service work, the practices of employment relations are changing, and so should its study.

It is not that employers no longer desire emotional labour in interactive services; rather employer strategies to address the transformation problem now also involve aesthetic labour: employee appearance, as well as their attitudes matter to employers. Thus as employer strategies to control workers' feelings complemented strategies to control workers' heads, these strategies are now complemented by other strategies centred on controlling workers' bodies. Recognition of the importance of aesthetic labour to employers highlights the continued dynamism of employment relations in terms of being a set of material practices and how these practices have developed recently within interactive service industries. It also opens up new issues of study within the employment relations of interactive services. Indeed, we have argued that aesthetic labour offers a new paradigm for analysing employment relations and identified how employers seek to address the transformation problem within the wage-effort bargain.

It needs to be emphasized, however, that even within interactive services, aesthetic labour is *a*, not *the*, new form of labour by which employers seek to create an efficacious service encounter and so generate more custom and profit through waged labour. As with other forms of labour before it, aesthetic labour will have contradictions, challenges and limitations for employers and so is likely in time to be complemented or superseded by other employer strategies. As Edwards (1979) noted by way of example, the technical control imposed by employers in manufacturing in the early decades of the twentieth century had facilitated the growth of industrial trade unions by mid-century, so then triggering employers' shift to bureaucratic control. With research of aesthetic labour still relatively new, these contradictions, challenges and limitations are yet to emerge – or at least be adequately identified and explored. However, what is apparent is that in weakly unionized industries, such as retail and hospitality, collective workplace employee responses to aesthetic labour are, as yet, difficult to discern. Two points emerge consequently. The first relates to employment relations practice; responses to aesthetic labour from outwith the workplace and by institutions other than trade unions – such as equal opportunities bodies – might emerge, backed by the state with anti-lookism legislation for example. To this end, as employee looks become more important in interactive services and beyond, it will be interesting to see whether other jurisdictions follow the example of Victoria in Australia and introduce legislation to proscribe employment discrimination on the basis of physical appearance. The second point relates to study – more research is needed that investigates employee attitudes to aesthetic labour, including whether employees self-select out of recruitment processes on the basis of their looks; prepare and accept aesthetic demands; or resist in subtle ways after appointment. Indeed, future research could further increase an understanding of the ways that employers mobilize and develop aesthetic labour, and identify employee resistance or acceptance of it. Such potential practice and research would also serve to emphasize the inherent dynamism of employment relations with interactive services.

Notes

1. For an update on labour process debate see Thompson and Smith (2010).
2. While this response rate is not high, it is within the range of commonly reported mail-out organizational surveys.
3. Unfortunately, the EOC Victoria destroys case files after seven years so that the research covers only the years after 1998–1999.

References

Ayto, J. (1999). *20th Century Words*. Oxford: Oxford University Press.
Bolton, S. (2005). *Emotion management in the workplace*. London: Palgrave.
Bourdieu, P., (1984). *Distinction: a social critique of the judgement of taste*. London: Routledge.
Braverman, H. (1974). *Labor and monopoly capital*. New York: Monthly Review Press.
Bray, M., Waring, P., & Cooper, R (2009). *Employment relations: theory and practice*. Sydney: McGraw-Hill.
Bunt, K., McAndrew, F., & Kuechel, A. (2005). *Jobcentre Plus Employer (Market View) Survey 2004*. Norwich: HMSO.
Callaghan, G. and Thompson, P. (2002) 'We recruit attitude': the selection and shaping of call centre labour. *Journal of Management Studies*, 39(2), 233–254.

Canny, A. (2002). Flexible labour? The growth of student employment in the UK. *Journal of Education and Work*, 15(3), 277–301.

Edwards, P. (1979). *Contested terrain*. London: Heinemann.

Edwards, P. (1995). From industrial relations to the employment relationship. *Relations Industrielles*, 50, 39–65.

Equal Opportunities Commission (EOC) (2003) 'Physical Features'. Retreived from http://www.eoc.vic.gov.au/materials/brochures/physical.html (accessed 15 December 2003).

Friedman, A. (1977). *Industry and labour*. London: Macmillan.

Gatta, M., Boushey, H., & Appelbaum, E. (2009). High-touch and here-to-stay: future skills demands in US low wage service occupations. *Sociology, 43*(5), 968–989.

Guest, D. E. (1997). Human resource management and performance: a review and research agenda. *International Journal of Human Resource Management, 8*(3), 263–276.

Hall, R. & van den Broek, D. (2011) *Economic and industrial democracy*. (Forthcoming.)

Hochschild, A. (1983). *The managed heart*. Berkeley: University of California Press.

Johnson, S., Podratz, K., Dipboye, R., & Gibbons, E. (2010). Physical attractiveness biases in ratings of employment sustainability: tracking down the 'beauty is beastly' effect. *Journal of Social Psychology, 150*(3), 301–318.

Kaufman, B. E. (2004). *Theoretical perspectives on work and the employment relationship*. Champaign, IL: Industrial Relations Research Association.

Korczynski, M. (2002). *Human resource management in the service sector*. Basingstoke: Palgrave Macmillan.

Leslie, D. (2002). Gender, retail employment and the clothing commodity chain. *Gender, Place and Culture*, 9(1), 61–76.

McDowell, L. (2009). *Working bodies: interactive service employment and workplace identities*. Chichester: Wiley-Blackwell.

McKinlay, A. (2009). *Banking, employment and masculinity, 1900–39: the peculiar case of Mr Notman*. Paper presented to the Management History Research Group Conference, University of York.

Mills, A. (2006). *Sex, strategy and the stratosphere: airlines and the gendering of organizational culture*. Basingstoke: Palgrave Macmillan.

Mills, C. W. (1951). *White collar*. New York: Oxford University Press.

Nickson, D., Warhurst, C., Commander, J., Hurrell, S.A., & Cullen, A.M. (2011). Soft skills and employability: evidence from UK retail. *Economic and Industrial Democracy* (forthcoming).

Nickson, D., Warhurst, C., Cullen, A.M., & Watt, A. (2003). Bringing in the excluded? Aesthetic labour, skills and training in the new economy. *Journal of Education and Work, 16*(2), 185–203.

Nickson, D., Warhurst, C., & Dutton, E. (2005). The importance of attitude and appearance in the service encounter in retail and hospitality. *Managing Service Quality*, 15(2), 195–208.

Nienhüser, N., & Warhurst, C. (2011). Comparative employment relations: definitional, disciplinary and development issues. In C. Brewster and W. Mayhofer (eds), *Handbook of research in comparative human resource management* Aldershot: Edward Elgar.

Nixon, D. (2009). 'I can't put a smiley face on': working class masculinity, emotional labour and service work in the 'new economy'. *Gender, Work and Organization*, 16(3), 300–322.

Pettinger, L. (2004). Brand culture and branded workers: service work and aesthetic labour in fashion retail. *Consumption, Markets and Culture*, 7(2), 165–184.

Pettinger, L. (2005). Gendered work meets gendered goods: selling and service in clothing retail. *Gender, Work and Organization*, 12(5), 460–478.

Thompson, P., & Smith, C. (eds). (2010). *Working life*. London: Palgrave Macmillan.

Tietje, L., & Cresap, S. (2005). Is lookism unjust? The ethics of aesthetics and public policy implications. *Journal of Libertarian Studies*, 19(2), 31–50.

van den Broek, D. (2010). Strapping as well as numerate: occupational identity, masculinity and the aesthetics of 19th century banking. *Business History*, Victorian Equal Opportunity & Human Rights Commission Annual Reports 1995–2009.

Victorian Equal Opportunity and Human Rights Commission (VEOHRC) (2006) *Victorian Equal Opportunity and Human Rights Commission Annual Report 2005/06*. Retrieved from http://www.humanrightscommission.vic. gov.au/index.php?option=com_k2&view=item&id=386:victorian-equal-opportunity-human-rights-commission-annual-report-2005/06&Itemid=690

Victorian Equal Opportunity & Human Rights Commission (VEOHRC) (2008). *2007/2008 Annual Report*. http://www.humanrightscommission.vic.gov.au/ publications/annual%20reports (accessed 11 December 2008)

Victorian Equal Opportunity and Human Rights Commission (VEOHRC) (2009) *Victorian Equal Opportunity and Human Rights Commission Annual Report 2008/09*. Retrieved from http://www.humanrightscommission.vic. gov.au/index.php?option=com_k2&view=item&id=384:victorian-equal-opportunity-human-rights-commission-annual-report-2007/08&Itemid=690

Victorian Equal Opportunity & Human Rights Commission (VEOHRC) (2010). eQuality in the workplace quality: dress and appearance in the workplace. http://www.equalopportunitycommission.vic.gov.au/pdf/Employer%20 Guide lines%20-%20Dress%20and%20appearance%20in%20the%20workplace.pdf

Walls, S. (2008). *Are you being served: gendered aesthetics among retail workers*. (unpublished doctoral thesis). University of Durham.

Warhurst, C., & Nickson, D. (2007). Employee experience of aesthetic labour in retail and hospitality. *Work, Employment and Society*, 21(1), 103–120.

Warhurst, C. & Nickson, D. (2009) 'Who's got the look?': from emotional to aesthetic and sexualised labour in interactive services. *Gender, Work and Organisation*, 16(3), 385–404.

Warhurst, C., Nickson, D., Witz, A., Cullen, A. M. (2000). Aesthetic labour in interactive service work: some case study evidence from the "new" Glasgow. *Service Industries Journal*, 20(3), 1–18.

Warhurst, C., van den Broek, D., Hall, R., & Nickson (2009). Lookism: the new frontier of employment discrimination? *Journal of Industrial Relations*, 51(1), 131–136.

9
Trust, HRM, and the Employment Relationship

Graham Dietz, Akinwunmi Martins, and Rosalind Searle

> Whatever matters to human beings, trust is the atmosphere in which it thrives
>
> Sissela Bok, 1978, cited in Baier, 1986, p. 231

> There is nothing less constant than interest, today it unites, and tomorrow it brings enmity
>
> Fox, 1974, p. 266

> Sometimes, it is not always possible for the business to do what is right
>
> Chris, HR Director; interviewee

Trust has long been considered a crucial determinant of people's experiences of work and the employment relationship (see, for example, Fox, 1974). Yet a commonplace argument holds that the increasing demands placed upon contemporary organizations (globalized market competition, de-regulation, and re-regulation), as well as trends in workforce composition (greater education levels, greater cultural diversity) and in the management of work (transactional contractual arrangements, increasing workloads and job-creep, information technologies), have heightened interest in trust among HR professionals (Hope-Hailey, Farndale, & Truss, 2005; Searle & Skinner, 2011; Sparrow & Marchington, 1998).

So too has the evidence of trust's impact on performance. Trusting relationships at work have been positively associated with higher job satisfaction and organizational commitment, discretionary effort on behalf of a wide range of stakeholders, knowledge sharing, and even customer satisfaction, sales, and profit (for reviews, see Colquitt, Scott, & LePine, 2007; Dirks & Ferrin, 2001). Some argue that trust can be a decisive source of sustainable competitive advantage (Barney & Hansen, 1994). The essential logic is this: for employees to perform optimally, they need to trust that their employer (specifically, their employer's representatives in management) will provide a positive working environment, support them in their efforts, and treat them fairly in matters of reward, welfare, and voice (Davis, Schoorman, Mayer, & Tan, 2000; Simons, 2002). Equally, high performance requires managers to trust employees to work responsibly, diligently, and effectively (Salamon & Robinson, 2008), reducing the need for unproductive and inefficient *excessive* monitoring. A level of appropriate two-way trust is needed.

Yet trust is a fragile commodity. It can take a long time to establish, and one misplaced or abusive act can destroy it. Many commentators point to faltering and insecure trust inside organizations (Edelman, 2009; Robinson, 1996; Thompson, 2003). Massive redundancy programmes and widespread perceptions of job insecurity, increased workloads and stress, the precarious status of pay and bonuses, and disparities in relative incomes can all be expected to damage trust in organizations.

These are HR policy domains, and HRM is among the most influential areas for trust development inside organizations (Whitener, 1997). The often-raised imperative for HR professionals is to build people management systems that deliver high levels of employee commitment and/or 'engagement' (CIPD, 2010). Trust dynamics – though seldom the explicit focus of these models – suffuse them all (see Searle & Skinner, 2011). Indeed, trust issues surface in almost every area of human resources (Robinson & Rousseau, 1994; Whitener, 1997) throughout the 'employee cycle' (Searle & Skinner, 2011). An organization's selected strategies and policies on HRM send out signals of intent to staff (Six & Sorge, 2008), while their implementation provides tangible evidence of the extent to which management's intentions are genuine and hence can be trusted (Skinner, Saunders, & Duckett, 2004). In short, trust plays a key role in the successes of HRM, as does mistrust in its failures (Whitener, 1997). Sparrow and Marchington's (1998) observation that trust-building might be 'the most fundamental base of knowledge' for HR professionals still applies more than a decade on.

Yet trust poses an acute challenge to HR professionals. They occupy a rather tricky and unenviable position in the relationship between employer and employee, often depicted as Janus-like (facing two ways, simultaneously). When facing the organisation, the HR professional's strategic partner/change agent roles (Ulrich, 1997) are to design policies and practices that secure productive employee inputs and outputs in pursuit of corporate and managerial interests. HR departments are entrusted by their employer to reflect the will of management and, by presumed extension, those of shareholders/budget-holders. Yet one of HR's other roles is as the 'employee champion/ advocate' (Ulrich, 1997), attending to the needs and welfare of staff, whether for its own sake, or because – following a service-profit chain model of management (Heskett, 1997) – corporate interests are understood to be best realized through satisfying employees' interests first. In navigating these potentially contradictory roles, HR professionals can face ethical, operational, intra-personal and inter-personal conflicts and dilemmas that must be resolved (Wright & Snell, 2005). Selecting the appropriate HR policy response on redundancies, appraisal systems, performance bonuses, and employee voice will have knock-on effects for the trust between employer and employee, as well as for the employer and employees' trust in the HR department. Several studies have shown how HR professionals can struggle with these conflicts (Caldwell, 2003; Francis & Keegan, 2005), especially when commercial imperatives take priority over employee welfare, or fairness concerns. Thus, senior HR leaders are in a unique position to comment on trust dynamics in the employment relationship, from both 'sides', as well as from their own viewpoint.

In exploring these dynamics and tensions, we have adopted a somewhat unconventional structure. We did not want to limit ourselves to an extended literature-driven commentary; we wanted to include real experience from HR practitioners to ground the debate in practice. So we conducted semi-structured interviews with a convenience sample of seven HR Directors and Managers known to the authors (six UK based, one Europe based).[1]

However, this chapter is *not* an empirical study; it is an opinion piece. The purpose of the interviews was confined to capturing compelling

Table 9.1 HR directors and managers interviewed for this chapter

Name	Industry
Andrea	Private HR consulting firm
Danny	Automobile manufacturing
Paul	Law firm
Chris	Telecommunications
Sally	Healthcare
Saskia	Construction
Sue	Retail

insights for the specific remit of this chapter. Thus, in terms of 'method' – or, more accurately, the origins of our practitioner inputs – we conducted telephone interviews in the summer of 2010, asking first for the practitioners' understanding of the employment relationship, then their insights into the nature of trust generally and within their workplace, and finally their thoughts on how HRM and HR departments help or hinder trust. The interviews were recorded, and we then went through them looking for compelling illustrative quotes that exemplified or countered the prevailing wisdom on trust and HRM. (The quotes have had to be edited for brevity and directness.)

The chapter proceeds as follows. The next section explains our primary construct, trust. We then examine the nature of the employment relationship, and our practitioners' takes on this. The third section reviews the practitioners' insights into trust in the workplace. In the final section, we explore how HRM can help or hinder trust in the employment relationship.

Trust

A broad consensus has now emerged on a three-stage process to trust (McEvily Perrone, & Zaheer, 2003). First, the foundations of trust arise from an assessment of the other party's trustworthiness. This consists of a set of subjective, aggregated beliefs – 'confident positive expectations' (Lewicki, McAllister, & Bies, 1998) – about their character and likely conduct, and one's relationship with them (Dietz & den Hartog, 2006). When these beliefs cross a threshold beyond hope and faith into something more confident, the trusting party makes the 'decision' to trust (Dietz & den Hartog, 2006). This decision reflects a 'willingness to accept vulnerability' (Rousseau, Sitkin, Burt, & Camerer, 1998), based on the preceding assessment of the other's trustworthiness. At risk for employees might be their job, workload, career, or personal status; for the employer, it might be the organization's operational effectiveness, sales, and reputation. For trust to be observed and truly verified, the trusting party must go on to rely on the other in a way that renders them vulnerable. This final behavioural stage involves a demonstration of their trust, such as allowing the other to have discretion over something of value (e.g. a budget, a decision, an employee's career progression), or making them privy to sensitive information (Gillespie, 2003). Without this risk-taking act, trust is 'cheap talk' (an 'empowered' employee whose work is micro-managed is not being trusted).

The antecedents of trust in an employing relationship are complex (see Searle, Weibel, & den Hartog, 2011). Mayer, Davis, and Schoorman's (1995) influential framework suggests that three trustworthiness factors are involved in interpersonal scenarios (the 'ABI' model of trustworthiness):

1. 'Ability' beliefs concern the perceived competence of the other party. In individuals, ability refers to their technical, cognitive, and communicative skills, while at the firm level, it encapsulates the organization's overall effectiveness, as realized via its managers and staff, and its access to resources.
2. 'Benevolence' perceptions reflect an assumption of benign, or at least non-detrimental, motives on the part of the trusted party. The trustor detects a positive orientation towards them from the other party. Benevolence implies a sincere concern for, and even a desire to enhance, the other party's well-being (Six & Sorge, 2008).
3. 'Integrity' focuses on adherence to a set of principles that the trustor finds acceptable. This not only implies a consistency between the trustee's words (intentions) and their deeds (actions), but also an assessment of moral character, including honesty and fair treatment of others. Examples would be keeping to each party's side of the 'psychological contract' bargain (Herriot, Manning, & Kidd, 1997; Robinson, 1996) such as employers fulfilling promises (e.g. on pay and rewards) and issuing clear and candid communications. For employees, integrity might include adherence to ethical codes of conduct, and admitting to errors or inadequacies in their performance.

Evidence for trustworthiness can come from direct encounters with others, observing their character, conduct, and performance. But indicators can also come via indirect sources, such as the obligations and constraints on people's behaviour implied by their role which render them predictable (e.g. doctors and train drivers). Similarly, we may trust another, by proxy, based on the presence of institutional constraints, such as legislation and regulations. Indeed, employees' trust can focus at the interpersonal level (e.g. with immediate bosses and colleagues), and at the organizational level, incorporating assessments of their senior leaders, and the various systems and policies the organization chooses to deploy (Gillespie & Dietz, 2009; Searle et al., 2011) – including its HRM policies. Awareness of these two sources for trust – interpersonal and systems – is necessary to understand more fully the precise dynamics of trust at work (Searle & Skinner, 2011). Although Mayer and colleagues'

'ABI' model is firmly established in interpersonal relations (Colquitt et al., 2007), Searle Den Hartog, Weibel, Gillespie, Six, & Hatzakis (in press) found only competence and benevolent intent to be discernible factors in employees' trust in their employer.

None of these trustworthiness attributes is sufficient on its own to generate trust; a minimum level of all three is needed for trust to emerge. Should there be a lack of convincing evidence in one or more attributes, trust is likely to be undermined. That said, people can compartmentalize and aggregate evidence, accommodating contradictions and errors within an overall positive assessment (see Lewicki et al., 1998).

Trust emerges through repeated interactions and exchanges of reciprocal obligations between parties (Lewicki, Tomlinson, & Gillespie, 2006), as depicted in social exchange theory (Whitener, Brodt, Korsgaard, & Werner, 1998). If obligations are met, and reciprocated, expectations are fulfilled and trust develops. But trust is damaged by either the failure to adhere to formal or social rules, or by disconfirmed expectations (Whitener et al., 1998). In this way, trust tends to evoke trust; distrust tends to evoke distrust (Fox, 1974, p. 67).

Put simply, then, the trust challenge at the heart of the employment relationship is this: can the trinity of trustworthiness attributes (ability, benevolence, and integrity) be delivered by both parties – employer and employee – in a credible, sustainable, and effective manner that allows both of them to take the decision to trust the other, and take productive risks at work? And how can HRM help this to happen?

Trust and the employment relationship

Hardin (1993) argues that it is useful to conceptualize trust as a three-part relation, involving the properties of a trustor, the attributes of a trustee, and the specific context in which trust is conferred. In the employment relationship, there is the individual employee, and her/his employer, but the latter role is represented by multiple agents including the employee's direct line manager, the HR department, and the senior managers, while the employee may be represented by a trade union. Thus, the exact profile of the dyad participants is vague. (This 'split responsibility' issue for the roll-out of HRM came out clearly in our interviews, of which more is discussed later.) The culture of the sector and the nations in which the employer operates, and the shifting demands of its markets, provide an idiosyncratic context.

In its simplest conceptualization, the employment relationship refers to the open-ended and dynamic series of interactions between an individual selling her capacity to work and the organization buying that labour capacity with a wage.[2] Managers' primary concern is to convert that capacity into a performance that brings tangible benefits to the organization's owners or custodians. Managers *may* choose to arrange the relationship in a manner that satisfies the aims and interests of the employees, but this is by no means a pre-requisite. Employees' primary interests, meanwhile, are to maintain a living and fair reward for their efforts, and a degree of autonomy over what happens to them at work (Herriot, Manning, & Kidd, 1997). Many may want to perform well, but this is not guaranteed.

Most academic commentators see the two sets of interests, or expectations, as potentially overlapping, but also potentially antagonistic (Blyton & Turnbull, 2007; Edwards, 1986). The relationship may be characterized by mutually productive trust, or mistrustful conflict, subject to changing circumstances, shifts in the parties' objectives, and fluctuating interpretations of the other's decisions and actions. (However, as we shall see, this is not a view shared by many practicing HR professionals.)

One way to address and resolve this fundamental tension is through the practices, activities, rules, duties, and obligations put in place to steer workplace interactions between managers and employees. HR policies and practices seek to shape employees' expectations regarding anticipated performance levels, their treatment at work (welfare, voice), and prospects for progression, among others. HR also seeks to create a climate and set of management procedures in which mutually beneficial reciprocal obligations between managers and staff, based on positive trusting expectations, can be realized. Clarity around the nature of the inducements and expectations, and the subsequent fulfilment of them both, build trust in the relationship (Korsgaard, Brodt, & Whitener, 2002; Tsui & Wu, 2005).

Examples of how HRM creates expectations and obligations include the following.

- creating an 'employer brand'/'employer value proposition', sending signals about the organization's trustworthiness to enhance applicant attraction;
- selecting candidates who endorse the organization's aims, and whose capacity is likely to deliver productive performance;
- helping to define what constitutes acceptable job performance, and design appraisal and reward schemes to achieve those targets;
- co-ordinating the distribution of information and communications, and formal provisions for employee voice;

- plotting career paths, and providing development opportunities to enable employees' ambitions to be realized, thereby enhancing the 'human capital' of the organization;
- overseeing the more antagonistic encounters, such as disciplinary cases, industrial disputes, or redundancies.

In short, HR policies may have positive trust assumptions and dynamics 'designed in', or not (Fox, 1974; Sparrow & Marchington, 1998). HRM fosters employer-employee trust, or undermines it (Searle & Skinner, 2011).

The assumptions of HR professionals on the nature of the employment relationship will influence how they design their policies. So we asked our interviewees for their general take on the employment relationship. Their answers tended towards a broadly unitarist frame of reference: that the ideal employment relationship – and in some cases, the reality – was of aligned interests between employer and employee, and hence the prospect of high levels of workplace trust. Sue described her non-unionized company in powerfully unitarist terms:

> *Sue:* We have a very, very positive relationship with our staff ... it's a family business, we are founder-led, it is viewed culturally as a 'family'. People tell us working here feels like working in a family, there is a shared sense of pride.

Chris, from a unionized setting, was more equivocal, but also aspired to a unitarist reality:

> *Chris:* The preferable scenario is where the employee wants to work for the organization, they have moral attachment, they enjoy what they do, the employer takes care of the employee, helps them to feel rewarded and fulfilled ... In an ideal world most people would say they would prefer to work somewhere they care about and have an interest in ... You can't expect people to be engaged and overtly dedicated to what you do all the time but at least whilst they are there working for you, you have a right to expect a certain level of performance.

Two others emphasized the need for a form of 'mutuality', albeit one directed by managers:

> *Andrea*: The smart way to do business is to say that people are a core part of delivering what the organisation needs and then you need to set up conditions of mutuality so that there are benefits for the

organization and the individual. In today's marketplace you need people to bring their passion and talent to the workplace. Creating a sense of meaning about what the organization is there to do helps develop an emotional connection so that employees give what they have willingly.

Danny: The employment relationship in my company is founded on mutual respect and clearly, the company expects the individual to work very hard and contribute to the business. And a part of the contract is that the company commits to provide career opportunities, safe working environment and hopefully to provide sustainable long-term employment opportunities ...

Few seemed prepared to acknowledge radicalist talk of 'inherent conflicts of interest', and 'structured antagonisms' (Edwards, 1986). They may even have regarded such notions as anachronistic relics. Only two felt that employer-employee conflict might be presumed, but again the primacy of the organization's interests was apparent:

Paul (Law firm): I think there is a conflict of interest in certain respects because it is not always possible to say that the employer has the interest of the employees at heart. Because the purpose of an organization, especially in the private sector, is to make profits. [But] I do not think there is any conflict that can never be reconciled ... Most employers want their employees to be happy and they try to do the right [HR-related] things ... A vast majority of employers know they have to treat their employees this way and they indeed do ... If there is a conflict, it can be managed ... and for the benefit of both parties. There has to be communication around issues, there has to be some kind of joint interest working for the benefit of the organization.

Saskia (Construction): The conflict of interest is always there at different levels, depending on who is involved ... The things you do as an organization, you have an obligation to do [them], it is difficult to provide a standard set [of HR policies; expectations]. Things just constantly change. If you have a financial crisis, everything that was, the way things are done, goes out of the window and everything goes back to bare productivity.

Our interviewees' preference for unitarist assumptions and intentions contrasts somewhat with Geare, Edgar, & McAndrew's (2006) survey of managers in New Zealand, who were broadly pluralist in the abstract, but tended towards unitarism when discussing their own organization. But our sample does echo the CIPD's 'official' standpoint on employee relations (Emmott, 2006).

These aspirations are hardly surprising: the HR profession's ambition, rightly, is to have a real strategic impact (Ulrich & Brockbank, 2005), and most see that to achieve this, they need to design and implement policies to align employer and employee interests and objectives. Few HR managers would want to accommodate the prospect of conflict and dissonance in their working lives. It reflects badly on them. So the default position of most of our HR practitioners as one of optimism on the likelihood of aligned interests, and hence of mutual trust, is understandable.

But this stance *is* problematic when viewed through a trust lens. Aligned interests should build trust, of course (Hurley, 2006), but many commentators, especially academics, see this as a Sisyphean task in the employment relationship, which contains within it a 'structured antagonism' between the two parties that, ultimately, will manifest itself at some point (Edwards, 1986) – whether in unjust appraisal and promotion decisions, or pay and bonus disputes, strikes, or redundancies. At some stage, as Saskia observed, these optimistic expectations of unity of purpose are likely to be dashed on the rocks of commercial expediency.

Clearly, many HR professionals disagree. Geare et al. (2006, p. 1191) argued that while normative ideology might reflect beliefs on what *should be*, a HR manager's empirical ideology considers *what is*. Chris' admirably frank contribution exemplified this. He works in a densely unionized company and, when asked, he sided, normatively, with a unitarist standpoint (see the quote on page 148). Yet when we asked about HRM in his firm, he was not only explicit about the rhetoric-reality gap first lamented by Karen Legge over twenty years ago, but he also seemed unapologetic about it:

> *Chris*: That is the propaganda. I sell that story to the people at work. I preach that egalitarian, unitary line very strongly but everyone recognises that some of the time, it is not possible. The practice [in his company] is towards a pluralist frame [i.e. an inherent conflict of interest resolved through negotiation and joint rule-making].

He expanded upon the reasons behind the rhetoric-reality gap:

> *Chris*: There are times the employer knows what the right thing to do for people at work is, but owing to pressures of business,

strategic priorities, financial priorities, the employer simply cannot do the right thing, and you have to explain why ... why certain tough decisions, which disengage people and don't live up to the employee contract or deal, have to be taken.

This mismatch in expectations – between signals and delivery – is a problem for trust, since trust is founded on positive expectations being fulfilled. Our concern is that the kinds of unitarist aspiration articulated by many of our interviewees and others (e.g. the CIPD) set a dauntingly high standard for HR professionals to achieve and maintain. We recognize, however, the paradox of the alternative: realistic job previews, less ambitious cultural programming (i.e. fewer grandiose claims of unity), and even the accommodation of inherent conflict may set reasonable and deliverable expectations, but perhaps not very attractive ones!

The HR practitioners' insights into trust

All of our interviewees hailed the centrality of trust in the employment relationship, their work, and the experiences of their colleagues. To take two illustrative quotes,

> *Chris (Telecoms)*: [Trust is] absolutely important, it is probably the most basic, most profound commodity of human transaction ...

> *Danny (Automotives)*: From the management perspective, if there is an absence of trust, then fundamentally, the capability of an organization is reduced ... If you have trust in the relationship and aligned goals, then you can move faster and be more dynamic and productive. Over the years in [his plant], managers have worked very hard to ensure that trust is evident for those reasons.

Rather than employees' trust in the firm, Sally saw managers' trust in their staff as being especially vital to her company's success:

> *Sally*: [Trust] is the ability of people to fulfil their role and responsibility on behalf of the company, representing the company how it wishes to be represented. Employees have to be trained and trusted to represent the company and go out to deliver. Management empowers employees to do their job and they trust them to do so. In the nature of our business, employees are trusted to go around doing their job without the company checking on them.

Most interviewees had a similar, quite accurate conception of the process of trust as being based on validated or disconfirmed expectations:

> *Andrea*: Trust is a concept based on whether my actual experience is in line with what was espoused to me and what I am experiencing. If these two things are in line, then an employee can trust the organization at large … Generally speaking, everybody knows that you have to deliver against what you say and if you do not, you lose credibility. There is a kind of 'say and do ratio': what you say and what you do. If you say a lot and do less, your ratio drops.

> *Chris*: From the employee point of view, it is whether or not the employer lives up to the promise of employment made initially. Do the practices and behaviours and the nature of the work match up to what was offered and what was priced?

> *Paul*: With trust, you expect to be treated fairly, given recognition for what you do, and be rewarded … It is having faith that you can rely on an organization to treat you well and impact positively in your life.

Thus, the centrality of trust is apparent, and the process is understood to be the demonstration of one party's trustworthiness, and of expectations being fulfilled or not. Implicit in several comments is an acknowledgement of an element of risk, although Chris rejected the notion of employee being required to render themselves vulnerable to their employer – a legacy, perhaps, of the latent unitarist assumptions held by many of our practitioners. All three highlight the importance of HR departments being able to set and deliver upon attractive employee expectations. But, to reiterate, these expectations need to be achievable.

Trust and the HR function

The interviewees were asked who should have responsibility for trust levels inside organizations. All argued that this cannot be the sole responsibility of HR:

> *Andrea*: Anybody that is in a leadership position, and every individual in the organization, has trust responsibilities … There are too many other players and so [HR] cannot be solely responsible. HR does have a leadership role in designing the 'architecture' within which the people side of things is brought to life.

Sue: The responsibility is with the senior leaders, and the line manager relationship [with employees] is crucial. Staff need to feel that managers care, and will also take their interests into consideration. They also need to feel that they will be recognised for doing well, and to be inspired and motivated.

Paul: The building of trust is everybody's responsibility, from the top to the bottom and vice versa, and those in the middle! ... It is not fair to leave the building of trust as a responsibility of HR.

Our interviewees argued strongly that HR's remit is to create the conditions for such trust to thrive, but it is up to managers, as 'owners' of their staff's psychological contract, to deliver on trust building and trust repair. The line manager is responsible for the immediate working environment around an individual employee, and senior management is responsible for the organization's wider culture. Saskia explained HR's guiding and cajoling role thus:

Saskia: It is the responsibility of the entire organization and senior management team. HR has the ability to provide advice, measurement and kick-start its strategy but ... HR cannot be responsible for organizational trust ... HR should be on the senior management table with the CEO providing guidance and advice in decision-making in terms of its impact of employees and productivity and engagement. They should also maintain two-way communications between management and employees so as to understand what the issues are with the workforce, [and] create and put in place strategies that build trust proactively rather than reactively.

Chris illustrated a systematic approach for how trust cascades from senior management through line managers to the workforce:

Chris: It is the responsibility first and foremost of senior management and leadership to create and role-model an environment where trust in management would thrive. It is the responsibility of middle and junior managers to then follow that through and to deal with their people in a way that reflects the trust and it's the responsibility of employees to live up to that and show a little bit of trust and less cynicism toward the organization ...

I think HR can help to build the environment for trust to thrive through policies and practices and things that encourage and build trust ... but it is the responsibility of people that work in various roles to build trust between themselves.

Danny illustrated how trust is built between a supervisor and employee in his industry:

> *Danny*: The relationship on a day-to-day basis is fundamentally between the employee and his frontline manager and it varies from function to function. The relationship is very strong and very team-oriented and so is the trust. The frontline supervisor looks after 20 people. He hires them, trains them, fires them, looks after their workstation and general well-being. That builds a very strong relationship between the employee and the frontline supervisors and that is where the clarity in expectations and objectives-setting take place ... If the company [including HR] doesn't invest and help the frontline supervisor with the clarity of information and doing what it says it would do, then it is impossible for him to engender trust in that relationship.

However, Paul offered some reflections on why this approach might prove problematic with these pen-portraits of typical management predispositions to trust that he had encountered:

> *Paul*: Your relationship with your employer is with a human being ... Some managers may start with a position of trusting their employees and giving them an opportunity to do the job without them getting involved. Only when employees step out of the line do they discipline them. Other managers may think employees cannot be trusted so they treat the whole workforce as not been able to be trusted. It is more of an individual psychological issue for a person and not because they are managers.

Devolving to line management of responsibility for the employment relationship (Francis & Keegan, 2005) and workplace trust (Whitener et al., 1998) fits with established strategic models of HR 'business partnering', which liberate HR practitioners for more 'value-added' activities as 'change agents' and 'strategic partners' (Ulrich, 1997). This is where they can have the greatest impact, and HR practitioners are correct to argue that line managers are closest to their staff, and therefore the right people to lead on people management.

But in trust terms, this approach might again place HR departments in a bind, for under this model, HR's impact and its own trustworthiness is refracted through, and determined by, the line managers. This mediated impact can work very well – Danny's justly lauded car plant and Sue's award-winning retail chain are notable examples – but HR professionals are essentially at the mercy of the whims and idiosyncrasies (e.g. levels of understanding, support, and dedication) of line managers for delivering on the expectations and obligations of trust HR has designed into their policies. Francis and Keegan (2005, p. 27) found that many managers have 'neither the time nor the training [nor, we would add, the inclination] to give HR the priority it needs'. As a result, the reputation of HR can become tainted unjustly. The next section explores how HR can address this second paradox.

HR policies and their presumed impact on trust

If trust is built on the basis of confident positive expectations regarding another's conduct being fulfilled, then the implications for the design of HR policies and practices are apparent. Six and Sorge (2008), in a study of two Dutch firms, identified four broad policies:

1. a relationship-oriented culture that values acts of benevolence;
2. unambiguous 'relational signalling' (on what is expected of everyone), both vertically and horizontally;
3. explicit socialization into the firm's values; and
4. mechanisms to manage, match, and develop professional competencies.

We asked our interviewees for examples of how their HR policies can help to build trust. Chris explained how trustworthiness is a core corporate and HR value:

> *Chris*: We have enshrined 'trustworthiness' in our people. It is one of our core values. Trustworthiness simply means do what you say you would, do not let people down. And we measure people against that in our activities ... The challenge is how to close 'the promise gap' [when the] espoused behaviours that attracted you to go work initially are not matched up by reality. The principal cause of employee disengagement is the gradual erosion of that trust.

In line with the literature (Korsgaard, Brodt, & Whitener, 2002), most interviewees argued for the importance of clarity as to what everyone is expected to aim for, and do:

Andrea: The fundamentals are that you are looking to espouse what the organization is about. You are looking to be clear on what the deal in the organization is ... Modern employment needs to create opportunities where people can fully bring themselves to the workplace and, in return for performance, get personal growth opportunities ... If you want people to bring their perspective, you have to share information. People have to understand why they need to do what you want them to do ...

HR makes very significant efforts. It ranges from setting standards, creating transparency and clarity, reinvesting in capability ... Outcomes should not just be for the benefit of the organization, but should be mutual. Being crystal clear on mutuality is fundamental in today's work environment.

Linked to this, several interviewees pointed to the notoriously nebulous concept of 'communication' as key to the transparency and clarity of expectations that builds trust:

Sally: We are very focused on being very transparent about performance management, and evaluations, and more face-to-face time with employees rather than emails. You cannot judge trust well from someone who writes something ... We have a lot of communication from senior management through video technology and blogs and it is very open ... There is no lock-down on what people can say. Senior managers interact and are involved with the lower levels in the organization.

Danny: My version of trust is built on transparency, and a two-way flow of communication. Clearly a management team that tells one story in its communication and doesn't do that in practice – where practical examples do not match the communication strategy – would have a real problem in sustaining trust within the working environment. From a company's perspective, clarity of communication, walking the talk and delivering what you say is important in building trust, and from an individual perspective, clarity of expectation levels and performance levels keeps the plant in the forefront of business. In the plant, the management team displays what is required very clearly and why the company is going in a particular direction and it does that through frequent communications at employee meetings, regular morning meetings, end of shift meetings, etc.

From the employee perspective, the whole performance appraisal process is underpinned by clarity and since there is no job description, you have to be clear about what you expect from someone. The expectations are made very clear and feed back is direct and positive. [Communication] is underpinned by reward and recognition. Recognition in the sense of career development and growth, and reward in both career development and promotion, and also telling someone they have done a good job.

Sue pointed to the value of employee voice as a way of fostering trust, although it is clear that her firm's network of staff forums, at store and regional and national levels, has a decidedly unitarist outlook and remit:

> *Sue*: We have a number of staff forums that are consultative; we use them to communicate changes, and about ways of improving the business. The forums are more about engagement than conflict resolution.

On other main HR policy domains, recruitment and selection came first (as it does chronologically, of course):

> *Chris*: People coming into graduate jobs go through psychometric tests so as [to] check how they measure up against the trustworthy values of the organization.

> *Sally*: For R&S we use psychometric tests, we make sure people know what we are. We let them know what is important to us in terms of competencies and from the get-go. People know when they join [the firm] what we look for in staff that we hire. Through induction we have open discussions with new hires and also get to know people's differences.

Chris argued for the importance of training and development to enhance managers' trustworthiness. But he hinted at the need sometimes for HR to challenge commercial imperatives and senior management strategies, in order to protect workplace trust:

> *Chris*: HR should be providing coaching and leadership development programmes. They should be providing direct feedback to senior managers as to what is good or bad [behaviour], how they are performing and how they can be better role models. HR can perform this function if there is the willpower to do it or the courage to do

it ... It comes down to HR directors: are they big or strong enough to go to top management and tell them they are not behaving in the right way, or setting good examples, and letting them know the impact on the employment relationship? ... You cannot have a company saying one thing and doing the other.

Paul outlined a similar role for HR in advocating and setting standards:

Paul: A good HR manager would try to influence the culture of the workplace by explaining why certain behaviours are important. It involves communication to explain why it is important for people to do things in a certain way ... Good HR managers should [also] explain the context within which the business operates. The idea is to make sure everyone is treated equally fairly. [This] helps to engender trust. Communication and education are key concepts that good HR managers should try to promote.

Sue described the following developmental policies in place in her retail firm:

Sue: We have a staff survey in which our employees can tell us how well they are being managed, and Area HR Managers then coach store managers on the results, and how to improve. We provide our store managers with training on how to get the best results from people: we encourage them to manage their staff as individuals. Regular 'People Reviews' are held with store managers, on what's going on and things to do [in HR matters]: succession planning, training, 'PDPs' ...

Sally noted HR's advisory and coaching role in disciplinary matters:

Sally: In HR we work one on one with managers on how to conduct themselves and where there is a breakdown in trust we are very much involved in trying to resolve that conflict.

This can be tricky terrain, too. Harrington and Rayner (2011) found that if HR staff are seen as partial in their treatment of employees in disciplinaries, they can lose line managers' trust, as well as that of employees: the strategic partner/employee champion conflict again (Caldwell, 2003).

Conclusion

This chapter has explored trust's importance in the employment relationship and HRM, and revealed some of the challenges and tensions involved for HR professionals in signalling and maintaining trust in the workplace.

One way of interpreting our practitioners' insights is that some trust tensions may, in part, be created by HR departments themselves, from fostering unrealistic or unsustainable expectations and obligations, the mediated impact of HRM on trust from the devolvement (partial surrender of influence?) of policy implementation to line managers, and the role-conflicts that can arise in balancing HR's multiple imperatives. Specifically, short-term commercial, or managerial demands may require, or inspire, actions from HR practitioners which can undermine staff expectations, and even be antithetical to trust. Examples include excessive promises in branding campaigns, forced ranking in appraisals, opaque bonus schemes, tacit if reluctant tolerance of discrimination. Thompson (2003) sees these breaches of trust as the inevitable consequence of the 'disconnected capitalism' of the modern age. How HR practitioners handle these trust dilemmas is an area for further research.

One solution that suggests itself is the continuing work to bolster HR's internal credibility (Boselie & Pauuwe, 2005; Guest & King, 2004; Sparrow & Marchington, 1998). Buy-in from senior and line managers, and securing political influence within the organization, is vital in supporting HR departments' insistence on doing what is right and fair, but also operationally sensitive and commercially viable. Credible HR functions, whose value is recognized by line and senior management, can find it easier to insist on best, rather than expedient, practice in people management. In other words, HR's own trustworthiness is a vital determinant.

Attention to the quality and capacity of line management is another area worthy of sustained focus from HR practitioners, to avoid trust pitfalls. Appraisal, reward, and training policies and interventions that develop managers' competence and character (i.e. their trustworthiness) can have a decisive impact on working relationships. Yet devising trust-inspired, comprehensive but user-friendly HR policies is a complex undertaking. Additionally, HR managers face multiple demands when designing policies (strategic, financial, legal, professional, moral – Wright & Snell, 2005), and multiple constituencies – not just employees, but line and senior management. We propose that a trust audit – what expectations are being set by this policy, and can our people deliver on them? And does this policy encourage confident risk taking, or stifle it? – would be a good place to start. We hope this chapter's insights into what builds trust can inform these designs.

Notes

1. We wish to thank the practitioners for their time and for their insights into this intriguing and vital aspect of their professional work. Each of them has endorsed the quotes attributed to them. Some names have been changed at the interviewee's request.
2. Although Rubery et al. (2002) have drawn attention to new forms of employment (sub-contracting, portfolio-style careers) that blur this essential structure, the majority of employment relationships are direct: the employee is paid to work by a main employer.

References

Baier, A. (1986). Trust and anti-trust. *Ethics, 96*(2), 231–260.

Barney, J. B., & Hansen, M. H. (1994). Trustworthiness as a source of competitive advantage. *Strategic Management Journal, 15,* 175–190.

Blyton, P., & Turnbull, P. (2007). *The dynamics of employee relations.* London: Macmillan.

Bok, S. (1978). *Lying.* New York: Pantheon Books.

Boselie, P., & Pauuwe, J. (2005). Human resource function competencies in European companies. *Personnel Review, 38*(5), 461–471.

Caldwell, R. (2003). The changing roles of personnel managers: old ambiguities, new uncertainties. *Journal of Management Studies, 40*(4), 983–1004.

CIPD (2010). *Creating an engaged workforce.* London: CIPD.

Colquitt, J. A., Scott, B. A., & LePine, L. A. (2007). Trust, trustworthiness, and trust propensity: a meta-analytic test of their unique relationships with risk taking and job performance. *Journal of Applied Psychology, 92*(4), 909–927.

Davis, J. H., Schoorman, F. D., Mayer, R. C., & Tan, H. H. (2000). The trusted general manager and business unit performance: empirical evidence of a competitive advantage. *Strategic Management Journal, 21,* 563–576.

Dietz, G., and Hartog, D. (2006). Measuring trust inside organisations. *Personnel Review, 35*(5) 557–588.

Dirks, K. T., & Ferrin, D. L. (2001). The role of trust in organizational settings. *Organization Science, 12*(4), 450–467.

Edelman, R. (2009). *Edelman Trust Barometer 2009.* London: Edelman.

Edwards, P. (1986). *Conflict at work: a materialist analysis of workplace relations.* Oxford: Basil Blackwell.

Emmott, M. (2006). *What is employee relations?* London: CIPD.

Fox, A. (1974). *Beyond contract: work, power and trust relations.* London: Faber and Faber.

Francis, H. & Keegan, A. (2005). Slippery slope. *People Management,* 30 June, 26–31.

Geare, A., Edgar, F., and McAndrew, I. (2006). Employment relationships: ideology and HRM practice. *International Journal of Human Resource Management, 17*(7), 1190–1208.

Gillespie, N. (2003). *Measuring trust in working relationships: the behavioural trust inventory.* Paper presented at the Academy of Management meeting, Seattle, August.

Gillespie, N., & Dietz, G. (2009). Trust repair after an organization-level failure. *Academy of Management Review, 34*(1), 127–145.

Guest, D., & King, Z. (2004). Power, innovation and problem solving: the Personnel Manager's three steps to heaven? *Journal of Management Studies, 41* (3), 401–423.

Hardin, R. (1993). The street-level epistemology of trust. *Politics and Society, 21*(4), 505–526.

Harrington, S. & Rayner, C. (2011). Whose side are you on? Trust and HR in workplace bullying. In R. Searle & D. Skinner (eds), *Trust and HRM.* Cheltenham: Edward Elgar.

Herriot, P., Manning, W., and Kidd, J. (1997). The content of the psychological contract. *British Journal of Management, 8*(2), 151–162.

Heskett, J. L. (1997). *The service profit chain: how leading companies link profit and growth to loyalty, satisfaction and value.* New York: Simon & Schuster.

Hope-Hailey, V., Farndale, E., and Truss, C. (2005). The HR department's role in organisational performance. *Human Resource Management Journal, 15* (3), 49–66.

Hurley, R. (2006). The decision to trust. *Harvard Business Review.* September, 55–62.

Korsgaard, M. A., Brodt, S. E., & Whitener, E. M. (2002). Trust in the face of conflict: the role of managerial trustworthy behavior and organizational context. *Journal of Applied Psychology, 87*(2), 312–319.

Lewicki, R., McAllister, D., and Bies, R. (1998). Trust and distrust: new relationships and realities. *Academy of Management Review, 23*(3), 438–458.

Lewicki, R., Tomlinson, E.C., & Gillespie, N. (2006). Models of interpersonal trust development: theoretical approaches, empirical evidence, and future directions. *Journal of Management, 32*(6), 991–1022.

Mayer, R. C., Davis, J. H., & Schoorman, F. D. (1995). An integrative model of organizational trust. *Academy of Management Review, 20*(3), 709–734.

McEvily, B., Perrone, V., and Zaheer, A. (2003). Trust as an organizing principle. *Organization Science, 14*, 91–103.

Robinson, S. L. (1996). Trust and breach of the psychological contract. *Administrative Science Quarterly, 41*(4), 574–599.

Robinson, S. L., & Rousseau, D. M. (1994). Violating the psychological contract: not the exception but the norm. *Journal of Organisational Behaviour, 15*(3), 245–259.

Rousseau, D. M., Sitkin S. B., Burt, R. S., & Camerer, C. (1998). Not so different after all: a cross-discipline view of trust. *Academy of Management Review, 23*(3), 393–404.

Rubery, J., Earnshaw, J., Marchington, M., Cooke, F. L., & Vincent, S. (2002). Changing organizational forms and the employment relationship. *Journal of Management Studies. 39*(5), 645–72.

Salamon, S. D., & Robinson, S. L. (2008). Trust that binds: the impact of collective felt trust on organizational performance. *Journal of Applied Psychology*, 93(3), 593–601.

Searle, R., & Skinner, D. (Eds.). (2011). *'Trust and HRM'*. Chichester: Edward Elgar.

Searle, R., Weibel, A., & Den Hartog, D. N. (2011). 'Employee Trust in Organizational Contexts'. In G.P. Hodgkinson & J.K. Ford (eds), *International Review of Industrial and Organizational Psychology*, vol. 23. Wiley.

Searle, R., Den Hartog, D., Weibel, A., Gillespie, N., Six, F., & Hatzakis, T. (in press). Trust in the employer: the role of high involvement work practices and procedural justice in European organizations. *International Journal of Human Resource Management*.

Simons, T. (2002). The high cost of low trust. *Harvard Business Review*, September, 18–19.

Six, F., & Sorge, A. (2008). Creating a high-trust organisation: an exploration into organisational policies that stimulate interpersonal trust building'. *Journal of Management Studies*, 45(5), 858–884.

Skinner, D., Saunders, M. N. K., & Duckett, H. (2004). Policies, promises and trust: improving working lives in the National Health Service. *International Journal of Public Sector Management*, 17(7), 558–570.

Sparrow, P. & Marchington, M. (1998). *Human resource management: the new agenda*. London: Financial Times.

Thompson, P. (2003). Disconnected capitalism: or why employers can't keep their side of the bargain. *Work, Employment and Society*, 17(2): 359–379.

Tsui, A. S. & Wu, J. B. (2005). The new employment relationship versus the mutual investment approach: implications for human resource management. *Human Resource Management*, 44(2), 115–121.

Ulrich, D. (1997). *Human Resource Champions*. Boston: Harvard Business School Press.

Ulrich, D. & Brockbank, W. (2005). *The HR Value Proposition*. Boston: Harvard Business School Press.

Whitener, E. (1997) The impact of human resource activities on employee trust. *Human Resource Management* Review, 7(4) 389–404.

Whitener, E., Brodt, S., Korsgaard, M., and Werner, J. (1998). Managers as initiators of trust: an exchange relationship framework for understanding managerial trustworthy behaviour. *Academy of Management Review*, 23(3), 513–530.

Wright, P. M. and Snell, S. A. (2005). Partner or guardian? HR's challenge in balancing value and values. *Human Resource Management*, 44(2), 177–182.

Part III

Employment Relations and the Society

10

Workplace Partnership and the Future Trajectory of Employment Relations within Liberal Market Economies

Tony Dobbins and Tony Dundon

Introduction

In this chapter we review the form, practice, and variable outcomes associated with *workplace partnership*. Enterprise or workplace-based partnership differs from national-level social pacts, in that in the former it is claimed that participants actively engage in dialogue leading to more informed decision making for the good of all stakeholders in the organization. In contrast, national-level *social partnership* is distant from the enterprise with a focus on broader macro-level social and economic policy, with gains accrued to citizens and the economy as a whole. However, the two are not mutually exclusive. National-level social partnership arrangements shape the institutional context in either supporting or hindering workplace practice. Tripartite systems of participation at a national level – involving government, employers, and unions – can be a precursor to the efficacy of workplace-level partnerships.

With the decline in collective bargaining and union density in most 'English-speaking' economies – such as Australia, the UK, USA, and Ireland – the concept of workplace partnership (WP) has attracted attention from scholars, practitioners, and policy makers. Moreover, the advent of intense and global competitive pressures has led many employers to demand higher levels of active cooperation and creative workforce engagement in order to compete successfully under new market conditions. This assumption has been particularly evident in Ireland, where workforce cooperation and innovation have figured prominently in academic and policy debates about enhancing national competitiveness (Wallace, Gunnigle, & McMahon, 2004; Roche, 2007; Dobbins, 2010; NCPP, 2010).

The Republic of Ireland therefore offers an interesting context for examining the extent to which workplace partnership has taken root. The Irish system of industrial relations is traditionally voluntarist, defined as a system of industrial relations based on voluntary settlements among employers, employees, and their representatives, rather than legal regulation (Flanders, 1970). But unlike the UK and the USA, Ireland developed a centralized bargaining system from 1987 , in which the social partners negotiated pay and other economic and social issues at national level (Hastings, Sheehan, & Yeates, 2007; Teague & Donaghey, 2009a&b). However, 'social partnership' broke down in early 2010 after a severe economic recession, and the Irish Government unilaterally introduced public sector pay cuts to help reduce the public deficit and support a failed banking system.

Since the mid-1990s national-level agreements have sought to engender more cooperative and innovative enterprise-level partnerships in Ireland. Successive centralized agreements adopted as public policy a set of guidelines on workplace partnership, defined in the *Partnership 2000* national pact (1997, p. 52) thus:

> Partnership is an active relationship based on recognition of a common interest to secure the competitiveness, viability and prosperity of the enterprise. It involves a continuing commitment from employees to improvements in efficiency and quality; and the acceptance by employers of employees as stakeholders with rights and interests to be considered in the context of major decisions affecting their employment.

The practices commonly associated with voluntary workplace partnership in countries like Ireland, the UK, and US include active cooperation between management and worker representatives, parallel direct employee involvement schemes, teamwork, and a range of complementary Human Resource Management (HRM) practices, notably financial incentives, employment security, and training. A key premise of workplace partnership expounded by its advocates is that it can deliver mutual gains for all stakeholders. The emphasis is on mutuality: management engage workers, both directly as individuals and indirectly through representatives, to pursue mutual gains through participation and upskilling that results in organizational performance outcomes (Kochan & Osterman, 1994; Guest & Peccei, 2001; Dietz, 2004).

The chapter considers the interplay between national social partnership and enterprise-based practices, and argues that the future prognosis for workplace partnership looks limited, although uncertain, due to extensive permissive voluntarism hindering rather than supporting cooperative industrial relations regimes. The argument is presented as follows. Next the historical context of workplace partnership is briefly outlined, followed by review of the prevalence of workplace partnership and its institutional context, in particular the impact of permissive voluntary employment relations regimes within liberal market economies (LME). Finally a number of robust and shallow partnership case studies from Ireland, the UK, and the US are presented before discussing future trajectories for workplace partnership in the context of global economic crisis.

The historical context of workplace partnership

Contemporary interest in workplace partnership evolved from historical debates on productivity bargaining (c. 1960s), industrial democracy (c. 1970s), employee involvement and participation, and human resource management (HRM) (1980s onwards), and then mutual gains and partnership (1990s onwards). Therefore, notwithstanding oversimplification and historical overlap, a number of different phases can be identified in order to locate workplace partnership in a contemporary context. Influenced by a requirement to accommodate growing trade union power, the 1960s were characterized by productivity bargaining between management and union representatives. Productivity bargaining has a long history in UK and Irish industrial relations, and the term was coined in the 1960s when the first productivity agreements were negotiated at the Esso oil refinery at Fawley in Kent (Flanders, 1964). Productivity bargaining is a form of collective bargaining leading to a productivity agreement in which management offers a pay rise in exchange for alterations to employee working practices designed to secure productivity gains. However, productivity bargaining took hold only in certain sectors and enterprises.

The 1970s witnessed debates over industrial democracy which emphasized worker rights to participate in the governance of industry. This was reflected in the UK by the 1977 Bullock Report on Industrial Democracy which addressed the question of how workers might be represented at board level (Bullock, 1977). This report was published in a context of strong union bargaining power and the Labour government's idea of a 'Social Contract' (which eventually crumbled as economic and industrial strife intensified in the UK). The Bullock Report was partly union-initiated, through the Labour Party, and based on collectivist principles which saw trade unions playing a key role in the governance of industry. Experiments with worker directors were initiated in the British Steel Corporation and the Post Office (Batstone, Ferner, & Terry, 1984). In Ireland, meanwhile, the Worker Participation (State Enterprise) Act 1977 provided for the appointment of 'worker directors' on the boards of state and semi-state companies.

However, in the UK, these industrial democracy experiments, along with the Bullock Report itself, were soon abandoned following the defeat of the Labour government and the subsequent election of the Thatcher Conservative government in 1979, which wanted to reduce rather than increase the role of unions in the governance of industry. Driven by new political circumstances and intensifying market pressures, the 1980s saw a very different agenda for workplace participation, one focused on reducing union power and promoting more individualistic, anti-collectivist employment relations philosophies. Influenced by the importing of management practices from overseas – notably from countries like Japan and the US – terms like 'involvement', 'communication', and human resource management (HRM) became more in fashion and were associated with managerial initiatives designed to elicit employee commitment. Therefore, from the 1980s the context for employee participation changed significantly in Britain and Ireland although Ireland retained board-level employee representation in those semi-state companies that were not privatized. The employment relations philosophy became much more overtly managerialist than pluralist. Second, the managerialist rationale for employee participation stressed direct communications with individual employees which, in turn, often bypassed or marginalized trade unions. Third, the new agenda for participation was anchored on business improvements and organizational performance through harnessing employee commitment. Unlike notions of industrial democracy, employee involvement during the 1980s stemmed from an economic efficiency argument. This new wave of involvement was neither focused on, nor indeed accommodated, robust employee participation in areas of managerial decision-making powers (Marchington, Goodman, Wilkinson, & Ackers, 1992). In effect, this was a period of employee participation on management's terms. As such, the objectives for employee participation can be seen as unitarist rather than pluralist in approach, often moralistic in tone, and predicated on the assumption that what is good for the business must be good for employees. The 1990s saw a consolidation of this unitarist consensus-oriented pattern. Many of the specific mechanisms to tap into labour as an organizational performance resource became crystallized in models of best-practice HRM and high commitment management largely originating in the US (Huselid, 1995; Pfeffer, 1998).

Finally, and also with significant origins in the US, from the 1990s there was increased interest in what Kochan and Osterman (1994) termed mutual gains bargaining between employers and unions/employee representatives. Therefore, workplace partnership, which is the subject of this chapter, became common parlance in countries like Ireland and the UK. Interest in partnership was also partially influenced by the emergence of increasing employment regulation at a European level – including the *European Directive on Employee Information and Consultation 2002*. It was also the case that many unions found partnership an attractive option as their power waned in the face of economic, labour market, and political pressures, and it became increasingly obvious to unions that many employers were not receptive to traditional adversarial collective bargaining. In some respects, mutual gains bargaining or workplace partnership resembles a return to 1960s productivity bargaining, in the sense that the emphasis is on management and unions/employee representatives collaborating to exchange wage rises (or other employee gains) for productivity improvements. However, as shown in the next section, workplace partnership remains a minority practice and exists alongside the much more prevalent tendency for managerial-led and dominated employee involvement and HRM practices.

The extent of workplace partnership

Despite the successes ascribed to Irish social partnership (Hastings, Sheehan, & Yeates, 2007; Teague & Donaghey, 2009a&b), workplace diffusion is rare, especially when employees' views are factored in (Roche, 2007; NCPP, 2010). In the most comprehensive survey of both employers and employees in Ireland to date, 16 per cent of private sector employer respondents in 2009 reported the presence of formal partnership, with 34 per cent of employers reporting they have some 'informal' arrangement (NCPP, 2010). Meanwhile, with regard to the employee survey conducted in 2009, substantial majorities of employees said they are not regularly provided key business or work-related information. For example, less than half of private sector employees are informed about the level of competition facing their firm, and less than one-third of private sector workers receive regular information about the organization's budget. Just over one-third of employees receive information about plans to change work practices. While just over 21 per cent of all employees reported the presence of formal partnership institutions at their workplaces, only about 4 per cent of all employees were personally involved in such forms of employee representation (down from 6 per cent when the same question was asked in 2003). Thus, there has been some decline in the incidence of workplace partnership between 2003 and 2009 (NCPP, 2010).

The trajectory of minimal workplace partnership is not unique to Ireland. In the UK, the Workplace Employment Relations Survey (WERS) found that management-union partnerships remain a rarity, with a consistent decline in the incidence of joint consultative arrangements to just 14 per cent of all workplaces (Kersley et al., 2006). On all issues that might form the basis for mutual gains activity, the extent of information and consultation tends to be limited (Guest, Brown, Peccei, & Huxley, 2008). Practices in smaller firms are similarly disappointing, with evidence showing that many owner-managers fall short of consultative practices commensurate with European regulations for employee voice (Wilkinson, Dundon, & Grugulis, 2007).

The institutional context of workplace partnership

It is important for scholars to learn more about how contextual conditions promote and prevent workplace cooperation – particularly the links between national industrial relations institutions and what happens at workplace level. Critics understate the potential for workplace coalitions around shared interests, suggesting collaboration is at odds with fundamental conflicts of interest in market economies (Allen, 2000; Kelly, 2004; D'Art & Turner, 2005; Danford Durbin, Richardson, Tailby, & Stewart, 2009). In contrast, advocates (Guest & Peccei, 2001; Ackers, 2002; Donaghey & Teague, 2007; Geary, 2008) often overestimate the upbeat nature of partnership and elevate the possibilities for mutuality in open economies like Ireland, the UK, and USA, which are more exposed to the volatilities of capitalism than regulated market regimes.

In this section we explore the conditions affecting the adoption and longevity of workplace partnership in Ireland. In so doing we place Ireland in a comparative context alongside other European economies. We review the 'varieties of capitalism' literature and outline three arguments to explain why – compared to more regulated market regimes – workplace cooperation is rare in Ireland. The first strand of the analysis is that workplace partnership is rare because the contextual conditions promoting cooperation are weaker than the conditions obstructing it, owing to the extent and legacy of the permissive blend of voluntarist industrial relations. The second argument is that despite the attempt in Ireland to diffuse partnership to enterprise levels, the objective has failed owing to the absence of what Streeck (1997) terms the 'beneficial constraints' of alternative regulated regime models. The third argument is that being located in a very open economy and exposed to global neo-liberal market forces makes it difficult for employers in Ireland to keep workplace bargains with employees (Thompson, 2003). In short, employer choice for more cooperative and innovative workplace practice is constrained by a globalized neo-liberal agenda.

Contradictions and the fragmentation of permissive voluntarism

The affect of a permissive voluntarist regime – such as in Ireland, the UK, Australia, New Zealand, and the USA (among others) – serves the interests of capital over labour. Although both Ireland and the UK have transposed European regulations for employee information and consultation, the actual legislation has been a minimalist interpretation of the European Commission's original intent (Geary & Roche, 2005; Dobbins, 2007). For example, regulations for indirect employee representation have been transposed with a preference for individualized employee information, with complex trigger mechanisms in order for workers to avail of such rights (Dundon,Curran, Maloney, & Ryan, 2006). In addition, Irish unions have no legal right to statutory recognition for collective bargaining purposes. Accordingly, in the context of Ireland's voluntarist traditions, employers retain sole authority to initiate enterprise partnership and shape its form. Moreover, collective bargaining, once the foundation of employment regulation in Ireland, is giving way to a highly fragmented system characterized by increased diversity and experimentation (Roche, 1998). The upshot is that WP is now one of several policy options for employers to consider: managerial unilateralism, collective bargaining, individualized HRM techniques, direct employee involvement, and a multitude of customized variations. Mutual gains relationships providing employee representatives with robust voice in company governance are uncommon, with few employers voluntarily choosing this path.

Voluntarism has constituted what can be termed a permissive system because it places few constraints, aside from a tendency towards minimalist regulations, on employer choice. In free market regimes such as Ireland, the UK, or the USA, the idea that employees can be company stakeholders goes against the grain of a deeply embedded ideological mindset that employers should have unilateral authority to make decisions, a situation exacerbated by the dominance of short-term shareholder capitalism rather than alternative (European) stakeholder variants (Hutton, 2002). The fact that permissive voluntarism places few constraints on labour market transactions renders Ireland more exposed than other, more regulated European economies to the structural contradictions of capitalism. These contradictions operate at macro and micro level. At the macro level, capitalism is subject to periodic volatility, and Ireland has fared particularly badly in the latest economic crisis (O'Toole, 2009). At the micro level, management actions are shaped by a drive to accumulate capital. But there are often contradictions: for instance, between pressures to cut costs on the one hand and invest in innovation on the other, and between flexibility and security or stability. In the employment relationship, management tends to gravitate towards pressures to control employee actions rather than invest in innovative and cooperative collaborations with labour (Cressey & MacInnes, 1980; Edwards, 2003). In this regard, partnership models imply a sharing of 'risk' by capital and labour (Martinez-Lucio & Stuart, 2005). However, the risks to workers, unions, and management are unequal. Thus the adoption of cooperative transactions remains risky and uncertain under conditions where institutional supports are lacking in laissez-faire market economies. These structural conditions serve to inhibit rather than promote workplace partnership, ultimately rendering the employment relationship potentially unstable and the generation of worker cooperation uncertain. Thompson (2003) argues that the contradictions associated with 'disconnected capitalism' mean that few employers adhere to workplace bargains made with employees.

The literature informs us that certain complementary clusters of specific conditions relating to product market, technology, and skill may promote workplace cooperation in voluntarist settings (Roche & Geary, 2000; Murray, Belanger, Giles, & Lapointe 2002; Belanger & Edwards, 2007). Workplace cooperation is most likely where competitive postures are oriented towards knowledge, innovation, and quality, and where employers introduce complementary 'bundles' of cooperative work practices that underpin value-added participation. Much of this links in with notions of best practice and best fit complementarity. Boxall and Purcell (2008) suggest that best practice principles like employee involvement can potentially be universally successful; however, the actual implementation of specific HR bundles depend on unique organizational circumstances and the mediating impact of internal and external variables. Competitive alternatives to value-added cooperation are heightened under permissive voluntarism. In liberal market economies, as Godard (2004) argues, unilateral management or weak employee involvement requiring fewer resources are more likely, given that cost minimization and labour-intensive practices are more common than quality competition. Arguably, robust (or strong) workplace partnerships will be adopted by employers in LMEs only when seen as economically advantageous. This challenges the 'universalistic' arguments of high performance work systems (HPWS) advocates (Huselid, 1995; Guthrie, Flood, Liu, & MacCurtain, 2009). Edwards and Wright (2001, pp. 570–575) observe that despite the trend of many recent quantitative studies to attribute a positive-sum cause and effect from adopting high involvement practices, the outcomes may be explained due to location or because of context-specific variables which are not reproducible elsewhere. HPWS along with the attendant collaborative relationships may be implemented in a multitude of ways and seldom adopted as a coherent or complete package. Indeed, it has been shown that such arrangements do not have the same uniformly positive impact for workers as for employers (Ramsey, Scholarios, & Harley, 2000). Furthermore, individual employer experimentation with high involvement management practice under permissive voluntarism reflects the need to create alternatives to simply controlling the wage-effort bargain.[1] According to Edwards (2008) and Godard (2004), workplace systems for inclusion remain fragmented, ad hoc, and hard to replicate due to the dominant effects of managerial prerogative under unfettered voluntary regimes.

Institutional constraints under liberal and coordinated market economies

In what is labelled the 'varieties of capitalism' (VoC) literature, Hall and Soskice (2001) distinguish between institutional contexts in 'liberal market economies' (LMEs) and 'coordinated market economies' (CMEs). The characteristic features of LMEs include the following: (1) the economy primarily operates according to free market principles and shareholder value; (2) there is little engagement of employers or worker representatives governing macro-economic issues; and (3) regulations promoting workplace cooperation are weak. The US, UK, Australia, and New Zealand are often described as adopting these liberalized tendencies. In contrast, CMEs include the likes of Austria, Belgium, Denmark, Finland, Germany, the Netherlands, and Sweden that have complementary linkages between institutions promoting cooperation across various levels. Hall and Soskice (2001) suggest that institutional complementarities are an important aspect of the distinction between

LMEs and CMEs: institutions are complementary if the presence of one institution enhances the efficiency of others. Some argue that Ireland is a hybrid in this regard. For example, Hamann and Kelly (2008, p. 144) suggest that Ireland has moved from a LME towards a more coordinated variant by adopting some CME-type strategies such as social partnership. Policy debates ask whether Ireland is closer to 'Boston or Berlin', invoking a contrast between the laissez-faire doctrines of American liberalization, or European social market regulation (Collings, Gunnigle, & Morley, 2008). Teague and Donaghey (2009b, p. 74) lend weight to the hybridization owing to an Irish blend of 'institutional complementarities' which created a particular symbiosis among traditionally competing social and economic institutions. Among other features, these included trade unions accepting wage restraint for employment growth, economic liberalization and market openness, the accommodation of foreign multinational capital, a minimalist welfare state, and the truncated adaptation of European employment rights. However, Ireland seems to lack what Hancke, Rhodes, and Thatcher (2007, p. 5) note is the all-important architecture of 'institutional comparative advantage', by which is meant an institutional complementarity across different levels rather than via a single, national system, in other words between labour relations actors, among corporate governance institutions, within and between training systems, and across inter-firm relations. These relationships determine the degree to which a political economy is 'coordinated' in pursuit of a redistribution of wealth and competitiveness. There are differences between institutional comparative advantage in LMEs and CMEs, which influence patterns of investment and the competitive standing of firms in response to market pressures. Generally speaking, high value-added and high-skill activities tend to be located in CMEs accompanied by strong rather than weak institutional coordination, whereas low-skill and low value-added activities tend to congregate in LMEs (Hancke et al., 2007). Although open to debate, Ireland displays tendencies of each but arguably gravitates more towards a voluntarist neo-liberal market system than a coordinated wealth distributing regime. One consequence is while Irish partnership displays elements of a corporatist model, the extent of laissez-faire capitalism results in an imbalance of benefits skewed to capital at the expense of labour.

Streeck (1997, 2004) takes the idea of institutional complementarity further by introducing the concept of 'beneficial constraints'. According to Streeck (1997, p. 197), contrary to neo-liberal arguments that economic performance improves the more that labour market constraints are removed, 'socially institutionalized constraints on the rational voluntarism of interest maximizing behaviour may be economically beneficial.' The notion is that beneficial constraints improve economic performance when society intervenes in market activity to limit the unfettered pursuit of profit maximization. Streeck (2004, p. 426) explains how 'institutions clearly not created with economic efficiency in mind, may turn out to be sources of superior economic performance and competitiveness.' Other evidence indicates that employers have found considerable utility when adopting worker participation schemes that were initially viewed as irrational, such as European Work Councils (Marchingtonet al., 2001). Streeck (2004) further cites examples of beneficial constraints such as minimum wages and the regulation of training in addition to statutory worker participation. To ensure stability, society requires a capacity to prevent interest maximizing employers from doing certain things they would by reflex prefer to do, by compelling them to do things they would normally avoid but which, ultimately, can be shown to be in their own interests. Given freedom of choice, and everything else being equal, Streeck (2004) observes that many employers tend to opt for low over high wages, prefer freedom to hire and fire workers rather than being constrained by employment protection rules, and prefer to make decisions unilaterally rather than by informing and consulting employees. Arguably, reliance on voluntarist workplace partnership provision by employers is impeded by contradictory pressures pushing management towards cost-cutting and unilateral actions. Even the most temporary alteration from cooperative relations can be counterproductive as employees question management credibility: 'the mere possibility of defection, as is by definition inherent in any voluntary arrangement, can damage the positive effects of workplace cooperation' (Streeck, 1997, p. 201).

It is noticeable that Northern European countries such as Finland, Germany, Sweden, Denmark, and the Netherlands possess institutional frameworks with beneficial constraints supporting value-added quality competition and consensus. Each of these countries has a different institutional arrangement, but all coordinate and support long-term compromise to a greater extent than countries with permissive voluntarist legacies like Ireland, the UK, or the USA. In Sweden, for example, the durability of consensus reflects institutional constraints through strong and independent trade unionism, the 1976 Co-determination Act, and the 1982 Development Agreement on co-determination. In Germany, Streeck (1997) cites five institutional features promoting quality competition and consensus in constraining managerial prerogative: strong proactive unions, employment protection legislation, a coordinated industry wage bargaining system, a statutory national vocational training system, and a set of binding rules enshrined in the Work Constitution Act 1972 providing for robust works councils. In addition, the Danish 'flexicurity' model successfully reconciles contradictory pressures for flexibility and security because beneficial constraints are placed on employers, for instance, by strong proactive unions (density is 80 per cent) and coordinated national and workplace dialogue. To this end, flexibilities are provided to employers while security protects workers during labour market transitions, which means both parties are willing and able to take 'risks' necessary for meaningful and genuine collaboration that helps to foster innovation and block off low-cost competition. Likewise, Finland has strong beneficial constraints including strong unions. Hutton (2002) notes, in contrast to neo-liberal expectations, the highly regulated Finnish institutional framework has contributed to a firm like Nokia becoming a globally successful entity on the basis of collaborative work relations and innovation (Steinbock, 2001).

These collaborative countries remain the most economically competitive *and* socially cohesive in the world, combining economic efficiency with equality, fairness, and voice by embedding institutional 'checks and balances' governing and channelling the power and interests of various groups (Hutton, 2002; Wilkinson & Pickett, 2010). In contrast, in laissez-faire voluntarist contexts such as the UK, North America, and Ireland, institutional conditions have historically encouraged adversarial relations, cost competition, and management prerogative more so than competitive collaboration. Arguably, Ireland's unprecedented economic boom during the 1990s coupled with its light touch regulation allowed neo-liberal preferences to percolate and surface with extreme vigour and conviction when recent economic conditions threatened the power of global capital. Given the enduring voluntarist legacy evident in Ireland (and elsewhere), Belanger and Edwards (2007, p. 713) conclude that conditions generating durable workplace compromise in liberal market economies are feasible but rare: stronger 'beneficial constraints' in the form of proactive state interventions are necessary if cooperation is to increase and, in particular, to disseminate practice to enterprise level.

How institutional disconnection in Ireland damages workplace bargains

The third argument concerns an analysis of the effect of market forces on employer outcomes, in terms of maintaining a stable bargain with employees (unions). As noted above, Ireland has an institutional complementarity that accords with both a liberal and coordinated market economy due to its recent history of corporatist peak-level social partnership, while at the same time actively promoting free market policies. On balance, the institutional configuration is tilted more towards LME doctrines than towards the beneficial or regulated constraints of CMEs noted above. Social policy tends to be subordinated to free market economic policies and individual employers have significant freedom to customize organization-specific employment relations, including sophisticated union avoidance options (Jacobson & Kirby, 2006; Lavelle, Gunnigle, & McDonnell, 2010). The Irish paradox, as noted earlier, is that despite Ireland's centralized agreements, durable micro cooperation is rare. Workplace partnership has been considered desirable by many as a means of enhancing Ireland's competitiveness. From this there stemmed various 'soft' non-prescriptive initiatives under successive national pacts, which sought to stimulate enterprise arrangement for workforce cooperation, while leaving significant scope to customize practices at workplace level. The State also signalled its support for workplace arrangements by establishing a specific institution, the National Centre for Partnership and Performance (NCPP), whose remit was to act as a voluntary catalyst for partnership. In 2007, An Taoiseach (the Prime Minister) launched various NCPP initiatives designed to deepen partnership across different sectors of the economy, established a formal Forum on the Future of the Workplace and created a Workplace Innovation Fund (WIF), influenced to a large degree by the Finnish experience (Alasoini, 2009). However, the NCPP was disbanded in April 2010 owing to government action to cut public spending.

Therefore, Ireland has tried but failed to promote workplace cooperation as part of a voluntarist system of social partnership, but without substantive regulatory constraints that can, arguably, lead to more cooperative and competitive benefits. Despite attempts to diffuse a national model to local level, Ireland does not have the comparatively strong coordinated institutional complementarities linking workplace governance with national arrangements (Teague & Donaghey, 2009a; Dobbins, 2010). In short, there is a disconnection between national level and workplace cooperation in Ireland. The Irish government has placed few constraints on individual employers, especially on the large inflow of multinational organizations setting up greenfield sites in the Republic, leaving managers free to decide whether and in what form to share power over workplace governance. Given the openness of

Ireland's economy and a concern to attract investment from powerful multinationals, Irish governments have pursued a paradoxical policy of promoting national partnership while blocking labour market policies to avoid upsetting multinational capital (Gunnigle, Collings, & Morley, 2005; Collings et al., 2008; Teague & Donaghey, 2009a). Being one of the most open economies in the world means Ireland is very exposed to market forces, and, in turn, employers are more likely to renege on workplace bargains struck with employees than in more insulated and regulated economies. This echoes Thompson's (2003, p. 360) view that there are 'powerful structural tendencies' in liberal market economies, driven by instability in capital markets, which are 'exacerbating disunity' between the domains of political economy, company governance, employment relations, and the labour process – thereby unravelling cohesiveness. Thompson (2003, p. 360–361) observes that actors within liberal market capitalism are 'finding it increasingly difficult to make connections between objectives in the spheres of work and employment, and simultaneously employers are finding it harder to keep their side of any bargain with employees.' The instabilities generated by what Thompson (2003) terms 'disconnected capitalism' are clearly evident in the Irish context, where the institutional configuration of social partnership and voluntarist workplace regimes serve to moderate rather than regulate or control the excesses of a global neo-liberal economic paradigm. Such tensions between minimal regulation and free market company governance mean that there is a high probability that employers will renege on workplace bargains with employees.

Case study examples

In this section, we draw on a number of studies to illustrate the variable forms and outcomes of workplace partnerships that have resulted from permissive voluntarism and adherence to a predominantly global free market ideology. While important quantitative data exists to chart the pattern and extent of enterprise partnerships, such studies are less suited for examining the complex dynamics of workplace cooperation and probing beneath surface level indicators of policy to reveal how actual practice is played out. We explore the latter through qualitative case-based evidence, drawing on some of our own research as well as other international evidence showing how contextual conditions affect the longevity of workplace partnerships in Ireland, the UK and the US (Kochan & Rubinstein, 2000; Oxenbridge & Brown,

2004; Roche & Geary, 2006; Dobbins & Gunnigle, 2009; Rittau & Dundon, 2010; Teague & Hann, 2010).

In two case studies of high-profile firms, Aughinish Alumina (AAL) and Waterford Crystal (WL), contextual factors mediated the form and strength of cooperative workplace relations (Dobbins & Gunnigle, 2009). Aughinish Alumina and Waterford Crystal introduced representative partnership forums providing unions with inputs into operational decisions and some element of corporate strategy. A crucial difference is that the partnership 'bundle' was more complete at AAL, including semi-autonomous teamwork, collective gain sharing, and employment security. In contrast, key partnership practices were absent at WC, which remained hierarchical coupled with embedded job demarcations. A conclusion from the two cases is that cooperation in a context of permissive voluntarism can deliver gains; however, the 'balance' varies according to context. At WC, the balance of mutuality favoured management. For example, while workers derived some benefits (notably extensive training) these were offset by negative experiences of change, work intensification, and outsourcing resulting in job insecurity. In comparison, partnership at AAL was perceived by workers as fair and robust owing to extensive arrangements for employee participation, especially the empowerment associated with semi-autonomous work teams.

The WC and AAL findings suggest that workplace cooperation in Ireland's permissive voluntarist context is vulnerable to breakdown, subject to both external and internal factors affecting the longevity of cooperative practice. For example, AAL faced competitive challenges but remained relatively insulated from market forces. In contrast, WC was more exposed to market turbulence and the demise of partnership was related to acute deterioration in competitive conditions, which ultimately led to the company closing in 2010. The collapse of partnership coincided with the senior managers responsible for inspiring a cooperative workplace regime all leaving the company, and new managers were less inclined to sustain cooperation. Meanwhile, key champions of partnership remained at AAL, and senior managers sought to vertically align partnership at AAL with other strategic functions. Finally, AAL's continuous process plant rendered relocation unlikely, but it was much easier to relocate production from WC, and relocation was a regular occurrence since 1990.

Another important finding from these two cases is that lack of beneficial constraints in Ireland – such as generalizable legal rights to information and consultation – meant that cooperation was not permanently institutionalized: the Waterford partnership committee fell into disuse and the AAL forum operates in an ad hoc way (the AAL unions wanted more structured representative voice). These cases illustrate that Ireland's accommodation of free market principles means employers are more likely to renege on workplace bargains than under regimes where managements' capacity to unilaterally exit from cooperative pacts is circumvented. At WC, the factors undermining the practice of partnership eventually became stronger than those supporting it, and management failed to maintain the explicit commitment to workplace cooperation. The fact that the AAL workplace compromise survives makes it rather unique in Ireland.

Roche and Geary's (2006) examination of partnership at the Irish airport authority Aer Rianta shows how apparent strong cooperative relations also broke down under permissive voluntarism. Partnership at Aer Rianta, known as the 'Compact for Constructive Participation', encompassed joint union–employee–management forums at strategic and operational levels. Major commercial challenges were tackled, notably by developing a joint strategy to deal with the company's future status and ending of duty-free sales. However, the experiment broke down after eight years, with the authors attributing this to weak internal institutional bulwarks, tensions between supporters and critics of partnership, a succession crisis after key management and union advocates retired, and failure to vertically align interlocking partnership practices by co-joining direct participation and complementary HR policies with representative forums. Partnership remained largely restricted to representative and indirect channels. These factors interacted with external obstacles, notably 'prolonged indecision and inaction by government on the future of Aer Rianta' (Roche & Geary, 2006, p. 252).

Rittau and Dundon (2010) report on the outcome of workplace partnerships on union stewards in five case study organizations in Ireland. The organizations were all heralded as leading exemplars of workplace cooperation by the government's support agency, the NCPP, and regarded as best practice evidence for the diffusion of cooperative arrangements at enterprise level. However, while union stewards were positively disposed towards the notion of mutual gains, the variability of practice meant that partnership is not a straightforward win-win concept in which all parties benefit. Rittau and Dundon (2010) suggest the debate about partnership processes and the way integrative problem-solving plays out is as important as the potential gains or losses. First, the interplay between structure and agency is important in determining how partnership processes are enacted at workplace level.

When comparing the cases on *structure*, three firms were described as robust (two manufacturing and one financial service firm), one shallow (hospitality company), and one collapsed (manufacturing organization). With regard to the *scope* of partnership, union stewards were on the whole able to voice members' concerns covering minor, operational, and more substantive issues. Across the cases, union stewards experienced increased information sharing and consultation, the result being a generally favourable posture towards partnership that helped legitimize union involvement. However, with regard to the *depth* of partnership, the picture was more complex. Deeper partnerships had a distinctive informal dimension coupled with openness to ring-fence conflictual issues as more appropriate to negotiation. In this way, partnership dealt with lower level matters, but was able to operate effectively on various issues of concern to union members. Informal roles of stewards were more developed in robust cases, which also helped to nurture collective bargaining as a parallel channel for resolving differences. Indeed, very little informal partnership was found in the manufacturing firm where partnership collapsed. A further outcome concerned the *independence* of stewards and their role with union members. A degree of independence from management was necessary to strengthen union-member relations. This was most apparent where stewards separated issues into those appropriate for collective negotiation, and those for a more cooperative arena. However, workers would become frustrated at lack of progress through partnership on issue of importance to them. In two of the case studies (a manufacturing firm and the financial services organization), employees pressurized union stewards to demand more tangible rewards from management and openly criticized partnership for failing to deliver promises.

Other case study evidence by Teague and Hann (2010) examined a workplace partnership that broke down at Bausch and Lomb, drawing on transaction cost economics to shed insights into why such arrangements are hard to sustain. They suggest that meaningful partnership requires trade unions and management to accept agency costs, which in practice involves ongoing compromise that was found wanting at Bausch and Lomb's Irish plant. Management failed to modify their right to manage while unions were reluctant to accept that issues normally addressed by collective bargaining could be delegated to partnership arrangements. The evidence of the case study is that neither management nor unions were prepared to incur such agency costs. The authors conclude that the trinity of meaningful partnership, collective bargaining, and management's right to manage is exceptionally difficult to operate in parallel, echoing Martinez-Lucio and Stuart's (2005) focus on the 'risks' associated with workplace cooperation for both parties.

The Irish cases can be contrasted with one of the most comprehensive studies of voluntary partnerships in the UK by Oxenbridge and Brown (2004), who concluded that managers and union representatives report mutual gains outcomes where cooperative relations are robust – primarily arising from the trust engendered by informal dialogue. However, they also observed that such arrangements are difficult to implement and sustain. Oxenbridge and Brown (2004) argue that cooperative relationships are most likely to be stable when employers accept and endorse an independent employee voice channel, especially where union density is high. Although one of their cases had successfully negotiated a second long-term partnership agreement, most had 'not yet been tested by time' (Oxenbridge and Brown, 2004, pp. 400–401). The authors make a distinction between 'robust' and 'shallow' arrangements, suggesting that 'cooperative relationships may develop as a relatively stable feature of those firms and sectors of the economy where employers perceive an advantage in a clear and independent employee voice', but 'cooperative relationships will be most likely where trade unionism already has deep roots ...' (Oxenbridge and Brown, 2004, pp. 400–401).[2]

Likewise, if we compare workplace partnership in the permissive voluntarist context of the United States, Rubinstein and Kochan (2001) identify mutual gains arising from innovations in cooperation at the American company *Saturn* (a General Motors (GM) subsidiary). The Saturn case has been praised for the extent to which unions were involved in co-management initiatives from shop-floor level up to corporate strategy, and workers participated in self-managed teams. Management also benefited from better product quality and customer service. But despite the equality of mutuality reported at Saturn, Rubinstein and Kochan identified contextual vulnerabilities, notably doubts over GM's commitment to the project. In addition, weak external institutional supports and America's corporate governance system were found to inhibit rather than sustain workplace partnership. If mutual gains enterprises are to endure in the US, Kochan and Rubinstein (2000, p. 384) argue, 'a change in the political environment from one that reinforces the ideology of unregulated capital markets and enterprises to one that legitimates other stakeholders is likely to be necessary to sustain these alternative organizational forms.' The very idea of cooperation and inclusion may have received a more recent endorsement through the values of President Obama; however the difficulties facing workplace cooperation have intensified after the American economy was recently hit by deep recession.[3]

Together, these empirical case studies of enterprise-level partnership forms show variable and uneven outcomes. Even strong or robust cooperation is vulnerable to erosion and collapse under permissive voluntary free market contexts which have a higher exposure to the volatility of capitalism compared to more coordinated and regulated economies elsewhere.

Future trajectory of workplace partnership?

Workplace partnerships under permissive voluntary regimes have focused on encouraging employers to voluntarily design their own arrangements, but there are limits to such experimentalism. To argue that there are no or few gains from partnership is an incomplete analysis. Elements of mutual gains are evident but they are also rare, and more often than not, remain heavily dependent on management and union actors to 'champion' the initiative. Much of our focus in this chapter has been on Ireland given its prominence in the extant literature as a country leading the way in collaborative partnerships (cf. Sabel, 1996). Yet Ireland has tried, but failed, to promote workplace cooperation as an embedded feature of a voluntarist system, lacking the generalizable beneficial constraints required for this to happen more widely. It appears under other LMEs also that employees and management do not always engage in mutually advantageous transactions, even if it may be in their self-interest to do so (Freeman & Lazear, 1995). Management tends to limit the requisite investment required to enable a distribution of power necessary for genuine participation as they seek to preserve their managerial prerogative. On the other hand, workers may demand more influence than deemed acceptable by employers. Without beneficial constraints along the lines of German works councils, most employers when left to their own choices will introduce weak employee voice systems. In turn, workers become sceptical and disillusioned when partnership-type practices are viewed as 'bolted-on', lacking integration with other people management policies and schemes are left to atrophy (Wilkinson & Dundon, 2010). This may not only result in a representation gap for employees but also produce sub-optimal performance outcomes for employers and for the economy as a whole (Streeck, 1997, 2004; Coats, 2004). In the absence of external institutional constraints, it is very difficult to balance the 'risks' underpinning a voluntary equilibrium between management's right to manage and employee demands for meaningful voice (Marchington et al., 2001; Martinez-Lucio & Stuart, 2005; Teague & Hann, 2010).

For the foreseeable future, especially viewed against the fall-out from the international recession, the prognosis for enterprise-based partnership under permissive liberal market economies does not look positive. The longevity of the partnership is likely to be tested further in Ireland (and elsewhere) owing to a depressed economic climate, with many employers engaging in retrenchment, restructuring, and cost-cutting. The structural contradictions inherent in managing employment relations have intensified with economic crisis, and survival, rather than partnership, is pre-occupying the thoughts of workplace actors. In Ireland, the state remains wedded to a largely neo-liberal economic agenda that is dependent on inward investment from US multinationals, and EU Central Bank and IMF financial aid. Arguably, this has left a deficiency in support for indigenous company innovation (Jacobson & Kirby, 2006), a message reinforced in a speech in Dublin by respected British analyst Will Hutton (2010). The importance of fostering an organizational innovation climate is illustrated in the recent NCPP (2010) workplace survey cited earlier, which identifies a clear association between participatory work practices/regularity of consultation and high performance output innovation in the form of new products and services. The eventual breakdown of social partnership in Ireland in early 2010, and the closure of the National Centre for Partnership and Performance, will further restrict oxygen for enterprise-based collaboration. The contradictions and tensions involved in attempting to operate a liberalized market policy alongside a social partnership consensus eventually contributed to the breakdown of the latter in a depressed economy – the government's decision in 2009 to unilaterally impose public service pay cuts in the face of union opposition was the knock-out blow for social partnership. This contradiction fits into the debate as to whether Ireland is closer to 'Boston or Berlin' in its policy direction. Part of the problem, according to David Begg, the General Secretary of the Irish Congress of Trade Unions (ICTU), is that social partnership in Ireland was based on foundations made of very soft sand (Begg, 2008, p. 54). So what implications might a continuation of this downbeat scenario have for unions, employers and the state in Ireland?

Trade unions: Even prior to the recession, unions in Ireland were struggling with declining density and organizational capacity, especially in the private sector. In the current difficult climate, and with employer associations refusing to concede statutory recognition rights for collective bargaining purposes, some union representatives may feel they have little choice but to cooperate with employers and engage in concession bargaining given the apparent marginalization of union legitimacy and declining membership. A problem for trade unions is that under permissive voluntarism there is heavy reliance on employer support for partnership. This is likely to add a higher degree of 'risk' for trade unions contemplating partnership while at the same time evaluating alternative workplace capacity around interests workers say they want fulfilled, such as upskilling and stronger voice (Freeman, Boxall, & Haynes, 2007). One option is to combine partnership and organize strategies to build independent workplace representative capacity (Heery, 2002). Unions have belatedly acknowledged this, with some commencing organizing campaigns. A problem facing Irish unions on this front, however, is that over the past 20 years there has been growing reliance on national tripartite bargaining to enhance union influence at this peak level. One consequence has been a diminution of the capacity of shop stewards to negotiate substantive issues at workplace level given the dominance of softer consultation through partnership. In other words, enterprise-based structures may no longer be effective in adjusting to decentralized bargaining demands in a depressed economic climate. Unions will have to respond to this diminution in workplace capacity in a difficult climate for recognition, bargaining, and a fundamentally different national model for social dialogue.

Employers: For employers, the take-up and longevity of workplace cooperation is often conditional on it adding value to firms, and even then the transaction costs, risks, and fragility of partnership means it is not guaranteed. On the face of it, it would appear to be in the interests of 'good' employers to embrace high-road value-added cooperative relations to prevent competitive undercutting by low-road employers. Some employers have seen the mutual benefits that collaborative networks with other employers, workers, and labour market institutions can generate. A significant example of an enlightened employer approach is the creation of a sector-level partnership forum for the Irish Print Industry in 2004, which all partners saw as adding value to a traditional ailing industry by addressing industry-level strategic issues. It is believed to be the first example of a sector-wide partnership in the private sector encompassing all main stakeholders: employers, unions, state bodies, and educational institutions. The Print Forum has generated a number of mutual gains through joint problem solving, most notably a redesigning of the apprenticeship system (Dobbins, 2009). But, for the most part, given the prevailing ideology of permissive liberal voluntarism, individual employers and employer associations' default position is to stave-off perceived challenges to managerial prerogative and to oppose labour market institutions that point to regulatory 'benefits'. For this to change, it would necessitate the Irish Government or European Commission compelling employers to do things they would ordinarily avoid, for example, robust employee consultation rather than minimalist or token-gesture communications.

The State: The liberal labour market trajectories of the like of Ireland, the UK, and the USA point towards the continuation of light touch regulation along with an increasingly individualized system of employment law. For the most part, government agencies and employer bodies within LMEs tend to view labour regulations and unions as something to be begrudgingly tolerated and akin to a negative constraint, rather than a beneficial springboard to generate performance and creative problem-solving systems between capital and labour (Freeman & Medoff, 1984; Kaufmann, 2009). The response of the government and employers to the EU information and consultation regulations illustrates this 'lowest common denominator' tendency (Geary & Roche, 2005; Dobbins, 2007). The best avenue for political support for collective enterprise-level cooperation seems to reside at European social policy level. But even here, European Commission labour market policy in recent times has gravitated towards 'softer' social dialogue edicts (mostly on individual workplace rights) that give Member States scope to transpose arrangements that suit their national circumstances – in Ireland and the UK that has translated into preserving voluntarism – rather than tighter regulations. Added to the mix are political struggles at the European level between neo-liberals and social democrats and the EU social partners, and the challenges associated with EU expansion and coordination. In short, not everyone is singing from the same hymnsheet of a social European model with stronger collective-based structures of inclusion and cooperation. National political development may further complicate future postures concerning workplace partnership. For example, it is difficult to see much extension of employee voice in the UK under a Conservative-Liberal coalition. In Ireland any subsequent major alteration in labour market institutions or regulatory rights for workers and unions appears unlikely under a new Fine Gael-Labour coalition government.

But this downbeat future trajectory is not necessarily set in stone. A more optimistic scenario is the possibility that more favourable conditions for enterprise partnerships could yet emerge internationally. For example, the EU Charter of Fundamental Rights and the re-cast 2010 European Works Council Directive provide opportunities for voice and participation. Additional international political developments could yet exert influence, notably if stronger rules regulating corporate governance and curbing short-term transactions in financial markets are agreed at international level, with impetus perhaps from the power blocs of the US and a Franco-German led EU.[4] In time, marginal restraints to neo-liberalism and the permissive dynamic of voluntarism may emerge in the form of EU-inspired stakeholder capitalism and trickle down to countries like Ireland and the UK. In addition, some kind of bottom-up backlash against free market liberalism and the dominance of corporate financiers and bankers cannot be discounted. For instance, in the UK, Wilkinson and Pickett (2010) note renewed interest in worker cooperatives and employee ownership.[5]

Notes

1. In more regulated European economies this collaborative employee participation function is served by generally applicable state-sponsored legally/ institutionally embedded rights to employee voice.
2. See Stuart and Martinez-Lucio (2005) and Johnstone, S., Ackers, P., & Wilkinson, A., (2009) for comprehensive reviews of workplace partnership in the UK.
3. See Kochan, T., Adler, P., McKersie, R., Eaton, A., Segal, P., and Gerhart, P. (2008) for recent review of workplace partnerships in the USA.
4. Under this scenario collaborative European stakeholder variants of capitalism would gain the ideological and political ascendancy over neo-liberal shareholder-driven capitalism.
5. See also Coats 2004; Edwards, 2008; Sisson, 2009 for UK overview of future trajectory of employment relations governance.

References

Ackers, P. (2002). Reframing employment relations: the case for neo-pluralism. *Industrial Relations Journal*, *33*(1), 2–19.

Alasoini, T. (2009). Strategies to promote workplace innovation: a comparative analysis of nine national and regional approaches. *Economic and Industrial Democracy*, *30*(4): 614–642.

Allen, K. (2000). *The Celtic tiger: the myth of social partnership in Ireland*. Manchester: Manchester University Press.

Batstone, E., Ferner, A., & Terry, M. (1984) *Consent and efficiency: labour relations and management strategy in the State enterprise*. Oxford: Basil Blackwell.

Begg, D. (2008) The mission of Unions is timeless. In T. Hastings (ed.), *The state of the Unions: challenges facing organised labour in Ireland*. Dublin: Liffey Press.

Belanger, J., & Edwards, P. (2007). The conditions promoting compromise in the workplace. *British Journal of Industrial Relations*, *45*(4), 713–734.

Boxall, P., and Purcell, J. (2008), *Strategy and human resource management*, Basingstoke and New York: Palgrave Macmillan and Macmillan.

Bullock, A. (Lord) (1977). *Report of the committee of inquiry on industrial democracy*. London: HMSO.

Coats, D. (2004) *Speaking up! Voice, industrial democracy and organisational performance*. London: The Work Foundation.

Collings, D. G., Gunnigle, P., & Morley, M. J. (2008). Between Boston and Berlin, American MNCs and the shifting contours ofiIndustrial relations in Ireland. *International Journal of Human Resource Management*, *19*(2), 242–263.

Cressey, P., & MacInnes, J. (1980). Voting for Ford. *Capital and Class*, 11, 5–33.

D'Art, D., & Turner, T. (2005). Union recognition and partnership at work: a new legitimacy for Irish trade unions? *Industrial Relations Journal*, *36*(2), 121–139.

Danford, A., Durbin, S., Richardson, M., Tailby, S., and Stewart, P. (2009). 'Everybody's talking at me': the dynamics of information disclosure and consultation in high-skill workplaces in the UK. *Human Resource Management Journal*, *19*(4): 337–354.

Dietz, G. (2004). Partnership and the development of trust in British workplaces. *Human Resource Management Journal*, *14*(1), 5–24.

Dobbins, T. (2007). Apathy reigns on information & consultation, despite Minister's move. *Industrial Relations News*, *12*, 3–4.

Dobbins, T. (2009). *The Print Industry fights back: the story of Ireland's print & packaging forum*. Dublin: National Centre for Partnership and Performance.

Dobbins, T. (2010). The case for beneficial constraints: why permissive voluntarism impedes workplace cooperation in Ireland. *Economic and Industrial Democracy*, *31*(4), 497–519.

Dobbins, T., & Gunnigle, P. (2009). Can voluntary workplace partnership deliver sustainable mutual gains? *British Journal of Industrial Relations*, *47*(3), 546–570.

Donaghey, J., and Teague, P. (2007). The mixed fortunes of Irish Unions: living with the paradoxes of social partnership. *Journal Labor Research*, *28*(1): 19–41.

Dundon, T., Curran, D., Maloney, M., & Ryan, P. (2006). Conceptualising the dynamics of employee voice: evidence from the Republic of Ireland. *Industrial Relations Journal*, *37*(5), 492–512.

Edwards, P. (2003). *Industrial relations* (2nd edn). Oxford: Blackwell.

Edwards, P. (2008). Workplace regimes and the governance of the employment relationship: re-establishing the connections in liberal market economies. *Paper for International Labour Process Conference*, Dublin.

Edwards, P., & Wright, M. (2001). High-involvement work systems and performance outcomes: the strength of variable, contingent and context-bound relationships. *International Journal of Human Resource Management*, *12*(4), 568–585.

Flanders, A. (1964). *The fawley productivity agreements*. London: Faber and Faber.

Flanders, A. (1970). *Management and unions*. London: Faber and Faber.

Freeman, R., & Lazear, E. (1995). An economic analysis of works councils. In J. Rogers and W. Streeck (eds), *Works councils: consultation, representation, and cooperation in industrial relations*. Chicago: University of Chicago Press.

Freeman, R., & Medoff, F. (1984). *What do unions do?* New York: Basic Books.

Freeman R., Boxall, P., & Haynes, P. (2007) *What workers say: employee voice in the Anglo-American workplace*. Ithaca, NY: ILR Press.

Geary, J. (2008). Do unions benefit from working in partnership with employers? Evidence from Ireland. *Industrial Relations, 47*(4), 530–69.

Geary, J., & Roche, W. (2005). The future of employee information and consultation in Ireland. In J. Storey (ed.), *Adding value through information and consultation*. London: Palgrave Macmillan.

Godard, J. (2004). A critical assessment of the high-performance paradigm. *British Journal of Industrial Relations, 42*(2), 349–378.

Guest, D., Brown, W., Peccei, R., & Huxley, K. (2008). Does partnership at work increase trust? An analysis based on the 2004 Workplace Employment Relations Survey. *Industrial Relations Journal, 39*(2), 124–152.

Guest, D.E. and Peccei, R. (2001). Partnership at work: mutuality and the balance of advantage. *British Journal of Industrial Relations, 39*(2), 207–236.

Gunnigle, P., Collings, D.G., & Morley, M. J. (2005). Exploring the dynamics of industrial relations in US multinationals: evidence from the Republic of Ireland. *Industrial Relations Journal, 36*(3), 241–256.

Guthrie, J., Flood, P., Liu, W., & MacCurtain, S. (2009). High performance work systems in Ireland: human resource and organisational outcomes. *International Journal Of Human Resource Management, 20*(1), 112–125.

Hall, P., & Soskice, D. (2001), *Varieties of capitalism: the institutional foundations of comparative advantage*. Oxford-New York: Oxford University Press.

Hamann, K., & Kelly, J. (2008). Varieties of capitalism and industrial relation. In P. Blyton, E. Heery, N. Bacon & J. Fiorito (eds), *The SAGE handbook of industrial relations* (pp. 129–149). London: Sage.

Hancke, B., Rhodes, M., & Thatcher, M. (2007). *Beyond varieties of capitalism: conflict, contradictions, and complementarities in the European economy*. Oxford: Oxford University Press.

Hastings, T., Sheehan, B., & Yeates, P. (2007). *Saving the future*. Dublin: Blackhall Publishing.

Heery, E. (2002). Partnership versus organising: alternative futures for British trade unionism. *Industrial Relations Journal, 33*(1), 20–35.

Huselid, M. (1995). The impact of human resource management practices on turnover, productivity and corporate financial performance. *Academy of Management Journal, 38*(3), 635–70.

Hutton, W. (2002). *The world we're in*. London: Little, Brown.

Hutton, W. (2010, May 12). *Building an alternative economic vision for Ireland*. Lecture presented for the Irish Congress of Trade Unions, Liberty Hall, Dublin.

Jacobson, D., & Kirby, P. (2006). Globalisation and Ireland. In D. Jacobson, D. Kirby and D. Broin (eds), *Taming the tiger: social exclusion in a globalised Ireland* (pp. 23–44). Dublin: TASC/New Island Publishing.

Johnstone, S., Ackers, P., & Wilkinson, A. (2009). The British partnership phenomenon: a ten year review. *Human Resource Management Journal, 19*(3), 260–279.

Kaufmann, B. (2009). Promoting labour market efficiency and fairness through a legal minimum wage: the Webbs and the social cost of labour. *British Journal of Industrial Relations, 47*(2), 306–326.

Kelly, J. (2004). Partnership agreements in Britain: labor cooperation and compliance. *Industrial Relations, 43*(1), 267–292.

Kersley, B., Alpin, C., Forth, J., Dix, G., Oxenbridge, S., Bryson, A., & Bewley, H. (2006). *Inside the workplace: findings from the 2004 Workplace Employment Relations Survey.* Oxford: Routledge.

Kochan, T., Adler, P., McKersie, R., Eaton, A., Segal, P., and Gerhart, P. (2008). The potential and precariousness of partnership: the case of the Kaiser Permanente Labour Management Partnership. *Industrial Relations, 47*(1), 36–66.

Kochan, T. A., & Osterman, P. (1994). *The mutual gains enterprise: forgoing a winning partnership among labor, management and government.* Harvard Business School Press: Boston.

Kochan, T., & Rubinstein, S. (2000). Toward a stakeholder theory of the firm: the Saturn Partnership. *Organization Science, 11*(4), 367–386.

Lavelle, J., Gunnigle, P., & McDonnell. A. (2010). Patterning employee voice in multinational companies. *Human Relations, 63*, 395–418.

Marchington, M., Goodman, J., Wilkinson, A., & Ackers, P. (1992). *New developments in employee involvement,* Research Paper No.2, London: Employment Department.

Marchington, M., Wilkinson, A., Ackers, P., & Dundon, T. (2001). *Management choice and employee voice.* London, CIPD Publishing.

Martinez Lucio, M., & Stuart, M. (2005). Partnership and new industrial relations in a risk society: an age of shotgun weddings and marriages of convenience. *Work, Employment and Society, 19*(4), 797–817.

Murray, G., Belanger, J., Giles, A., & Lapointe, P. A. (2002). *Work & employment relations in the high-performance workplace.* London: Continuum.

National Centre for Partnership and Performance (NCPP) (2010), *NCPP 2009 national employee workplace survey and national employer workplace survey.* Dublin: NCPP.

O'Toole, F. (2009). *Ship of fools: how corruption and stupidity sank the celtic tiger,* New York: Faber and Faber.

Oxenbridge, S., & Brown, W. (2004). Achieving a new equilibrium? The stability of cooperative employer-union relationships. *Industrial Relations Journal, 35*(5), 388–402.

Partnership 2000 (1997). Dublin: Department of the Taoiseach.

Pfeffer, J. (1998). *The human equation: building profits by putting people first.* Boston: Harvard Business School Press.

Ramsey, H., Scholarios, D., & Harley, B. (2000). Employees and high-performance work systems: testing inside the Black Box. *British Journal of Industrial Relations, 29*(2), 112–125.

Rittau, Y., & Dundon, T. (2010). The roles and functions of shop stewards in workplace partnership: evidence from the Republic of Ireland. *Employee Relations, 32*(1), 10–27.

Roche, W. K. (1998). Between regime fragmentation and realignment: Irish industrial relations in the 1990's. *Industrial Relations Journal, 29*(2), 112–125.

Roche, W. K. (2007), Social partnership and workplace regimes in Ireland, *Industrial Relations Journal,* 38(3): 188–209.

Roche, W. K., & Geary, J. (2000), Collaborative production and the Irish boom: work organization, partnership and direct involvement in Irish workplaces. *Economic and Social Review, 31*(1), 1–36.

Roche, W. K., & Geary, J. F. (2006). *Partnership at work: the quest for radical organizational change.* London: Routledge.

Rubinstein, S., & Kochan, T. (2001). *Learning from Saturn.* Ithaca, NY: ILR Press.

Sabel, C. (1996). *Ireland: local partnerships and social innovation.* Paris: OECD.

Sisson, K. (2009). Why employment relations matter. *Warwick Papers in Industrial Relations,* no. 92.

Steinbock, D. (2001). *The Nokia revolution: the story of an extraordinary company that transformed an industry.* New York: Amacom.

Streeck, W. (1997). Beneficial constraints: on the economic limits of rational voluntarism. In J. Hollingsworth, J. Rogers & R. Boyer (eds), *Contemporary capitalism: The embeddedness of institutions* (pp. 197–219). Cambridge: Cambridge University Press.

Streeck, W. (2004). Educating capitalists: a rejoinder to Wright and Tsakalotos. *Socio-Economic Review, 2*(3), 425–437.

Stuart, M., & Martinez-Lucio, M. (2005). *Partnership and modernisation in employment relations.* London: Routledge.

Teague, P., & Donaghey, J. (2009a). Why has Irish social partnership survived? *British Journal of Industrial Relations, 47*(1), 55–78.

Teague, P., & Donaghey, J. (2009b). Social partnership and democratic legitimacy in Ireland. *New Political Economy, 14*(1), 51–71.

Teague, P., & Hann, D. (2010). Problems with partnership at work: lessons from an Irish case study. *Human Resource Management Journal, 20*(1), 100–114.

Thompson, P. (2003). Disconnected capitalism: or why employers can't keep their side of the bargain. *Work, Employment and Society, 17*(2), 359–378.

Wallace, J., Gunnigle, P., & McMahon, G. (2004). *Industrial relations in Ireland* (3rd edn). Dublin: Gill & Macmillan.

Wilkinson, A., Dundon, T., & Grugulis, I. (2007). Information but not consultation: exploring employee involvement in SMEs. *International Journal of Human Resource Management, 18*(7), 1279–1297.

Wilkinson, A., & Dundon, T. (2010) Direct employee participation. In A. Wilkinson, P. Gollan, M. Marchington and D. Lewin (eds), *Oxford handbook of participation in organizations* Oxford: Oxford University Press.

Wilkinson, R. and Pickett, K. (2010), *The spirit level: why equality is better for everyone.* London: Penguin.

11
The Global Financial Crisis and Employment Relations

David Peetz, Stephane Le Queux, and Ann Frost

Introduction

In an expensively decorated office high above Wall Street, financier Charles Smith sat down to read all the documentation surrounding the 'CDO squared' (CDO^2) he was about to purchase. The CDO^2 was a privately issued bond; the underlying assets backing it were a multitude of collateralized debt obligations (CDOs) – bonds issued against mixed pools of assets, mostly loans. Each of the underlying CDOs was 200 pages long, so in order to understand the CDO^2, worth many millions of dollars, Mr Smith had to read through 1.1 billion pages of text associated with 94 million mortgages and other instruments within that CDO^2. He sat with his coffee and commenced reading on 2 January 2008, and with meal and coffee breaks had finished by 7 August 2863.[1]

This, of course, is a fictional story – because no one ever read *all* the documentation associated with a CDO^2. So nobody buying them understood the risks involved, aside from a small number of individuals who had read *enough* to sense 'that lenders had lost it' (Michael Burry quote in Lewis 2010). Liberalization of financial markets, over nearly three decades from the Reagan administration onwards, delivered neither the free flow of perfect information necessary to make the textbook model work, nor the improvements in human life expectancy necessary to enable such information to be synthesized by mere mortals. As the late Craig Littler (2009, p. 16) pointed out, the finance sector experienced 'deknowledging': 'this was not the "knowledge economy"... it was more like "blind man's bluff"'. And so when badly performing loans formed much of the assets behind CDOs purchased by investors ranging from the City of London to municipal councils in Norway, the House of Cards that was the liberal market economy model of modern capitalism came crashing down. Or so, at least, it appeared to the millions of people who lost their jobs. In the United States, the number of unemployed rose by 8 million between December quarter 2007 and December quarter 2009, more than doubling in that time. In the European Union, 6 million were added to the rolls of the unemployed.

Yet the story of the global financial crisis is not just a story of impenetrable money trails and indolent investors. Less still is it a story of individual indiscretions and illegalities. Delicious headlines were made through scams by people like Bernie Madoff – the former chair of the NASDAQ stock exchange who embezzled around USD 60 billion of investors' funds – yet remarkably few people went to jail for their part in the destruction of millions of jobs and billions of dollars of value. The story of the crisis is one of systemic failures: failures so large as to raise issues about methods of human resource management, state regulation, and even economic organization, as well as labour responses, failures that followed three decades of neoliberal policies that promised a new prosperity but delivered so little. Between 1950 and 1973, annual per capita GDP growth averaged 3.9 per cent in Western Europe and 2.4 per cent in North America and Australasia; over the following two decades the performance was barely half of that (Maddison, 1995), and OECD annual per capita GDP growth was only 2 per cent over the 1995–2005 period (Organisation for Economic Cooperation and Development, 2006). Yet across 17 countries between 1990 and 2005, the ratio of the profits of the financial sector to the wages of *all* private sector workers rose from 32 per cent to 40 per cent (Freeman 2010). In this chapter we focus on the employment relations aspects of the global financial crisis with special attention to these issues. Our analysis is cross-national but, for space reasons, confined to developed nations, where the causes and effects of the crisis have been most directly observable. We consider the experiences in North America, Europe, and Australia.

Human resource management in the crisis

The global financial crisis exposed some major failings in the performance reward systems facing employees, managers, and chief executives in the finance sector, and led to major public debate about the remuneration of CEOs in particular. It also emphasized the need for *humane* resource management policies by firms in the face of such crisis. So we commence with analysis of the implications of the crisis for human resource management.

Corporations facing a drop in demand had choices as to how to respond: how much labour to dismiss, how much to hoard and how much to redeploy. In response to the economic crisis, average employment in the US fell by 3.8 per cent between 2008 and 2009, over double the fall in EU employment of 1.7 per cent. Yet GDP fell by considerably more in the EU (4.2 per cent) than in the US (2.4 per cent) (Organisation for Economic Cooperation and Development, 2010b). The different employment outcomes were not a result of underlying differences in productivity growth trends – between 1987 and 2007, average labour productivity growth in the US was only 0.1 percentage points above that of Europe's (Organisation for Economic Cooperation and Development, 2010a). The different employment outcomes resulted principally from very different approaches to the retention or abandonment of labour.

In the US, corporations responded to falling demand by sacking employees. In the EU, while layoffs were still common, more effort was put into finding alternatives to retrenching labour through redeployment or simply by hoarding labour, albeit on reduced hours. Certainly, there were instances of brutal corporate behaviour in Europe: in April 2010, European automobile equipment multinational Continental sent a letter to 600 out of 1120 dismissed staff offering job relocations in Tunisia for 137 Euros a month, saying that by doing so they were complying with their legal obligations to relocate staff in existing operations within the company (soyoutv.com, 2010). Still, there were national case-by-case examples of employers taking up 'positive' initiatives, for example in Romania (Eurofound, 2008; see also Eurofound, 2009c for an account of European initiatives). Special deals in industry collective agreements were also indicative of commitment by some large employers to job protection and job recovery. Company level agreements often contained provisions for flexible reduction of working time or work sharing with partial compensation of income losses financed by public funds (e.g. at Fiat and Indesit in Italy, Scania and Volvo in Sweden, Daimler and Schaeffer in Germany, and Danfos and Grundfos in Denmark) (Glassner & Keune, 2010). Some of such agreements provided for full rather than partial compensation (e.g. Renault in France and DAF Trucks in the Netherlands). Some focused on internal restructuring through redeployment of labour (e.g. Powertrain and Indesit in Italy). Some also focused on restructuring of labour through training (e.g. Peugeot in France and Telecom Italia) (Glassner & Keune 2010).

The contrasting approaches taken by corporations in the US and EU were partly a function of different corporate cultures among the decision-making elites, but these in turn reflected important differences in legislative frameworks. The US model of 'employment at will' contrasts sharply with the prevalence of employment protection legislation in the EU as well as national short-time working schemes provided for under legislation in countries such as Germany, Austria, France, Belgium, Netherlands, Italy, Poland, Bulgaria, Romania, Slovenia, and Hungary, or in national level collective agreements in Sweden and Denmark (Glassner, 2010; Glassner & Keune, 2010). Thus not only is the role of the state critical in the HRM responses of corporations to the financial crisis; at least as important is the role of organized labour. It is no surprise that the progressive responses most prominently occurred through collective agreements negotiated with unions. Without both a facilitative state and powerful unions – both lacking in the US, where union density remains around 12 per cent (Bureau of Labor Statistics, 2010) – there is neither the means nor the pressure for firms to implement innovative and humane HRM responses to the labour crisis that arose from the financial crisis. We turn in more depth to the roles of the state and organized labour shortly. But first, we look at some of the HRM *contributions to* the financial crisis.

The rise of unsafe lending and purchasing practices through such mechanisms as sub-prime loans, derivatives, and CDO^2s could not be solely attributed to innovative thinking on the part of some 'masters of the universe' from Tom Wolfe's *Bonfire of the vanities*. It relied upon the existence of incentive systems that prioritized growth in book value at the expense of more efficient or productive investments. And so it was that the performance appraisal and performance reward systems in the finance sector distorted behaviour in ways that made the crisis inevitable. A number of reports (summarized in Kirkpatrick, 2009) have argued that remuneration systems rewarded returns from high-risk activity without taking account of the potential or actual losses also incurred through high risk-taking. One of us interviewed a former Australia-based employee of a large transnational bank, who described the contradictions in the remuneration and reward systems there:

> They commensurated their sales people in gross sales with no eye to how much that business was consequently costing them. So as soon as [the sales area] were writing business we were closing it almost as quickly down in the bank branch – and yet the sales people were the lauded ones! I had six sales people reporting to me and I was trying to push this notion that you just can't [do that]. I wasn't in control of how they were remunerated though, so they were just reacting to how they were being remunerated and just went out and flogged

business. Crazy stuff. [With] no long term sustainability at all and no accountability or responsibility for how those loans then came down ... The sales people in the retail bank were also highly remunerated, to the extent that the highest paid employee in Australia was a sales person, not the CEO of the company ... Certainly those remuneration packages were highly questionable.[2]

The experience of the financial crisis demonstrated one of the ever-present dangers of any performance reward scheme: the possibility, unless carefully designed, that they will distort behaviour away from matters important to the organization that are not covered by the reward scheme, and to narrower behaviours that maximize individual gain but undermine organizational objectives. In effect, employees gained the benefit from risk taking without incurring the costs. The costs were instead borne by the organization, though eventually these were externalized to the broader community through bailout packages, bank closures, and job losses. Moreover, as behavioural experiments by Richard Freeman and Alexander Gelber (2010) demonstrated, increasing financial incentives increased the incentives for people to misreport their performance, one of the problems behind several collapses such as AIG. The size of remuneration itself helped bring about the financial crisis.

Among remuneration systems that failed, those that stood out most were for senior executives and chief executive officers (CEOs). Levels of executive compensation became a hot-button topic in American public discourse. In 2008, the S&P 500 CEOs took home pay that was 344 times higher than that of the average worker (Anderson, Cavanagh, Collins, & Pizzigati, 2008). Excess persisted despite the financial crisis and continued high levels of unemployment and wage stagnation for the working class. US elected officials responded with several attempts to secure 'say on pay' legislation. The original Emergency Economic Stabilization Act of 2008, that established the Troubled Asset Relief Program (TARP) to bail out a number of financial institutions, required shareholders at companies with outstanding funds from TARP to have a non-binding vote on executive pay (Donovan, 2009). In June 2009, additional legislation was brought forward that would authorize the Securities and Exchange Commission to require 'say on pay' regulations at all companies – not just at those with outstanding funds from TARP (Ellis, 2009). Eventually, this culminated in the 'Corporate and Financial Institution Compensation Fairness Act of 2009' that was brought forward in July 2009. This bill included a 'say on pay' feature for all public institutions and a provision for a shareholder vote on golden parachutes, and was passed by a 2 to 1 majority by the House of Representatives (Drum Major Institute for Public Policy, 2009). At time of writing it was under consideration by Senate committees. In 2009, 25 per cent of the companies that had reduced executive pay in 2008, reinstated or increased those salaries (O'Rourke, 2010). That many of these companies had not repaid TARP bailout funding was enough to anger President Obama (O'Rourke, 2010). Within a year, large and, in most eyes, excessive bonuses were again being paid to finance sector executives and CEOs in corporations that had only survived through state intervention.

Concern about executive pay was not restricted to the US. Executive pay caps were also a matter of concern and outrage throughout Europe. Across Europe, Australia, and the US, four-fifths of people believed that business leaders in their countries were paid too much and most supported caps through regulation (Harris Interactive, 2009; Ferguson, 2009). Legislative responses occurred in some countries, and there was widespread debate throughout the continent. In France, a report was adopted by the Parliament in July 2009 (Eurofound, 2009b). Following this report, the CEOs of the six major banks (BNP Paribas, Société générale, Crédit mutuel, Crédit agricole, Banques populaires and Caisses d'épargne) and of the four major car manufacturing companies (PSA, Renault, Renault Trucks–Volvo, and Iveco) were legally forbidden from receiving free stock options. The government also imposed a cap on their bonuses till the end of 2010. Financial institutions whose deposits had been fully guaranteed by the Irish government were asked to limit the pay of top-level executives to €500,000 a year (Eurofound, 2009a). In Canada, a recent study found that the 100 highest compensated CEOs earned 174 times the average Canadian worker (Mackenzie, 2010). This ratio too has risen over the past decade but in part is held in check (relative to the US) by higher minimum wages and higher unionization rates. In Australia, concern about CEO excess led to the Labor Party government commissioning an inquiry by the Productivity Commission, a conservative economic advice agency. The report erroneously argued that the growth of CEO pay largely reflected company performance (Productivity Commission, 2009; Peetz, 2010) and recommended the creation of some muted 'say on pay' rights and improvements to board governance, which were mostly adopted by the government. The recommendations did little to overcome the core problem of executive remuneration: the concentration of power and resources in the hands of CEOs, who share the social and economic milieu of the people with whom they 'negotiate', ensuring that in place of arms-length bargaining there is a steady accumulation of resources regardless of company performance (Ang, Nagel, & Yang, 2007; Bebchuk & Fried, 2004; Crystal, 1991; House of Commons Treasury Committee, 2009; Shields, O'Donnell & O'Brien, 2003, 2004; RiskMetrics Australia, 2009). Nor did they deal with what Torres referred to as the first of two 'root problems' of the financial crisis: inappropriate incentives affecting both risk-taking and pay of bank executives and traders (Torres, 2010).

The remuneration systems for top executives as well as senior and middle ranking employees in turn created cultures that not only privileged risk but also discouraged dissent. Innovation in the creation of complex and risky financial products was not matched by internal debate on the merits of such activities. The employee of a large transnational bank we quoted earlier saw 'culture as a serious problem' as 'they wouldn't listen to dissent', a situation which was 'just a set up for disaster' (interview A, 2009). What Willmott (1993) referred to as 'culturism' – the deliberate creation of corporate cultures in the image of top management in order to maintain stability and control – has in the end undermined organizational stability. As Stanley Milgram's obedience experiments in the 1960s suggested, in the absence of dissenting voices, even intelligent and ethical people will often engage in dubious or unethical acts if the predominant culture encourages them (Milgram, 1963). Morck (2004) used the Milgram experiments to explain why, even when the CEOs were demonstrably misperforming, corporate boards were typically acquiescent to CEOs, but they equally provide insight into why individuals in corporations would engage in activities that were potentially dangerous.

The global financial crisis has demonstrated some failures in HRM practices. As Freeman (2010) argues, 'a new compensation system that rewards finance for contributing to the real economy and that penalizes financial misconduct and rent-seeking is a necessary part of any reform agenda.' The challenges for HRM are to develop models of performance management and remuneration for top and middle ranking executives and models of cultural management that go beyond culturism and emphasize diversity.

The state in crisis

As we saw in the case of executive pay, the failure of HRM practices and governance during the financial crisis invited greater state action. The immediate priority of the state in every country was to prevent massive job losses and the dislocation that follows over many years. The challenges facing the state were greater than at any other time during the post-war period. We saw this in the extensive state interventions, showing unprecedented coordination, within and across national boundaries (Organisation for Economic Cooperation and Development, 2009a). These interventions represented a refutation of the orthodoxy that had dominated economic policy making for nearly three decades (Quiggin, 2010). They were, however, much more extensive in terms of their call upon government budgets – and ultimately, the taxes paid by wage and salary earners – than in effectively regulating the causes of the crisis.

When what became known in North America as the Great Recession hit the US in the fall of 2008, it almost immediately resulted in deep job cuts and unprecedented numbers of home foreclosures as the banking system was driven to its knees. In the US, the unemployment rate immediately rose to 6.6 per cent in October 2008 from 6.2 per cent the month before, and was 10.0 per cent a year later in December 2009 (U.S. Bureau of Labor Statistics, 2010). More stringent banking regulation in Canada prevented the worst excesses seen south of the border, but Canadian unemployment still rose rapidly, peaking at 8.4 per cent in 2009, (Statistics Canada, 2010). By early 2009, governments of both countries had acted to resist recession. In January 2009, the US federal government announced an $819 billion stimulus package – much of it in health and human services, labour, and education. In addition to spending on programmes and infrastructure, a sizeable amount was directed towards individuals especially in unemployment assistance, continuation of health insurance benefits for the unemployed, and payments to Medicaid. The US government used TARP to bail out institutions such as Bear Stearns ($30 billion), Fannie Mae/Freddie Mac ($400 billion), and AIG ($180 billion). The auto industry also received a $25 billion low interest loan package to build more fuel-efficient, environmentally friendly cars. In October 2008, the US Congress passed the Emergency Economic Stabilization Act that provided $700 billion to help buy up troubled financial assets (for example, Bank of America received $142 billion and Citigroup $280 billion) (propublica.org). After decades of extolling the virtues of private ownership for everyone else, US banks were, in effect, nationalized.

The Conservative Canadian government announced a $50 billion economic action plan in January 2009, which included immediate spending to build infrastructure, stimulate new housing construction, tax credits for enhanced energy efficiency, social housing, as well as a

Canada Skills and Transition Strategy for those most affected by the economic downturn requiring job retraining and enhancements to Employment Insurance (Canada's Economic Action Plan, 2010). The plan also provided $7.5 billion targeted at specific sectors and regions, particularly automobiles, forestry, and manufacturing. Fortunately, as Canadian banks were more tightly regulated and had more conservative lending practices (Richburg, 2008), only 1 in 20 Canadian mortgages granted between 2004 and 2006 were rated subprime compared with nearly 1 in 4 in the US. Correspondingly, the foreclosure rate in Canada stood at 0.27 per cent in October 2008 compared with 4.5 per cent in the US (Kay, 2008).

Across the Atlantic, the EU Commission in Autumn 2008 recommended a €200 billion stimulus package (around 1.5 per cent of GDP). Individual member states were to provide €170 billion and the remaining €30 billion would come from the European budget. The EU-27 agreed on the package in December. Legislation on a €26 billion package was voted in France at the end of January (BBC, 2009). As in Germany, it included support to low income earners, infrastructure investments, and tax reductions for working families and businesses. A key state contribution to moderating the rise in unemployment was the financial underpinning of short-time work schemes developed under collective agreements mentioned earlier. The financial crisis generated several government initiatives and industry collective agreements often supported by the state to find solutions to keep people at work through partial unemployment, job sharing, and flexitime agreements. This agenda (Eurofound, 2009c) represented a change from the situation before the financial crisis, when the EU labour agenda was focused on 'flexicurity', the idea originating in Denmark that optimal labour market outcomes are based on a combination of low employment protection legislation and active employment adjustment policies (although in practice policy makers' discourse had appeared to focus mainly on the 'flexi' component rather than 'security') (e.g. Madsen, 2002). In Europe, as in the US, the disasters created by the unwarranted expansion of private sector debt were averted only by the explosion of public sector debt, which represents a brake on growth (governments must be fiscally conservative and therefore slow down their economies in the face of excess debt), imposing real costs in terms of persistent unemployment and depressed wages growth (Torres, 2010). In some cases, such as Greece, excess public sector debt led to crisis and the imposition of very extensive costs on workers (through such mechanisms as cuts in pensions, jobs, and public sector pay). In Ireland, bailing out failed banks led the Irish state to take on a debt burden per capita ten times that of the US, one that is likely to exceed that of Greece (Kelly, 2010). The citizens of Iceland, whose banking system totally collapsed after a period of heady expansion, refused to bail out the banks or repay debts the failed banks owed to British and Dutch investors. After falling for eight quarters after September quarter 2008, it showed signs of recovery with growth in September quarter 2010, and seems to be outperforming Ireland, which propped up the banks on employment (Jolly, 2010; Gurdgiev 2011). Around the developed world, the cost of the excess and failure in remuneration and governance in the finance sector were borne by workers and will be felt until at least 2015, the earliest that a return to pre-crisis unemployment levels is projected (Freeman, 2010).

Moves to impose a 'Tobin tax' – a tax on international transactions (Tobin, 1978), designed to discourage global financial instability and generate funds for economic development, but small enough not to damage trade flows, gained substantial support in Europe. The Tobin tax had been discussed, but not implemented, by the French National Assembly several years earlier, and later won sponsorship from other governments. It also obtained backing from the International Labour Organisation and international trade union bodies as well as global justice lobbyists such as ATTAC (Association for the Taxation of Financial Transactions and Aid to Citizens) in France (e.g. ETUC, 2010). Discussions on prohibiting tax havens also gathered momentum at EU level.

Australia was one of only two OECD countries to experience economic growth between June 2008 and June 2009 or to maintain positive annual economic growth through 2008 and 2009. The Australian government's response to the financial crisis was rapid, effective and yet contradictory. In October 2008, within a month of the Lehmann Brothers collapse, it announced an AUD 10 billion stimulus package focusing on transfer payments, followed shortly by an AUD 42 billion package focusing on infrastructure, housing, and schools. It had the largest expenditure package in the OECD as a proportion of GDP and the third largest total package (other countries focusing more on tax cuts, which have less direct effects) (Organisation for Economic Cooperation and Development, 2009a). The government also moved quickly to guarantee all bank deposits, without which the oligopolistic banking system would have disintegrated. A number of financial institutions collapsed, but no banks, due to the history of stronger financial regulation in Australia than in the US. Two significant banks, however, were taken over by larger competitors. The government put in place other measures to support the construction industry. Illustrating the shift from previous thinking, Prime Minister Kevin Rudd even published a major essay decrying the failures of neoliberalism (Rudd, 2009). Yet the government resisted calls for more forceful regulation of executive remuneration or the financial system, dodged around European proposals for a Tobin Tax, and showed little sign of following up the Rudd critique and developing an alternative vision for the economy. On industrial relations legislation, the government adopted a decidedly centrist approach, repudiating and replacing the predecessor government's anti-union 'WorkChoices' laws but leaving several restrictions on union activity including industrial action in place, and failing to rescind laws denying normal civil rights to unionists in the construction industry.

In the US, industrial legislation was similarly contentious, with calls for labour law reform emerging as the economic situation of American workers worsened with the financial crisis and resistance by employers intensifying. (By contrast, the financial crisis had little impact on debate on industrial legislation in Australia as labour law had already been a decisive factor in the election that defeated the previous conservative government.) At the centre of the US debate was the Employee Free Choice Act (EFCA). It sought three major revisions: enabling a union to be certified through a simple majority signing union membership cards (rather than a ballot, frequently vigorously opposed by employers), allowing compulsory arbitration where negotiations for a first contract fail (currently less than one in five newly certified bargaining units ever manages to negotiate a first contract (Ferguson & Kochan, 2008), and imposing stiffer penalties for labour law violations. EFCA was reintroduced in Congress in March 2009 and referred to committee in April 2009. With a small number of Democrat Senators vacillating, the fate of the EFCA was in limbo for some time, but it was eventually killed off with the mid-term elections in 2010.

But perhaps the most notable aspect of the role of the state that emerged from the financial crisis was the failure of three decades of neoliberal policies aimed at increasing the 'flexibility' of labour markets and, in effect, transferring power from labour to capital. The US experienced a worse deterioration in employment than Europe. The greater labour market flexibility in the US that was meant to protect employment ended up more readily destroying it. In 2009 the OECD found no evidence that structural reform policies to promote flexibility had made labour markets 'less sensitive to severe economic downturns than was the case in the past' and recommended governments improve income support and unemployment insurance benefit systems, which had previously said would decrease flexibility (Organisation for Economic Cooperation and Development, 2009b, p. 40). As Freeman concludes,

'Financial markets can destroy economies whereas labour markets cannot.' So it was that Torres (2010) identified the second cause of the crisis as inadequate and incomplete regulation. Policy makers' focus on labour market and employment relations reform as the keys to prosperity have not only failed to deliver gains that would enable labour markets to painlessly adapt to recessions, but it also diverted attention from the causes of recessions.

Labour and the crisis

Unions responded around the world to the depth and extent of the current financial crisis. In North America, union priorities were on protecting the wellbeing of working people generally, but especially the unemployed and those employed in threatened industries. In Canada, many unions sought pension guarantees from the government (Townson, 2010), as corporations on the brink of financial ruin threatened current and future pension benefits owed to members. Canadian labour organizations – such as the Canadian Autoworkers, the United Steelworkers, the Canadian Union of Public Employees, and the Canadian Labour Congress (Canadian Labour Congress, 2009) – were also concerned with the level of unemployment benefits and their eligibility criteria. Whereas in the previous major recession 80 per cent of the unemployed qualified to receive unemployment benefits, this time less than half of laid off workers qualified. This was because many more people found themselves working part time, on temporary contracts, or as self employed – none of which qualified for coverage under the Employment Insurance programme. The Canadian Labour Congress in particular was vocal about the government's diverting funds from the Employment Insurance Account (which had accumulated an estimated $54 billion surplus) into general deficit reduction rather than extending unemployment benefits at a time when coverage of benefits had narrowed and duration of unemployment increased.

In the US, as in Canada, fewer than half of laid off workers qualified for unemployment insurance benefits. Retrenched workers often also lost their health care coverage. The AFL-CIO organized protests against the tax system. On 15 April 2010 (the day US income taxes were due), activists held rallies at banks and post offices across the country to highlight the need for new good jobs. The AFL-CIO also supported a Tobin-style tax on financial speculation (Acosta, 2010).

The North American labour movement was relatively mild in what it called for as a new paradigm to govern the post-financial crisis economy. In the US both peak councils – the AFL-CIO and Change to Win – emphasized investments in infrastructure, health care, the reregulation of the banking sector, and the passage of the EFCA to facilitate union organizing (Tilly, 2010). In Canada, the leader of the Canadian Labour Congress, Ken Georgetti, called for the overhaul of Canada's financial system, new public investments to create jobs, and changes to unfair trade agreements (Canadian Labour Congress, 2010). None of this was any different than what one might have observed a decade ago. Australian unions also reiterated some long-standing calls for a more interventionist state, and strongly supported the Rudd government's stimulus package against conservative critique. While unions sought different approaches in some areas including executive remuneration and financial regulation (Australian Council of Trade Unions, 2009), media coverage focused on their concern about preventing Australian jobs being lost overseas (e.g. AAP, 2009).

In Europe, national level unions were responding to pressures for wage flexibility, in some cases negotiating clauses in collective agreements that phased wage increases with potential for temporary suspension in case of company difficulties, provided for short-time work or provided for enhanced training and skill enhancement to enable redeployment of labour in return for employment guarantees. Wages growth slowed and in Germany became negative (Glassner, 2010). Yet unlike some previous crises, there was little in the way of systematic moves towards greater decentralization in wage bargaining structures, as IR systems seemed flexible enough to allow firm level adjustments. Ireland appeared to be the only country where substantial pressure in this direction was likely to bear fruit, due to policy directions by government and the largest employer organization (Glassner, 2010). In some isolated instances, local labour reactions to the crisis were explosive, with a wave of bossnapping in France when corporations sought to close down workplaces. It reached a peak of at least one case a week in Spring 2009, in corporations such as Logistic, Molex, Sony, Scapa, 3M, Fauressia, and Caterpillar, where several bosses were sequestrated for days. Majorities of respondents to a French opinion poll indicated that radical social actions such as factory occupation and bossnapping were justified and opposed legal sanctions against bossnappers (BVA, 2009). Neither the US nor Canada experienced the financial crisis-related protests and violence that erupted in many European countries over 2009 or 2010.

At the *regional*, pan-European, level there has long been a tension between, on the one hand, the incorporation of European trade union bodies within the broader institutional superstructure of Europe and, on the other hand, the growing resistance to neoliberal policies embodied in social movements, some of which also opposed the social-liberal model of European integration (Bieler, 2008). European labour showed an initial reluctance to shift attitudes towards protest movements (Le Queux, 2008). At demonstrations in Brussels in March 2005 against the Bolkestein Directive (enabling multinational firms to hire workers on the pay and conditions in their home rather than host countries), the union leadership at the head of the procession carried slogans of 'yes' to social Europe, while the tail of the procession was made up of tens of thousands of activists, shouting 'no' to the European Constitution and 'no' to an anti-social Europe (Le Queux, 2005). The focus of the ETUC is on institution-building rather than mobilization (Goetschy, 1996), on 'structure before action' (Martin and Ross, 1999). Although, according to Groux (2004, p. 46), the ETUC's institutional strategy has enabled it to establish its presence as an important social actor on the European stage, many observers are sceptical because it was difficult to gain popular support for a 'social liberal' Europe embroiled within a rationale of 'comitology' (governance by committees) (Hyman, 2004); it could not directly mobilize people, relying on recruitment for demonstrations by national trade unions and civil society; and its negotiating capacity was caught up in and hemmed in by the European social dialogue, to occlude social conflict (Gobin, 1997). At best, as stressed by Braud (2004), it attempted to build bridges with civil society while at the same time maintaining a safe distance.

In the lead up to and during the financial crisis, and under the new lead of the International Trade Union Confederation (ITUC), the ETUC moved closer to establishing new transnational alliances with non-union actors, especially the global justice movement. The ETUC initiated a campaign, 'fight the crisis – and win the aftermath', alongside the 2009 ETUC Paris declaration (McKay, 2009), the first time that the ETUC leadership took such a stance towards mobilization. For trade unions these alliances 'represent opportunities to reach out to a new public, to act in innovative ways and to strengthen its mobilization capacity, in particular transnationally' (Keun & Schmidt, 2009, p. 17). Mounting reaction to restructuring – for example the loss of 6,000 European jobs in General Motors over several years (Gajewska, 2008) – led to increased cross-border solidarity campaigning and protests. Sometimes, though, massive job losses or threats on jobs resulting from the economic downfall speared sentiments of exacerbation and despair, leading to violent outbursts and xenophobic reflexes, and exposing cracks within the European social-liberal model, presenting major solidarity challenges for the ETUC.

Beyond these national and regional actions, there is the question of *global* union responses to the financial crisis. Global unions arose as a response to the rise of multinational corporations, and they operate at a level at which they can contemplate challenging the problems arising from global financial capital. Bieler et. al. (2008) discuss the strategic importance of building alliances with new social movements among top priority actions for global solidarity, including cross-border campaigning and organizing the informal sector (where the bulk of labour in developing economies is often to be found). Campaigning activities of the ITUC revolved around the 'Decent Work for a Decent Life' global agenda (http://www.wddw.org), launched at the 2007 World Social Forum (WSF) in Nairobi in association with militant organizations from the civil society such as Social Alert, Solidar, and the Global Progressive Forum and taken up by the ETUC, though not without divisions between it and radical unions (Bieler, 2007). 'Decent Work' thus signalled a qualitative shift in global labour politics, a step away from bureaucracy and diplomacy (Hyman, 2005) and a step closer to the global justice movements that emerged in protest against globalization at the turn of the 21st century. The Decent Work campaign reached a new height and a new turn with the financial crisis. It aimed at building a greater convergence between unions and social movements as well as bridging the Global North and Global South. For the ITUC general secretary, 'the creation of decent work will have to be put at the heart of the new financial architecture and economic governance that we have to build (Guy Ryder as cited in ITUC, 2009a), while the assistant general secretary called for 'an economic model based on redistribution, respect for the environment and fair relations between rich and poor countries' (M. Cissé as cited in ITUC, 2009c).

The financial crisis provided momentum for global unions to bolster their agenda as they warned the November 2008 G-20 meeting in Washington: 'Half measures will not fix a broken global economy.' The subsequent April 2009 *Global Unions London Declaration*, a Statement to the London G-20 summit, laid down a detailed programme for reformed global governance, demanding a coordinated international recovery and sustainable growth plan, new rules for global financial markets and an end to wage deflation and the 'crisis of distributive justice' (ITUC, 2009b). Global unions' response to the financial crisis was articulated around three fronts: mobilization for social justice and mounting pressures to the G20, a call for a more inclusive model of global governance, and a call for a Global New Deal involving a 'global jobs pact', an initiative supported by the ILO but now seemingly threatened by G20 commitments to halve public debt by 2020 (ITUC, 2010b, 2010a). Yet the global unions' impact in public debate has been limited, beyond the generalized dissent of the anti-globalization protests. International institutions and corporations will pay more attention if international unions can engage in co-ordinated action. Some global union federations (representing particular industries) have negotiated transnational agreements with multinational corporations, but the challenge remains for unions to make their presence felt on the international stage and to force the state and capital at that level to respond to it.

Towards a new vision

Each of the parties to employment relations faces new challenges as a result of the global financial crisis. For management, a key challenge is to overcome the failures of human resource management practices that helped precipitate the crisis. Principal among these were inadequate performance management and remuneration systems in the finance sector, along with the demonstrated pitfalls of allowing the development of organizational monocultures that accepted and encouraged inappropriate lending, marketing, and purchasing practices. These failures in the finance sector point to likely weaknesses in other sectors as well, but it is in the finance sector that their effects have been devastating beyond the boundaries of one industry and caused damage throughout the economy – not just within a nation, but across the international economy.

For the state, there has been the rediscovery of the potential, and limits, of Keynesian stimulus policies, and particularly the benefit of rapid, co-ordinated responses. The policy legacy of nearly three decades of neoliberalism has been found severely deficient. Policies to create labour market flexibility, the holy grail of policy makers, did nothing to prevent the crisis and, as shown in the US example, exacerbated rather than ameliorated its effects. Instead, active intervention by unions and governments, negotiating and facilitating firm-level agreements for adjustment, helped moderate the effects of a crisis created elsewhere. And the liberation of capital markets from government controls and consequent promotion of financialization has been an economic disaster. State bailouts enabled finance capital to externalize the costs onto the rest of society, especially onto workers through lost jobs, higher liabilities, and lower economic prospects.

The state relied on economists' models, and the economics profession focused on models that ignored real world processes as modellers failed to communicate the limitations of their models and potential misuses of their research (Colander, Föllmer, Haas, Goldberg, Juselius, Kirman, Lux, & Sloth, 2009). Key theorems and assumptions underlying existing policy models were revealed as false (Quiggin, 2010). The efficient markets hypothesis, under which markets would always determine the 'correct' price for a product, was demonstrably and spectacularly wrong. Similarly, the idea that markets 'self-correct', and find stable equilibrium, was wrong. The idea of 'trickle down', or 'a rising tide lifts all boats', by which everyone would benefit from the increased wealth of the rich, was likewise falsified. The idea that markets are able to accurately assess risk and returns, and therefore most efficient at allocating resources – an idea underpinning the rationale for privatization, a practice with typically adverse implications for workers' jobs and conditions (Quiggin, 1995) – was also shown to be bogus. Yet a couple of years into the crisis, policy makers carried on much as before, as no consensus about a coherent alternative had emerged. The above ideas had been killed, yet they were still alive – as Quiggin (2010) calls it, they were 'zombie ideas'. Policy makers must now seek and embrace a new paradigm for understanding the modern capitalist economy, and devise new policies. One part of this requires giving policy priority not to further liberalization of labour markets, but to new regulation of financial markets. And so another part means ensuring that the problems with remuneration practices in the financial sector are resolved. It might be feasible that top management of financial corporations may recognize it is in their interests to reform the remuneration policies affecting those below them – though the resurgence in bonus payments in 2010 (Freeman, 2010) suggests this is unlikely. Experience indicates there is *no* prospect of CEOs repairing their own remuneration practices. Policy inaction will lead to history being repeated.

For trade unions, part of their task is to build their capacities for negotiating adjustment deals when firms are in crisis and a just share of profit when they are not. If bonuses of workers were tied to bonuses of their CEOs, some restraint at the top might start to materialize. But all problems cannot be resolved on an enterprise by enterprise basis. To achieve more influence, unions must 'win back their legitimacy' (Hyman, 2007, p. 207), and a major way of achieving this is by defining 'alternative ways of connecting economy and society, work and life'

(Hyman, 2007, p. 208). If a new, coherent paradigm is to emerge to influence policy makers, unions will likely need to play a role in devising, or at a minimum effectively advocating, an alternative model. The problems identified by the unions cannot be solved without the cooperation of mainstream international institutions like the IMF and WTO, and unions were simultaneously railing against, but pleading for the support, of these bodies. If unions are to effectively push for the adoption of a new model, they will need greater power through mobilization.

There has been an unusually coordinated union response to the financial crisis, though aimed more at preserving capitalism in a modified form than overthrowing it. The rising prominence of 'Decent Work' signals that international labour is developing a new vision and narrative, and it has significantly moved towards the global social justice agenda. The need to build alliances with civil society has been widely acknowledged. A key issue is how this idea cascades down at national level, for example in countries like Canada and Australia. On the streets of Europe and to some degree elsewhere, there is a sense that this is not the workers' crisis, so why should they pay for it in ever worsening ways? As the cost of recovering from the crisis is increasingly felt by workers, the tensions arising from working within the constraints of the existing economic structures intensify.

As Scherrer (2010) pointed out, there is nothing inevitable about what follows the financial crisis. As the Great Depression demonstrated the failure of the classical economics of the day, there were several possible outcomes, including Fascism and Stalinism. It was only the Second World War that resolved the matter finally, and led to the great post-war accommodation and its development of the welfare state over nearly three decades of prosperity that subsequently has been unrivalled and unravelled. Now the range of possible outcomes, if nothing much changes, includes a global ecological crisis (Burawoy, 2010). How corporations, the state, and unions respond to the crisis – and how well the academy provides them with the tools to respond – will shape the future of the labour market and employment relations, and in many respects the global economy for decades to come.

Notes

1. This is not a typo. For source of the calculation see Haldane, A. G. (2009). Rethinking the financial network. *Speech delivered at the Financial Student Association*. Amsterdam, Bank of England. CDO^2 is a short-hand term for a CDO of asset-backed securities CDOs.
2. interview A, conducted by David Peetz & Georgina Murray, NSW, February 2009.

References

AAP. (2009, March 5). Pacific Brands refuses to reverse job losses. *Herald-Sun*. Retrieved from http://www.heraldsun.com.au/news/victoria/pacific-brands-wont-budge-on-jobs/story-e6frf7kx-1111119038036

Acosta, A. (2010, April 15). It's April 15: time to tax Wall Street. We need good jobs now. [Blog]. Retrieved from *AFL-CIO Now Blog News*: http://blog.afl-cio.org/2010/04/15/its-april-15-time-to-tax-wall-street-we-need-good-jobs-now/

Anderson, S., Cavanagh, J., Collins, C., Pizzigati, S., & Lapham, M. (2008). *Executive excess 2008: how average taxpayers subsidize runaway pay*. Retrieved from Institute for Policy Studies and United for a Fair Economy, Washington, DC: http://www.faireconomy.org/files/executive_excess_2008.pdf

Ang, J., Nagel, G., & Yang, J. (2007). *Is there a social circle premium in CEO compensation?* SSRN Working Paper.

Australian Council of Trade Unions (2009, 25 November). *ACTU Congress 2009 Policies and Resolutions*. Melbourne: Australian Council of Trade Unions.

BBC (2009, February 2). France unveils stimulus package. Retrieved from *BBC*: http://news.bbc.co.uk/2/hi/business/7864942.stm

Bebchuk, L., & Fried, J. (2004). *Pay without performance: the unfulfilled promise of executive compensation*. Cambridge: Harvard University Press.

Bieler, A. (2007, February 27). Labour at the World Social Forum 2007 in Nairobi/Kenya. [Blog]. Retrieved from http://www.choike.org/nuevo_eng/informes/5380.html

Bieler, A. (2008). *Transnational solidarity or conflict? Trade unions and neo-liberal restructuring in Europe*. CSSGJ working paper, WP001: August.

Bieler, A., Lindberg, I. & Pillay, D. (2008). *Labour and the challenges of globalization: what prospects for transnational solidarity?* London: Pluto Press.

Braud, M. (2004). Après le congrès de la CES, quelle stratégie et quelles actions syndicales européennes? *Chronique Internationale de l'IRES, 86*, 43–52.

Burawoy, M. (2010). From Polanyi to Pollyanna: the false optimism of global labor studies. *Global Labour Journal, 1*(2), 301–313.

Bureau of Labor Statistics (2010, January 22). *Union members 2009 news release USDL-10–0069*. Retrieved from Department of Labor: http://www.bls.gov/news.release/pdf/union2.pdf

BVA (2009, April 15). 55% des Français jugent 'justifiées' les séquestrations de patrons. *l'Express.fr*. Retrieved from http://www.lexpress.fr/actualite/economie/55-pourcent-des-francais-jugent-justifiees-les-sequestrations-de-patrons_754055.html

Canada's Economic Action Plan (2010). Government of Canada. http://www.actionplan.gc.ca/eng/feature.asp?featureId=4

Canadian Labour Congress (2009). Fix employment insurance now. http://www.canadianlabour.ca/national/news/fix-employment-insurance-now

Canadian Labour Congress (2010). The 'Great Recession': from a financial crisis to a jobs crisis, to a new labour market model. http://www.canadianlabour.ca/news-room/publications/great-recession-financial-crisis-jobs-crisis-new-labour-market-model

Colander, D., Föllmer, H., Haas, A., Goldberg, M., Juselius, K., Kirman, A., Lux, T., & Sloth, B. (2009). *The financial crisis and the systemic failure of academic economics*. Discussion Paper No 09–03. Copenhagen: Department of Economics, University of Copenhagen.

Crystal, G. (1991). *In search of excess: the overcompensation of American executives.* New York: Norton.

Drum Major Institute for Public Policy (2009). H. R. 3269 Corporate and Financial Institution Compensation Fairness Act of 2009. In Corporate Accountability, Executive Compensation, Shareholder Rights. http://www. themiddleclass.org/bill/corporate-and-financial-institution-compensation-fairness-act-2009

Ellis, D. (2009). 'Say on Pay' Moves Full Speed Ahead. http://money.cnn. com/2009/07/28/news/companies/compensation_executives/index.htm

ETUC (2010). *The economic crisis: new sources of finance Brussels, European Trade Union Congress: 9–10 March.* Retrieved from http://www.etuc.org/a/7052? var_recherche=ceo#nh6

Eurofound (2008). *Employer organisations seek response to economic crisis.* Retrieved from EIROnline: http://www.eurofound.europa.eu/eiro/2008/11/articles/ ro0811029i.htm

Eurofound (2009a). *Finance minister seeks to cap pay of top bankers.* Retrieved from EIROnline: http://www.eurofound.europa.eu/eiro/2009/03/articles/ ie0903029i.htm

Eurofound (2009b). *Parliament adopts report on executive pay in bid to curb abuse.* Retrieved from EIROnline: http://www.eurofound.europa.eu/eiro/2009/08/ articles/fr0908029i.htm

Eurofound (2009c). *Tackling the recession: employment-related public initiatives in the EU Member States and Norway: August.* Retrieved from http://www.euro-found.europa.eu/emcc/erm/studies/tn0907020s/index.htm

Ferguson, A. (2009, September 23). Executive salary anger puts spotlight on commission report. Retrivede from *The Australian:* http://www.theaustralian. com.au/news/executive-lifestyle/executive-salary-anger-puts-spotlight-on-commission-report/story-e6frga8o-1225778362634

Ferguson, J. P. and Kochan, T. (2008). 'Sequential failures in workers' right to organize', MIT Sloan School of Management Institute for Work and Employment Research, http://www. americanrightsatwork.org/dmdocuments/sequential_failures_in_workers_right_to_organize_3_25_2008.pdf

Freeman, R. B. (2010). It's financialization! *International Labour Review, 149*(2), 163–183.

Freeman, R. B., & Gelber, A. M. (2010). Prize structure and information in tournaments: experimental evidence. *American Economic Journal: Applied economics, 2*(1), 149–164.

Gajewska, K. (2008). The emergence of a European labour protest movement? *European Journal of Industrial Relations, 14*(1), 104–121.

Glassner, V. (2010). Social partner responses to the economic crisis in Europe: why collective bargaining makes a difference. *Global Labour Column, 21.*

Glassner, V., & Keune, M. (2010). *Collective bargaining responses to the economic crisis in Europe. ETUI Policy Brief 1/2010, European Economic and Employment Policy.* Brussels: European Trade Union Institute.

Gobin, C. (1997). *L'Europe syndicale: entre désir et réalité.* Bruxelles: Labor.

Goetschy, J. (1996). The European trade union confederation and the construction of European trade unionism. In P. Leisink, J. Van Leemputt & J. Vilrokx (eds), *The challenges of trade unions in Europe* (pp. 253–265). Cheltenham: Edward Elgar.

Groux, G. (2004). La montée en puissance d'un acteur social européen. *Alternatives internationales, 2,* 46–47.

Gurdgiev, C. (2011). Ireland v Iceland: Economy, part 2, True Economics. http:\trueeconomics.blogspot.com\2011\02\28022011-ireland-v-iceland-economy-part.html

Haldane, A. G. (2009). *Rethinking the financial network.* Speech presented for the Financial Student Association, Bank of England, Amsterdam.

Harris Interactive (2009). *Six-country Financial Times/Harris Poll shows how badly economic crisis has hurt reputation of business leaders.* Retrieved from Secondary Harris Interactive.: http://www.harrisinteractive.com/news/FTHarrisPoll/HI_FinancialTimes_HarrisPoll_EconomicCrisis_Apr15_09.pdf

House of Commons Treasury Committee (2009). *Banking Crisis: reforming corporate governance and pay in the city.* Retrieved from Secondary House of Commons Treasury Committee: http://www.publications.parliament.uk/pa/cm200809/cmselect/cmtreasy/519/519.pdf

Hyman, R. (2004). *Trade unions and the politics of the European social model. Organised labour – An agent of eu democracy?* Trade Union Strategies and the EU Integration Process, European Conference. Dublin: University College of Dublin.

Hyman, R. (2005). Shifting Dynamics in International Trade Unionism: Agitation, Organisation, Bureaucracy, Diplomacy, *Labor History,* 46(2), 137–154.

Hyman, R. (2007). How can trade unions act strategically? *Transfer – European Review of Labour and Research,* 13(2), 193–210.

ITUC (2009a, January 29). *Decent work decent life campaign acts on financial crisis in world social forum.* Retrieved from ITUC OnLine 013/290109: http://www.ituc-csi.org/decent-work-decent-life-campaign.html

ITUC (2009b). *Global unions London declaration. Statement to the London G20 Summit.* Retrieved from International Trade Unions Confederation, Trade Union Advisory Committee to the OECD, and Global Unions: http://www.ituc-csi.org/IMG/pdf/No_16_-_G20_London_Declaration_FINAL.pdf

ITUC (2009c, January 28). *World social forum: trade unions call for a new growth model.* Retrieved from ITUC Onlines 012/280109: http://www.ituc-csi.org/world-social-forum-trade-unions.html?lang=en

ITUC (2010a, June 7). G20 finance ministers risk tipping global economy back into recession. Retrieved from ITUC OnLine: http://www.ituc-csi.org/g20-finance-ministers-world-unions.html?lang=en

ITUC (2010b, October 26). G20 finance ministers: world unions warn of complacent attitude and ask 'where are the jobs?'. Retrieved from ITUC OnLine: http://www.ituc-csi.org/g20-finance-ministers-world-unions.html?lang=en

Jolly, D. (2010, December 7). Iceland emerged from recession in 3rd quarter. Retrieved from *New York Times:* http://www.nytimes.com/2010/12/08/business/global/08icecon.html

Kay, J. (2008). The financial crisis for dummies: why Canada is immune from a U.S.-style mortgage meltdown. *National Post,* 2 October. http://network.nationalpost.com/np/blogs/fullcomment/archive/2008/10/02/the-financial-crisis-for-dummies-why-canada-is-completely-immune-from-the-u-s-mortgage-meltdown-kind-of.aspx

Kelly, M. (2010, May 22). Burden of Irish debt could yet eclipse that of Greece. Retrieved from *The Irish Times:* http://www.irishtimes.com/newspaper/opinion/2010/0522/1224270888132.html

Keun, M., & Schmidt, V. (2009). Global capital strategies and trade union responses: towards transnational collective bargaining? *International Journal of Labour Research, 1*(2), 9–26.

Kirkpatrick, G. (2009). The corporate governance lessons from the financial crisis. *Financial Market Trends 2009/1*(OECD).

Le Queux, S. (2005). New protest movements and the revival of labour politics – a critical assessment. *Transfer – European Review of Labour and Research, 11*(4), 569–588.

Le Queux, S. (2008). Acting together for another world? Anti-globalisation and labour organisations. *International Journal of Social Inquiry, 1*(2), 135–154.

Lewis, M. (2010). *The big short: inside the doomsday machine.* New York: W. W. Norton.

Littler, C. (2009). The current global financial crisis as a context for labour and industry in the twenty-first century. *Labour and Industry, 19*(3), 5–28.

Mackenzie, H. (2010). A soft landing: recession and Canada's 100 highest paid CEOs. Ottawa: Canadian Centre for Policy Alternatives, http://www.policyalternatives.ca/publications/reports/soft-landing

Maddison, A. (1995). *Monitoring the World Economy, 1820–1992.* Paris: OECD.

Madsen, P. K. (2002). The Danish model of "flexicurity" – a paradise with some snakes. Interactions between labour market and social protection. Brussels: European Foundation for the Improvement of Living and Working Conditions.

Martin, A. and G. Ross (1999). *The brave new world of European labor.* New York: Berghahn.

McKay, S. (2009). Europe's trade unions respond to crisis. Retrieved from http://www.eurofound.europa.eu/eiro/2009/06/articles/eu0906029i.htm

Milgram, S. (1963). Behavioral study of obedience. *Journal of Abnormal and Social Psychology, 67,* 371–378.

Morck, R. (2004). *Behavioral finance in corporate governance – independent directors and non-executive chairs.* NBER Working Paper No. w10644 Organisation for Economic Cooperation and Development (2006). *OECD Productivity Database, September 2006.* Paris: OECD.

Organisation for Economic Cooperation and Development (2009a). *The effectiveness and scope of fiscal stimulus. Economic outlook interim report.* Paris: OECD.

Organisation for Economic Cooperation and Development (2009b). *Employment Outlook.* Paris: OECD.

Organisation for Economic Cooperation and Development (2010a). *OECD productivity database.* Paris: OECD.

Organisation for Economic Cooperation and Development (2010b). OECD StatExtracts. Retrieved from http://stats.oecd.org/

O'Rourke, M. 2010. Compensation controversy, *Risk Management: New York.* 57(2), March. http://news-business.vlex.com/vid/compensation-controversy-205950699

Peetz, D. (2010). Asymmetric reference points and the growth of Executive remuneration, Centre for Work, Organisation and Wellbeing, Griffith University, Brisbane, Working Paper Series, September.

Productivity Commission (2009). *Executive Remuneration in Australia*. Melbourne: Productivity Commission.

Quiggin, J. (1995). Does Privatisation Pay? *Australian Economic Review, 28*(2), 23–42.

Quiggin, J. (2010). *Zombie Economics*. New Jersey: Princeton University Press.

Richburg, K. (2008). Worldwide financial crisis largely bypasses Canada. The *Washington Post*, 15 October, http://www.washingtonpost.com/wp-dyn/content/article/2008/10/15/AR2008101503321.html

RiskMetrics Australia (2009). *Submission to productivity commission inquiry into executive remuneration*. Melbourne: RiskMetrics.

Rudd, K. (2009). The global financial crisis. *Monthly, February*, 20–29.

Scherrer, C. (2010). Finance capital will not fade away on its own. *Global Labour Column, 17*.

Shields, J., O'Donnell, M., & O'Brien, J. (2003). *The bucks stop here: private sector executive remuneration in Australia*. Labour Council of New South Wales.

Shields, J., O'Donnell, M., & O'Brien, J. (2004). *The bucks stop here: executive pay and company performance*. Proceedings of the 18th AIRAANZ Conference, Noosa, Qld. Association of Industrial Relations Academics of Australia and New Zealand.

soyoutv.com (2010, April 1). Continental propose des postes en Tunisie rémunérés 137 euros par mois: les députés dégoûtés! Retrieved from http://www.lepost.fr/article/2010/04/01/2014297_continental-propose-des-postes-en-tunisie-remuneres-137-euros-par-mois-les-depuets-degoutes.html

Statistics Canada (2010). Table 282-0087 Labour force survey estimates (LFS), by sex and age group, seasonally adjusted and unadjusted, monthly (persons unless otherwise noted), CANSIM (database), Using E-STAT (distributor). http://estat.statcan.gc.ca/cgi-win/cnsmcgi.exe?Lang=E&EST-Fi=EStat/English/CII_1-eng.htm

Tilly, C. (2010). An opportunity not taken...yet: U.S. labor and the current economic crisis. Paper prepared for the 2010 Global Labour University conference, Berlin, 15–16 September. http://www.global-labour-university.org/fileadmin/GLU_conference_2010/papers/95._An_opportunity_not_taken_yet_U.S._labor_and_the_current_economic_crisis.pdf

Tobin, J. (1978). A proposal for international monetary reform. *Eastern Economic Journal* 4(3–4), 153–159.

Townson, M. (2010). Options for pension reform Canadian Centre for policy alternatives. Ottawa: Canadian Centre for Policy Alternatives. http://www.policyalternatives.ca/sites/default/files/uploads/publications/reports/docs/Options%20for%20Pension%20Reform.pdf

Torres, R. (2010). *Global financial crisis 2.0*. Retrieved from Global Labour Column: http://column.global-labour-university.org/search/label/Financial%20Crisis

Willmott, H. (1993). Strength is ignorance; slavery is freedom: managing culture in modern organizations. *Journal of Management Studies, 30*(4), 515–552.

12
Sustainability and HRM: A Model and Suggestions for Future Research

Ina Ehnert

Introduction: Sustainability on the HR agenda

Sustainability is on the agenda of many organizations worldwide and has recently raised interest from human resources management (HRM).* Climate change, water shortages, the problem that the world population consumes more resources per year than are produced, education, demographic developments, and increasing strains from business activities on employees has given reason to criticize widespread assumptions about how organizations can be managed in the long term (for example, Bansal, 2005). Focusing on the market model which is successful for short-term economic success fails with regard to long-term effects on the environment and the wider system (Dunphy and Griffith, 1998). One reason is an over-occupation with efficient exploitation of natural, social, and human resources in organizations (see Docherty et al., 2008; Wilkinson, 2005) coupled with a lack of effort to sustain the companies' resource base as long as this is not regarded as economically rational (Ehnert, 2009a).

This becomes problematic when human and social resources that are desperately needed to implement corporate strategies are not available, or, when highly talented employees and executives suffer from side effects of work such as work-related health problems because they are being exploited or exploiting themselves. Both problems beg consideration about how companies treat their resources and to explore what needs to be done to sustain the company's (human and social) resource base and its origin (see also Wilkinson, 2005).

Corporations such as L'Oreal have started using the notion of sustainability in the context of managing human resources (Ehnert, 2009a). PriceWaterhouseCoopers (PWC, 2007) emphasize in their reports on 'Managing tomorrow's people' that one scenario for the future of work includes companies with a strong focus on sustainability, green management, and social responsibility. Topics related to sustainability and HR-related issues are, for example, recruiting and retaining top talent, developing critical competencies, employability, lifelong learning, aging workforces, maintaining employee health and safety, quality of life, work-life-balance, and corporate social responsibility – issues going beyond those discussed in the (mainstream) HRM and performance discourse (see also Hartog et al., 2008; Ehnert, 2009b). Scholars dealing with the topic suggest that 'sustainability' can be used as a new paradigm for HRM which helps developing a fresh view on how to manage social and human resources.

Currently, little research exists on sustainability and HRM (for exceptions see Ehnert, 2009a, 2009b; Gollan, 2005; Mariappanadar, 2003; Zaugg, 2009; Zaugg et al., 2001). This chapter addresses this gap and provides answers to the following questions: (1) What is the meaning and importance of sustainability for HRM? (2) How can sustainability be linked systematically to HRM? (3) What are the key elements and characteristics of 'Sustainable HRM'? (4) Which issues deserve further exploration regarding sustainability and HRM? The objective of this chapter is to examine the idea of sustainability for HRM and to make suggestions for future research. In the second section, the relevance of sustainability for HRM is described, and a typology of sustainability interpretations is proposed. Next, research using the idea of sustainability for HRM is compared. In conclusion it is suggested that 'Sustainable HRM' is an emerging concept and drivers which help understanding why sustainability is a new topic for HRM are identified. Hence, the characteristics of Sustainable HRM are described on the basis of integrative systems thinking and a model for Sustainable HRM is proposed. Finally, this chapter offers implications for future research.

Importance of sustainability for HRM

Defining sustainability – a history

Sustainability is one of the key terms in the 21st century for politicians, business managers, and academics. A large variety of sustainability definitions have emerged in management practice and research after the World Commission on Environment and Development (WCED) or Brundtland Commission defined sustainable development as 'a development that meets the needs of the present without compromising the ability of future generations to meet their own needs' (WCED, 1987,

p. 43). This definition addresses inter- and intra-generational justice concerning the ability of people living on this planet to have equal and fair access to its resources.

Elkington (1994) transferred this societal concept of sustainable development to the corporate business level and argues that ecological and social bottom lines have to be integrated with the traditional bottom line that is financial performance. The proponents of this concept assume that the three 'sustainability principles' economic prosperity, environmental integrity, and social equity are necessary but not sufficient conditions for economic sustainability (Bansal, 2005).

The Brundtland Commission's definition has led to a large number of sustainability definitions and competing concepts (see Anand and Sen, 2000; Gladwin et al., 1995) and to an increasing interest in concepts such as corporate sustainability (CS), corporate social responsibility (CSR), or corporate social performance (CSP) (for an overview, see Montiel, 2008). About a decade ago, this trend reached HR-related research (for example, Ehnert, 2009a; Zaugg et al., 2001).

Before the Brundtland Commission's report, sustainability was applied by environmentalists and development aid specialists concerned with the over-exploitation of natural resources, the earth's limited carrying capacity, and the limits of uncontrolled economic and population growth (for example, Daly, 1973; Meadows, Meadows, Randers, and Behrens, 1972). From the 12th century, the term sustainability was used in the European forestry and fishing industry (Leal Filho, 2000) on the basis of the idea that the consumption and reproduction of economically necessary resources must be balanced. In Europe, the term can even be traced back to ancient Greece, where Aristotle offered his concept of a self-sustaining household (Greek *'oikoi'* or *'oikos'*). It is important to understand that various meanings and interpretations of sustainability have emerged which can be useful for HRM but which offer different explanations and implications that require careful consideration.

Meanings of sustainability for HRM and underlying rationalities

Three interpretations of sustainability for HRM come to the fore which provide different explanations for why and when companies commit themselves to sustainability in HRM that is a responsibility-oriented, an efficiency-/innovation-oriented, and a substance-oriented understanding (see Table 12.1).

The *responsibility-oriented* understanding is based on the implicit assumption that 'needs' and 'equity' are generalizable, universal values across different generations and cultures (see Anand and Sen, 2000).

The objective of the responsibility-oriented understanding is a social, ecological, and economic development that is inter- and intra-generationally fair and legitimated by society. Implications for HRM from a social-responsibility understanding of sustainability are to treat people in organizations in a socially responsible, humane way (see also Boxall and Purcell, 2003; Paauwe, 2004), to reduce side and feedback effects from corporate actions on employees and the society (for example, Mariappanadar, 2003) and to care for the well-being, health, and quality of life of employees (for example, Docherty et al., 2008) – *because* it is an ethical, moral duty to do so (see Table 12.1).

The strength of this understanding of sustainability is that it highlights the importance of the business-society relationship for today's HRM and of the active role that companies are expected to take in this process. Additionally, this understanding helps to identify a problem: our traditional economic model fosters an organizational behaviour which produces externalities for corporate natural, social and human environments and individuals even at the risk of their destruction. But companies depend on these environments and on the legitimacy of their activities ('licence to operate') within them. To continue exploring this idea for HRM, this debate can be easily linked to the Harvard approach (Beer et al., 1984) and HRM research influenced by the Human Relations movement. However, several limitations of this understanding of sustainability need to be considered. First, the concept of 'needs' is very difficult to operationalize when choices are related to the preferences of future generations or stakeholders (see Anand and Sen, 2000). Second, this understanding reflects a societal vision of what is desirable, and this is insufficient to legitimize sustainability at the corporate and HRM level because this often becomes a matter of 'belief'. Third, it is critical if sustainability is regarded as 'good' in general and if social-responsibility behaviour is imitated in HRM without reflecting about the underlying motifs, objectives, values, and interests served.

Proponents of an *efficiency/innovation-oriented* understanding try to buffer these limitations by interpreting sustainability as a new business opportunity (for example, Dean and McMullen, 2007; Porter and Van der Linde, 1995) and by offering a link between sustainability and traditional economic thinking. The World Business Council of Sustainable Development (WBCSD) introduced the concept of 'eco-efficiency' (see DeSimone and Popoff, 2000), defining it as the ratio of economic value added by a firm to its environmental impact. In analogy, 'socio-efficiency' has been defined as the ratio of value creation and social impact and refers to minimizing 'negative' social impact of business activities on societies (Bansal, 2005; Hockerts, 1999). This kind of thinking could also be transferred to HRM. The objective of the efficiency/innovation-oriented understanding is to reduce resource consumption (and costs) or to increase the efficiency of resource exploitation (and value creation) via innovation. Implications of the efficiency-oriented understanding of sustainability for HRM are, for example, to reduce the impact on human resources and to decrease the 'utilization' of human resources (see Table 12.1). However, limitations of this understanding of HRM become rapidly apparent.

The first limitation is that the mental model (efficiency) remains the same as the one causing the problems (see Ehnert, 2009a). Second, based on the Brundtland Commission's work in sustainability research the assumption is advanced that win-win-win solutions can be created for business, society, people and nature (for example, Bansal, 2005). However, some authors have argued that win-win-win solutions are rare and that this approach is insufficient to advance corporate sustainable development because it does not suggest how to *develop* resources when they are scarce or not available (for example, Müller-Christ, 2001).

The *substance-oriented meaning* of sustainability builds on Aristotle's understanding of a self-sustaining household, on the definition of sustainability from old European forestry laws, on a systemic corporate perspective (Luhmann, 1995) and co-evolution theory (for example, Bateson, 1972). Sustainability is defined as 'resource reproduction divided by resource consumption equals one' (Müller-Christ and Remer, 1999, p. 70, translated by the author). This ideal also changes the mental model and thinking about sustainability for HRM because sustainability and efficiency are interpreted as contradictory oppositions (see Ehnert, 2009a). The objective is to sustain the corporate and human resource base ('substance') and hitherto the company itself by balancing resource consumption and reproduction. Organizational environments are interpreted as 'sources of resources' (for example, labour markets, education systems, or families), and it becomes a 'survival strategy' to invest actively in the survival of these environments (Müller-Christ, 2001). The main implication of this approach for HRM is to ask what organizations have to do in their environments to have durable access to human and social resources (Sustainable Human Resource Management) (Müller-Christ and Remer, 1999). In HRM practice, several examples can be found where companies have started going in this direction (Ehnert, 2009b; see also Table 12.1).

The advantage of the substance-oriented logic is that it can be applied to corporate decision making by differentiating between choices

Table 12.1 Sustainability interpretations, objectives, implications, and explanations for HRM

Interpretation of sustainability	Sustainability as an ethical, moral value (social responsibility)	Sustainability as a business opportunity	Sustainability as a rationality to sustain the corporate resource base
Justification	Companies are responsible for their employees ('normative')	Economic self-interest ('efficiency-oriented')	Economic self-interest ('substance-oriented')
Objectives	Social justice, social fairness, social legitimacy ('licence to operate'), accountability, reputation, risk management	Cost reduction, economic value creation	Durable access to human resources and to the HR base (the 'origin' of HR), organizational viability
Resource problem	Willingness of organizational environments to provide HR (problem of legitimacy)	Efficient and effective HR deployment, increase and sustain performance (problem of efficiency)	Ability of organizational environments to provide HR (problem of sustaining substance and access to resources)
Key theoretical frameworks	for example, Resource dependence approach, Institutional theory, Stakeholder approach	Strategic HRM theories such as the Resource-based view	for example, Social systems theory, Co-evolution theory, Economic ecology, Salutogenesis, Paradox theory
Key paradox	Tensions between shareholder vs. stakeholder positions	Paradoxes and tensions are ignored (belief in win-win-win solutions)	Paradoxes of efficiency vs. substance; short vs. long-term effects

continued

Table 12.1 continued

Implication for treating HR and examples from practice	Treat HR socially responsible (for example, support in job-loss situations, foster socially responsible employer image)	Attract talents by becoming employer of choice (for example, fostering working environment, possibilities to participate)	Invest in the 'origin' of HR and sustain access to HR today and in the future (for example, education)
	Reduce impact on HR (for example, foster ergonomic workplace conditions)	Reduce impact on HR (for example, reduce risk of accidents)	Reduce impact on HR and on relevant organizational environments (for example, reduce impact on employees' families)
	Foster employee well-being, health and quality of life (for example, improve quality of working place)	Invest in qualification of today's workforce (for example, lifelong learning, foster career development)	Foster HR regeneration and health (for example, foster a healthy life style, work-life-balance, and the ability of employees to perform and regenerate)
		Make best use of HR, Decrease utilization of HR	Develop mutual resourcing partnerships (for example, cooperations with universities, schools, NGOs)

Source: Own elaboration, extended from Ehnert (2009b, p. 424).

contributing to efficient resource consumption or to sustainable resource reproduction in organizations (Ehnert, 2009a, 2009b). The difficulty for HR executives is that this ideal idea of sustainability and of sustaining the resource base for the future cannot be maximized simultaneously with efficient and effective approaches to HRM today. Instead, paradoxes, dilemmas, and tensions become visible which need addressing and lead to challenges for HRM. To survive and to be successful on a long-term basis, companies need to become efficient and effective as well as sustainable. This is the strategic potential of sustainability because this thinking encourages questions about the origin of human resources and about what becomes necessary to sustain the long-term availability of the human resource (Ehnert, 2009a).

Ehnert (2009a) assumes that all three interpretations of sustainability have their respective merits for HRM because they provide partial solutions to the problem of sustainable development (see Table 12.1).

Sustainability and HRM: linking concepts

Sustainability and HR issues are discussed under the labels 'Sustainable Works Systems' (for example, Docherty et al., 2008; Kira, 2003), 'Sustainable HRM' (for example, Ehnert, 2009a, 2009b; Zaugg, 2009; Zaugg et al., 2001), 'Green HRM' (for example, Renwick et al., 2008), or adapted into Strategic HRM (SHRM) (for example, Schuler and Jackson, 2005). Social responsibility- or efficiency-oriented understandings dominate and substance-oriented thinking is rare.

Social responsibility and sustainability in Strategic HRM

The notions of 'sustainability' and 'social responsibility' have been used in Strategic HRM research before. The terms 'sustainable' or 'sustainability' are applied in the sense of sustaining competitive advantage or economic success. 'Social responsibility' appeared in one of the early Strategic HRM models from Beer and colleagues (1984). Recently, however, SHRM scholars have started incorporating ideas from sustainability research, the Brundtlandt Report, and also CSR research into their writings – which makes the boundaries between previously separate research fields become blurred, which changes meanings and applications of the terms sustainability and social responsibility, and which in the author's experience can lead to misunderstandings about what sustainability refers to. Additionally, research has started linking sustainability and HRM more systematically (for example, Docherty et al., 2008; Ehnert, 2009a, 2009b; Kira, 2003; Gollan, 2005; Zaugg, 2009).

Different approaches of Sustainable Work Systems (SWS) have emerged (for example, Docherty et al., 2008; Kira and Forslin, 2008; Moldaschl and Fischer, 2004). The objectives of SWS are the prevention of negative outcomes from intensive HR deployment; improvement of employee health and development; the regeneration, learning, and development of employees in cooperative, trustful, and constructive industrial relations; a balance of working life quality and organizational performance and sustainable change processes. In short, SWS focuses on exploring how roles, responsibilities, and (employment) relationships need to be designed in a sustainable way.

In parallel, authors active in the HRM and performance field have (re-)discovered social legitimacy, employee health, and individual well-being as objectives for HRM going beyond traditional financial performance objectives (see Boxall and Purcell, 2003). Referring to this source from Boxall and Purcell, Paauwe (2004) proposes a relational rationality (humanism) for HRM in addition to a 'pure' economic rationality (instrumentalism). Legge (2005) observed that ethical considerations concerning stakeholders have become more important in the recent HRM debate because of stock markets and NGOs speaking 'in the language of the "triple bottom line"' (p. 4). Schuler and Jackson (2005) integrate their understanding of sustainability as a social responsibility towards stakeholders on the basis of the Brundtland Commission's definition of sustainability into their SHRM framework. Boudreau and Ramstad (2005) have suggested sustainability as a new paradigm for HRM and apply it to talent pools and sustainable employment relationships. Iles (1997) suggests incorporating ideas from environmentalism (sustainable development) into career development research and advances a 'sustainable career development'.

Others, however, go one step further and point towards the importance of recognizing HRM (and organizations) from a wider systems perspective (for example, Dunphy and Griffiths, 1998). Mariappandar (2003) proposes a 'Sustainable Human Resource Strategy' and a broader view of HRM which recognizes that organizations and HRM do not act in a 'societal vacuum' but that their activities have a large number of implications for the communities surrounding them. Wilkinson et al. (2001) outlined the relevance of managing human resources in the context of companies striving for ecological, social, and economic sustainable development. Renwick and colleagues (2008) have addressed the third sustainability dimension, the ecological one, by shedding light on 'the HR aspects of environmental management (EM)' labelled 'Green HRM'. Pfeffer (2010) proposed giving human sustainability as much attention as ecological sustainability when building sustainable organizations.

These scholars see a commonality between two challenges for today's organizations: many organizations feel external pressures to use all their resources efficiently and cost effective and to become more ecologically and socially sustainable. Simultaneously, internal pressures on people in organizations shift the attention to the problem of human sustainability (for example, Gollan, 2005; Wilkinson et al., 2001). The concept of 'Sustainable HRM' follows these ideas more systematically.

Emergence of a new concept: Sustainable HRM

The first systematic, extended work on 'Sustainable HRM' has been proposed by Robert Zaugg and colleagues (Zaugg, 2009; Zaugget al., 2001). The Swiss approach of Sustainable HRM focuses on the following problems: (1) shortage in the supply of skilled and motivated people, (2) stress-related absence of employees and work-related health problems, and (3) more demanding workforces because of changing work values (Zaugg, 2009). The objectives of this approach address needs of the organization (that is to sustain competitive advantage based on the shortage of competence in Sustainable HRM, long-term supply with skilled and motivated people) and its workforce (that is to sustain well-being, employability, self-responsibility, work-life-balance, and a better quality of life) (Zaugg, 2009). Conceptually, the approach builds on Sustainable Work Systems (for example, Docherty et al., 2002; Kira, 2003), the Brundtland Comission's definition of sustainability, Strategic HRM theory (for example Pfeffer, 1998), and a qualitative empirical exploration of best practices in Sustainable HRM (Zaugg et al., 2001).

Thom and Zaugg (2004) define Sustainable HRM as 'those long-term oriented conceptual approaches and activities aimed at a socially responsible and economically appropriate recruitment and selection, development, deployment, and downsizing of employees'. (p. 217; translated from German by Ehnert, 2009a, p. 73). Zaugg (2009) assumes that companies, employees, and society are mutually responsible for Sustainable HRM activities and that all stakeholders benefit from sustainability (win-win assumption). He suggests that the following principles need to be realized simultaneously: flexibility, employee participation, value orientation, strategy orientation, competency and knowledge orientation, stakeholder orientation as well as building mutually trustful employer-employee relationships.

Following those authors proposing that the win-win assumption is *not* very likely, Ehnert (2009a) introduced an integrative substance-oriented approach of Sustainable HRM. This is seen as integrated into the broader context of an organization's sustainable management of natural, social, human, and economic resources. Sustainable HRM is defined as

> Sustainable HRM is the pattern of planned or emerging human resource strategies and practices intended to enable organisational goal achievement while simultaneously reproducing the HR base over a long-lasting calendar time and controlling for self-induced side and feedback effects of HR systems on the HR base and thus on the company itself (Ehnert, 2009, p. 74).

From an ideal point of view, the role of Sustainable HRM is to foster regeneration and development of the workforce and HR base (the origin of human resources) today and in the future. This kind of thinking fuels ideas about what HR executives and leaders need to do in their corporate environments to sustain access to skilled human resources. The approach focuses on three HR problems: (1) labour shortage of supply with skilled, motivated people, (2) problems caused by the impact of work on employees (for example, health problems), and (3) the relationship between HRM and its environments. The organizational objective of this approach is to foster organizational viability by keeping supplies coming with talented people, by sustaining the viability of the 'origin' of these resources while simultaneously balancing this with economic, social, and ecological requirements – even if these are contradictory.

Conceptually, the approach builds on insights from literature on sustainability and HRM, Sustainable Resource Management (Müller-Christ, 2001), Strategic HRM, and a paradox perspective from organization theory (for details, see Ehnert, 2009a). Ehnert's Sustainable HRM approach applies sustainability to extend the understanding of strategic success in HRM and points towards the importance of reconciling tensions between co-existing rationales such as 'social responsibility' versus 'economic rationality' (see also Paauwe, 2004) as well as 'efficiency' versus a 'substance-oriented' understanding of sustainability.

Based on the assumption that sustainability means that HRM needs to develop long-term HRM-environment relationships to resource-providing organizational environments such as schools, universities, or families, four generic sustainability strategies are recommended to maintain an organization's resource base over time (see Ehnert,

2009a): first, particular emphasis is given to develop the ability of HRM to develop and maintain an organization's resource base that is the origin of HR ('sources of resources') from within the organization. Second, controlling dysfunctional effects (the 'impact') of HR strategies and activities on employees, on organizational environments, and finally on the organization itself become a 'survival strategy' for organizations. Third, developing mutual trustful resource exchange relationships or 'resourcing partnerships' by understanding and considering the specific conditions of human resource development, care and regeneration. The fourth generic sustainability strategy is to sustain social legitimacy (that is the 'licence to operate'). Paradoxes and tensions which arise from the effort of sustaining the resource base must be balanced and coped with while simultaneously deploying human resources efficiently and effectively.

To conclude, Sustainable HRM is a broader concept than Strategic HRM and needs to be viewed in the context of a corporate sustainable management strategy interested in sustaining the organization and its resources by sustaining and developing the corresponding organizational environments which becomes necessary to ensure corporate viability.

Model of 'Sustainable HRM': fostering the ability of HRM to sustain access to resources

An initial model is developed in this section by identifying drivers for and links between sustainability and HRM to guide future research (see Figure 12.1). The focus of this discussion is on HRM in developed countries, and it is assumed that drivers and characteristics for HRM in other parts in the world can be different.

Drivers for sustainability in HRM

Several indicators fuelling the emergence of sustainability in the context of HRM are identified here. Instead of linear cause and effect relationships, it is assumed that these factors are connected by multiple interdependent relationships.

Internationalization and globalization

Jones Christensen and colleagues (2007) surveyed the *Financial Times* top 50 global business schools in Europe and the US, and found that after having established international programmes, universities and business schools have started to integrate sustainability and CSR topics

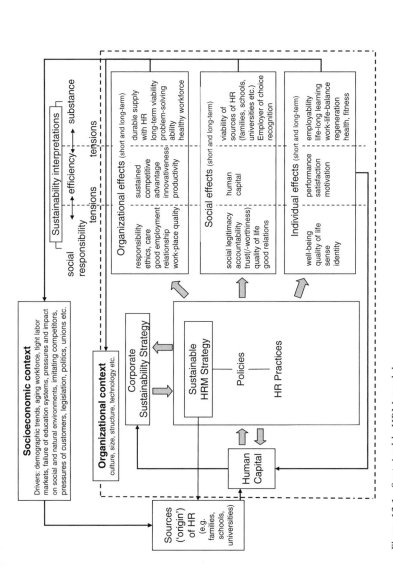

Figure 12.1 Sustainable HRM model

Source: Ehnert (2009, p. 172), extended from Martín-Alcázar (2005, p. 651).

into their curricula. After internationalization and globalization, sustainability is one of the key challenges for HRM especially for companies with an origin in countries where sustainable development is appreciated by stakeholders because internationalization and globalization point towards the boundaries of current resourcing and deployment strategies and practices (see also Muller-Camen et al., 2010). The task is to identify what needs to be done to develop a Sustainable HRM at a global versus local level and to balance their global integration as well as their local diversification.

Demographic trends and aging workforces

In Western societies, demographic trends influence the lack of highly qualified staff. For example, birth rates in many EU countries are low with an average of 1.5 children per woman and especially low with highly qualified females (see Marcu, 2009). The demographic trends bring up several challenges for a Sustainable HRM. First, ageing workforces must remain healthy, fit, and well educated. Second, from a global perspective, demographic developments in countries like China or India come into play which will have an effect on human resourcing strategies in multinational or transnational organizations.

Tight labour markets and insufficient quality of education

While demographic trends are reducing the population in Western countries, labour markets in some countries are becoming tight with regard to certain professions and qualifications (local demands may differ). According to OECD surveys (see OECD, 2004 and 2005) some countries cannot keep up with providing their children the necessary skills in reading, writing, maths, and natural sciences. It seems to be becoming increasingly difficult for HRM to provide the necessary qualifications in time. From a sustainability point of view, the key challenge for HRM is to become more independent from local labour markets by developing a more proactive and long-term approach in resourcing, for example by identifying the key competences needed for work in the future (such as social or cross-cultural skills and competences for building sustainable organizations) and by investing actively into today's and future human resources.

Changing employment relationships

The 'new employment relationship' (Roehling, Cavanaugh, Moynihan, and Boswell, 2000) is – in comparison to the previous understanding of employment relationships, where employees were rewarded for their loyalty to employers with a long-term or life-long relationship – a contract-like economic exchange with employers arguing that they can no longer guarantee for their employee's jobs (Tsui and Wu, 2005). In this process, employees have learned that they are responsible for their careers, they need to sustain their employability (for example, Baruch, 2001; Fugateet al., 2004), and that they must be mobile and flexible. This has created the problem that highly qualified staff is very hard to retain and less loyal towards their employers (see, for example, Tsui and Wu, 2005). The key challenge for HRM from a sustainability perspective is to develop an alternative which fosters employability and sustainable employment relationships.

Changing work values and employee expectations

Employees today often expect more from their employees than a good salary. For example, employees expect new qualities from their employers such as support in their work-life-balance and that work does not make them sick. It is expected that employers act in a socially responsible and environmentally sustainable way, and that they are provided with the opportunity to exhibit socially responsible behaviour at the workplace (for example, Hartog et al., 2008; PriceWaterhouseCoopers 2007). From a sustainability perspective, the key challenge for HRM is to attract and maintain talent, for example, to become employers of choice and 'great places to work' by supporting the regeneration and development of their human resources. For all companies which do not develop themselves as attractive employers, the risk is to lose the competition for talent.

Impact of business activities on human, social, and natural resources

Side and feedback effects of work and business activities probably cannot be avoided completely. However, from a sustainability perspective on HRM it becomes necessary to understand that financial performance is not enough – instead ecological and social effects need to be kept in check and the idea of employees taking on responsibility for their health fostered. The challenge for HRM is to make conscious choices about the underlying motifs and justifications and about the impact of business activities which need to be monitored.

Characteristics of a Sustainable HRM concept and research

Several characteristics can be identified which can make sustainability a fruitful concept for HRM. These aspects indicate why it could be useful for the HRM field to establish 'Sustainable HRM' as an alternative approach (Ehnert, 2009a) and as a potential umbrella term for activities and strategies linking sustainability and HRM.

Exploring short-term as well as long-term effects as well as side and feedback effects

Research on sustainability suggests that organizations need to consider both a short- and a longer-term perspective when making corporate decisions and measuring their effects (Ehnert, 2009a). Sustainable HRM can help with what Evans (1999) has called 'building the future into the present'. Sustainability research argues that it is neither socially responsible nor economically rational to ignore side and feedback effects of work processes, work intensity, and corporate decisions on employees and managers, organizational environments, and organizations themselves. Risks of destroying valuable resources or their origins by externalizing costs must be reduced – in particular when these resources are scarce. HRM operates in a macro-social context with multiple mutual and interdependent relationships. This can be achieved, for example, by reducing the risk of work accidents, injuries, fatalities, by offering ergonomic workplace conditions and stress prevention and reduction programmes. Sustainability extends the role and boundaries of HRM systems and shifts the attention to the survival strategy of sustaining (human and social and if applicable also ecological) resources and their 'origin' in its organizational environments.

Extending the notion of success by considering economic, social, and ecological objectives

Focusing on excellence in financial performance is considered necessary but not sufficient to sustain long-term corporate viability. Instead, the idea of sustainability takes an integrative view of the economic, ecological, and social dimensions of business activities with the objectives of sustaining social legitimacy, access to human/social resources, and of guaranteeing the functioning of the organizational environments delivering these resources. Sustainable HRM focuses at least on the economic and social, wherever applicable and necessary also on the ecological dimension. Sustainability can become an indicator for strategic success in HRM and can contribute to choosing new corporate goals and objectives as well as new means to achieve them.

Considering moral, ethical positions as well as economic arguments

In the second section of this chapter, it has been argued that ethics are not necessary to justify sustainable business behaviour. Despite this, the author of this chapter assumes that *some* choices concerning human resources cannot be made without ethical considerations. Even a substance-oriented view on sustainability does not prevent decision makers from applying this logic in an immoral way. Ethical considerations are not only a question of economic survival – it is also a question of how people in organizations want to work with each other, in what kind of employment relationships, with which corporate culture, and how this shapes the common future of businesses and societies. Treating people in a socially responsible manner can become visible in a caring attitude towards employees or in offering support in job-loss situations. Ethics and values, however, are culture dependent, and tensions between social and economic arguments must be balanced.

Fostering the ability of HRM to develop and sustain the HR base and environments from within

The substance-oriented understanding of sustainability has made the case that sustaining critical resources and their origins as well as developing them is an important strategic organizational task (Ehnert, 2009a). 'Administrating' labour shortages is regarded as insufficient for a company's long-term success and viability. Instead, the task of HRM is extended to caring for relationships to the sources or 'origins' of human resources such as families, labour markets, or education systems. From a corporate perspective this can be done, for example, by creating mutual resourcing relationships, by investing in education, apprenticeships, scholarships, life-long learning, co-operations with schools or universities, and by enabling the regeneration of organizational workforces by promoting a healthy lifestyle or work-life-balance. Important tasks of a Sustainable HRM are also to foster employee well-being and health as well as attracting talent and being recognized as an employer of choice.

Balancing paradoxes, dualities, dilemmas, and tensions

From a sustainability point of view, one challenge for HRM is to balance the tensions between, for example, faster and shorter financial market and production cycles and long-term human resource development cycles (see Gratton et al., 1999). Second, another challenge is tensions between 'human resource efficiency' and 'human resource sustainability'. Third, tensions between 'social responsibility' and 'economic rationality' must be balanced. Decision makers need the competence to deal actively with paradoxes and tensions in order to thrive on their dynamic potential.

Illustration of a Sustainable HRM Model

When resources are scarce it becomes economically rational for companies to contribute to sustaining their human resource base, to sustain even the 'origin' of their resources, and to control the impact of their activities and strategies on the resource base and the corresponding environments (see Ehnert, 2009a). Based on theory and on a website analysis (Ehnert, 2009a and 2009b) Martín-Alcazár's (2005) integrative model of Strategic HRM has been extended towards a model for research on Sustainable HRM (see Figure 12.1). This model includes the drivers for and key characteristics of sustainability for HRM as well as potential outcomes of Sustainable HRM. Of course, contextual differences need to be recognized because what might be good for one organization in terms of sustainability might not work for another.

Future research challenges and conclusions

This chapter has shed some light on the link between sustainability and HRM and on the boundaries of a potentially new concept 'Sustainable HRM'. This area of research crosses research boundaries and focuses on the long-term ability of organizations to develop, regenerate, and maintain human resources and their origin. The remainder of this section is dedicated to highlighting three topics which deserve more scholarly attention and effort. Some research on these issues is already underway, but, it is suggested that more effort is needed.

Key issues and future directions

First, conceptual models for studying Sustainable HRM and for explaining why organizations engage in Sustainable HRM and how they do it must be improved and linked back to existing knowledge in HRM research. This chapter indicates that conceptualizations on linking sustainability and HRM are diverse depending on the author's field of origin and on the emphasis of social, human resource, or ecological issues. However, the author of this chapter assumes that these different approaches can help stimulate much more sophisticated research on sustainability and HRM and that it is worth trying to integrate findings from different fields – in particular from HRM to CS and CSR research and vice versa. The chapter indicates that there are several challenges for future theory development. For example, research on Sustainable HRM must be built on theoretically grounded conceptualizations and measures. Conceptualizations have been provided, for example, from Zaugg (2009) and Ehnert (2009a); however, the conceptual development of 'Sustainable HRM' is in its early period and should be extended by future research. As Sustainable HRM is a complex concept it might be necessary to supplement this concept with a 'complex' theory such as social systems theory (Luhmann, 1995). The model that has been introduced in this chapter is only a puzzle piece in the conceptual foundation of Sustainable HRM, and the author is convinced that it is helpful in conducting future research.

The second issue concerns the current gap that research on sustainability and HRM is mainly descriptive and that mostly qualitative studies have been conducted based on corporate websites and sustainability or social responsibility reports and not in organizations themselves. This is partly due to the problem that companies have only recently started deliberately using sustainability as a concept for managing people (for example, Ehnert, 2009b). Initially, the majority of organizations focused only on environmental aspects of sustainability (see also Pfeffer, 2010). However, from the author's observation, an increasing number of business managers and HR executives have become interested in Sustainable HRM. These managers understand that people are their most important resource and that financial success is no long-term guarantee to have access to the qualifications and motivations needed in the future. This interest can be sustained only if first conceptualizations are complemented by fruitful empirical research and efforts to measure effects of 'sustainable' HR practices and strategies. For example, it is possible to look at HRM in different cultural or organizational contexts and compare sustainability practices and strategies advanced in HRM (see also Muller-Camenet al., 2010). This is recommended because the literature reviewed in this chapter largely stems from a Western scholarly background. However, future research should also look at sustainability issues in Asia, India, and so on.

The third issue involves the increasingly important topic of sustainability reporting that will sooner or later affect HRM. Organizations have increasingly made use of sustainability and corporate social responsibility reporting to communicate with their stakeholders (for example, Kolk, forthcoming). KPMG (2010) assures that the international trend goes towards integrating financial reporting and sustainability reporting initiatives – whereas in the beginning different reports have been made for different stakeholders. This reporting issue is relevant for HRM because future employees inform themselves via internet or company reports about their potential employers. Of course, many more issues can be thought of for an emerging field, however, these three are perceived as being the most rewarding ones.

Conclusion

Managing people efficiently and effectively is challenging. Managing them at the same time in a sustainable manner is even more challenging. The literature reviewed in this chapter has pioneered the application of the notion of sustainability to HRM. The circle has been closed between approaches considering economic, social, and ecological sustainability and the paradoxes and tensions this may create have been addressed. In this chapter, the importance of sustainability for HRM has been recognized and three sustainability interpretations, their underlying rationalities, and different implications for HRM have been discussed. Next, the chapter has offered an overview on the literature from different areas that have made first attempts to link sustainability and HRM. This research is characterized by conceptual variety and empirical paucity – which is normal for an emerging concept in a field or even for the emergence of a new stream of research but should be motivating for future research. A conceptual model which allows understanding the drivers for sustainability in HRM, the links between both concepts and the challenges for HRM practice and research has been presented and discussed. There is the possibility for future research to contribute and make a 'Sustainable HRM' field grow. The author assumes that future research should focus on the following aspects: (1) theoretical foundation and link to existing knowledge in HRM, (2) (comparative) empirical research on Sustainable HRM, and (3) considering the issue of sustainability reporting and HRM.

* The author would like to thank Wes Harry and the editors of this volume for their valuable comments on an earlier draft of this chapter.

References

Anand, S., & Sen, A. (2000). Human development and economic sustainability. *World Development, 28*(12), 2029–2049.

Bansal, P. (2005). Evolving sustainably, longitudinal study of corporate. *Sustainable Development, 26*(3), 197–218.

Baruch, Y. (2001). Employability: A Substitute for Loyalty, *4*(4), 543–566.

Bateson, G. (1972). *Steps to an ecology of mind: collected essays in anthropology, psychiatry, evolution, and epistemology.* Chicago: University Of Chicago Press.

Beer, M., Spector, B., Lawrence, P. R., Mills, D. Q., & Walton, E. R. (1984). *Managing human assets.* New York: The Free Press.

Boudreau, J. W. & Ramstad, P. M. (2005). Talentship, talent segmentation, and sustainability: A new HR Decision Science Paradigm for a new Strategy Definition, *Human Resource Management, 44*(2), 129–136.

Boxall, P. & Purcell, J. (2003). *Strategy and human resource management.* Basingstoke: Palgrave Macmillan.

Daly, H. E. (1973). *Towards a steady state economy.* San Francisco: Freeman.

DeSimone, L. D. & Popoff, F. (2000). *Eco-efficiency: the business link to sustainable development.* Cambridge: MIT Press.

Dean, T. J. & McMullen, J. S. (2007). 'Toward a theory of sustainable entrepreneurship' reducing environmental degradation through entrepreneurial action, *Journal of Business Venturing, 22*(2007): 50–76.

Docherty P., Forslin J. & Shani, A. B. R. (eds) (2002). *Creating sustainable work systems: emerging perspectives and practice.* London: Routledge.

Docherty, P., M. Kira & Shani, A. B. (2008). *Creating sustainable work systems: developing social sustainability,* 2nd edn. London: Routledge.

Dunphy, D. & Griffiths, A. (1998). *The sustainable corporation: organisational renewal in Australia.* Sydney: Allen & Unwin.

Ehnert, I. (2009a). Sustainable human resource management: a conceptual and exploratory analysis from a paradox perspective. *Contributions to management science,* Heidelberg: Physica, Springer-Verlag.

Ehnert, I. (2009b). 'Sustainability and human resource management: reasoning and applications on corporate websites'. *European Journal of International Management 3*(4): 419–438.

Elkington, J. (1994). 'Towards the sustainable corporation: win-win-win business strategies for sustainable development.' *California Management Review 36*(2): 90–100.

Evans, P. A. L. (1999). 'HRM on the Edge.' *A Duality Perspective 6*(2): 325–338.

Fugate, M., A. J. Kinicki & B. E. Ashforth (2004). '"Employability": A psychosocial construct, Its dimensions, and applications'. *Journal of Vocational Behavior, 65*(1): 14–38.

Gladwin, T. N., Kennelly, J. J. & Krause, T-S. (1995). 'Shifting Paradigms for Sustainable Development.' *Implications for Management Theory and Research 20*(4): 874–907.

Gollan, P. (2005). 'Voice and non-union workplace'. *Employee relations: the international journal, 27*: 92.

Gratton, L., Hope Hailey, V., Stiles, P. & Truss, C. (1999). 'Linking individual performance to business strategy: the people process model'. *Human Resource Management 38*(1): 17–32.

Hartog., Morton, C., et al. (2008). 'Corporate social responsibility and sustainable HRM'. In Muller-Camen, M., Croucher, R., and Leigh, S. (eds). *Human Resource Management: A Case Study Approach.*London: CIPD, 467–488.

Hockerts, K. (1999). 'The sustainability radar - a tool for the innovation of sustainable products and services'. *Greener Management International 25*: 29–49.

Iles, P. (1997). 'Sustainable High-Potential Career Development.' *A Resoure-Based View 2*(7): 347–353.

Jones Christensen, L., Peirce, E., Hartmann, L. P., Hoffman, W. M. & Carrier, J. (2007). 'Ethics, CSR, and Sustainability Education in the Financial Times Top 50 Global Business Schools'. *Baseline Data and Future Research Directions 73*(2007): 347–368.

Kira, M. (2003). 'From Good Work to Sustainable Development'. *Human Resource Consumption and Regeneration in the Post-Bureaucratic Working Life.* Stockholm, Sweden.

Kira, M. and Forslin, J. (2008). 'Seeking regenerative work in the post-bureaucratic transition'. *Journal of Organizational Change Management 21*(1): 76–91.

Kolk, A. (forthcoming). 'Trajectories of sustainability reporting by MNCs'. *Journal of World Business*(in press).

Leal Filho, W. (2000). 'Dealing with Misconceptions on the Concept of Sustainability'. *International Journal of Sustainability in Higher Education 1*(1): 9–19.

Legge, K. (2005). *Human Resource Management: Rhetorics and Realities.* Hampshire, Palgrave Macmillan.

Luhmann, N. (1995). *Social Systems.* Stanford, CA: Stanford University Press.

Marcu, M. (2009). 'The EU-27 population continues to grow: population statistics in Europe'. Eurostat.

Mariappanadar, S. (2003). 'Sustainable human resource strategy': the sustainable and unsustainable dilemmas of retrenchment, *International Journal of Social Economics, 30*(8): 906–923.

Meadows, D. H., Meadows, D. L. et al. (1972). *The limits of growth.* New York: Universe Books and Potomac Associates.

Moldaschl, M. and D. Fischer (2004). 'Beyond the Management View': A Resource-Centered Socio-Economic Perspective Special Issue, *15*(1): 122–152.

Montiel, I. (2008). 'Corporate social responsibility and corporate sustainability separate pasts, common futures.' *Organization & Environment 21*(3): 245–269.

Muller-Camen, M., Parsa, S., and Roper, I. (2010). The Sustainable Business and Human Resource Practices: What is the Link? *Presented at British Academy of Management Conference (BAM).* April 22nd 2010.

Müller-Christ, G. (2001). *Nachhaltiges Ressourcenmanagement.* Marburg: Metropolis-Verlag.

Müller-Christ, G. and Remer, A. (1999). Umweltwirtschaft oder Wirtschaftsökologie? *Vorüberlegung zu einer Theorie des Ressourcenmanagements.* Berlin u. a., Springer: 69–87.

OECD (2004). Learning for Tomorrow's World: First Results from PISA 2003. Accessed via http://www.oecd.org/dataoecd/1/60/34002216.pdf

OECD (2005). Problem Solving for Tomorrow's World: First Measures of Cross-Curricular Competencies from PISA 2003. Accessed via http://www.oecd.org/dataoecd/25/12/34009000.pdf

Paauwe, J. (2004). *HRM and Performance.* New York: Oxford University Press.

Pfeffer, J. (1998). 'The human equation: building profits by putting people first'. Boston: Harvard Business School Press.

Pfeffer, J. (2010). 'Building sustainable organizations: the human factor'. *Academy of Management Perspectives,* (February), 34–45.

Porter, M. E. (1980). *Competitive Strategy.* New York: Free Press.

Porter, M. E. and van der Linde, C. (1995). 'Green and Competitive: Ending the Stalemate'. *Harvard Business Review 73*(5): 120–134.

Renwick, D., Redman, T. & Maguire, S. (2008). Green HRM: a review, process model, and research agenda. *Discussion Paper Series,* University of Sheffield Management School. Discussion Paper No. 2008.01.

Roehling, M. V., Cavanaugh, M. A. et al. (2000). 'The Nature of the New Employment Relationship: A Content Analysis of the Practitioner and Academic Literatures'. *Human Resource Management 39*(4): 305–320.

PWC (2007). 'Managing tomorrow's people - The future of work to 2020', http://www.pwc.ch/de/dyn_output.html?content.cdid=11724&content. vcname=publikations_seite&comeFromOverview=true&comefromcontainer=& collectionpageid=29&containervoid=49&containervoid2=%containervoid%& SID=cda9d29f5597905d8d580b06c26343ec

Schuler, R. S. and Jackson, S. E. (2005). 'A Quarter-Century Review of Human Resource Management in the U.S.' *The Growth in Importance of the International Perspective 16*(1): 11–35.

Thom, N. and Zaugg R. J. (2004). Nachhaltiges und innovatives Personalmanagement: Spitzengruppenbefragung in europaeischen Unternehmungen und Institutionen. In Schwarz, E. J. (ed) *Nachhaltiges Innovationsmanagement. Gabler,* Wiesbaden, pp. 215–245.

Tsui, A. S. and Wu, J. B. (2005). 'The New Employment Relationship versus The Mutual Investment Approach'. *Implications For Human Resource Management 44*(2): 115–121.

WCED (1987). *Our common future.* Oxford: Oxford University Press.

Wilkinson, A. (2005). 'Downsizing, rightsizing or dumbsizing? Quality, human resources and the management of sustainability'. *Total Quality Management & Business Excellence 16*(8/9): 1079–1088.

Wilkinson, A., Hill, M. & Gollan, P. (2001). 'The sustainability debate'. *International Journal of Operations & Production Management 21*(12): 1492–1502.

Zaugg, R. J. (2009). *Nachhaltiges Personalmanagement: eine neue Perspektive und empirische Exploration des Human Resource Management.* Wiesbaden: Deutscher Universitätsverlag.

Zaugg, R. J., Blum, A., & Thom, N. (2001). 'Sustainability in human resource management'. Working paper No. 51, Institute for Organisation und Personell. Bern: University of Bern.

13

Corporate Governance
Systems and Industrial Relations

Chris Brewster, Marc Goergen, and Geoffrey Wood

The individualization of industrial relations and the general decline of
unions over the past two decades have neither been a uniform nor an
uncontested process.* In some contexts, the practice of industrial relations
has remained persistently collectivist, while unions retained a prominent
role in some national settings. While it can be argued that much of this
uneven nature of systemic change reflects strategic choices by social
actors, the range of options and outcomes reflects structural realities.
The latter encompass the sources of firm finance, corporate governance,
and embedded formal and informal rules and norms. In this chapter we
review the alternative institutional explanations for persistent variations
in national industrial relations practice, and test these explanations in the
light of large scale trans-national survey evidence, provided by the Cranet
survey (Cranet is a survey of HR practices in private and public sector
organizations across Europe and the rest of the world). Given the chapter's
central coverage of corporate governance, we focus on those institutional
accounts that place governance at the centre of their analysis: this includes
both rational incentive accounts and the socio-economic account of Hall
and Soskice (2001), rather than approaches (see Amable, 2003) that see
governance as only one of many formative institutional features, or more
mainstream contemporary regulationist thinking. However, we return to
the relevance of such accounts in our concluding sections.

Institutions and industrial relations: alternative accounts

Persistent difference has prompted a revival of interest in the effects
of institutions and practice. By "institutions" we mean the embedded
sets of rules and practices that impact on – and in turn are remoulded
by – socio-economic behaviour. Classical accounts by writers such

as Durkheim saw institutions as providing the underpinnings for sustainable collective action, and hence, economic activity (Prosser, 2006). The hegemony of neo-liberal ideologies in the 1980s and 1990s (and their continued influence) led to a dominant focus on the effects of rational action. As the proponents of globalization-driven convergence were gradually discredited by empirical realities, writers such as North (1990) sought to reorient the broad paradigm to take account of institutional consequences. Given the central attention accorded to rational economic man, North (1990) saw institutions as providers of incentives, and disincentives, to rational actors.

This line of thinking permeated both economics and finance, and managerial theory. One of the more influential examples of the latter was Powell and DiMaggio (1991) who focused on the effects of institutions as drivers of homogeneity within national settings; generally absent from this rather intellectually impoverished account was attention to systemic change or, indeed, the nature of institutions themselves. Within the economics and finance literature, debates focused on the role of institutions as providing the foundations for economic growth (La Porta, Lopez-de-Silanes, Shleifer, & Vishny, 1997; North, 1990). A general – and predictably conservative – consensus emerged that when property rights were strongest, growth was likely to be the most robust.

Law, property rights, and industrial relations

A focus on property rights led La Porta et al. (1997) to consider the effects of legal system. Since an abiding concern within common law legal systems was the right to private property, it was suggested that countries that come closest to this model were likely to perform the best. In contrast, the civil law tradition has placed a stronger emphasis on social order and coherence (Prosser, 2006), which, in turn, has made for weaker property rights. Within the latter broad category, La Porta et al. (1997) argued that French civil law represents the archetype, with weaker or more mixed forms of civil law found in Germany and Scandinavia. La Porta et al.'s (1997; 1998) analysis of the effects of law on economic growth does work, as long as the dysfunctional civil law systems of West Africa are included in the analysis. However, a closer scrutiny reveals that a number of civil law systems (e.g. Sweden) outperformed liberal markets even during the heyday of neo-liberalism in the late 1990s and early 2000s.

If legal tradition affects the rights of property owners and shareholders, how does it affect the rights of employees? La Porta et al. (1997)

argue that only owners have sunk capital in the firm, they bear the risk and should have the rewards (see also Djankov, Glaeser, La Porta, Lopez-de-Silnes & Shleifer, 2003). As a result, they tend to see owner and employee rights as a "zero-sum game"; greater power to the former means the latter must lose out and vice versa. This would suggest that employee rights are stronger in civil law countries. There are three basic reasons for this. First, there is the direct effect of the law: individual (e.g. job protection) and collective (e.g. union and bargaining) employment rights tend to be stronger in civil countries. Second, where the rights of owners and shareholders are weaker, managers have more room to "empire build", which, for interests of prestige and resource access, they have a natural inclination to do – what is referred to as the agency problem (ibid.; Roe, 2003). Empire building is likely to be more successful in collusion with employees, who, in turn, will extract concessions from management; in any event, larger organizations are associated with more generous terms and conditions of employment and job security (Roe, 2003). Third, there is the nature of common law. Legislation tends to be rather broad in such contexts, with much being left to the courts to interpret and fill out the broad intent of legislators; in contrast, rights and obligations in civil law systems are more clearly delineated (Wood, Harcourt, & Harcourt, 2004). This means that in common law systems, employees are more likely to have to resort to litigation to secure their rights. This process is, of course, a relatively high risk one, as action against one's employer is likely to be detrimental to the future employment relationship: the employee typically has only one employer while the employer has many employees making for a persistent imbalance. Hence, it is easier for the employer to retaliate over the long term in subtle ways that may not always be remediable via further legal action (Wood, Harcourt, & Harcourt, 2004).

The effects of electoral system on industrial relations

A second dominant institutional feature could be electoral systems. Within more representative systems, parties are often forced to forge coalitions, bringing together the interests of more than one grouping in society. And, in forging such coalitions, it is easier to focus on the interests of large groupings with arguably homogeneous preferences, such as workers (Pagano & Volpin, 2005). While the resultant coalitions may be beneficial to the managerial class, they are less likely to suit the interests of owners (Pagano & Volpin, 2005). In first-past-the-post systems, political parties concentrate their efforts on a relatively small pool of floating voters, a grouping that does not have strong preferences of their own (Pagano & Volpin, 2005). It is likely that the propertied classes will have greater resources to bring to bear in swaying this grouping, which, in any event, is not likely to have the homogeneous preferences that would lend itself to coalition building with the less advantaged.

The effects of politics on industrial relations

Roe (2003) notes that right-wing governments are more sympathetic to property owners. Hence, under right-wing governments the interests of the latter grouping will be more closely and directly served; in turn, this would mean that workers will inevitably lose out. The latter would include both greater constraints on wages (resources which instead will be returned to owners) and worker rights; as unions challenge the allocation of resources within the firm, owners will, if given greater room for manoeuvre, inevitably seek to move against them.

In line with La Porta et al. (1997), Roe (2003) argues that any improvement in worker pay or rights simply worsens the agency problem. Conceptually speaking, a limitation with this argument is that closely reining in management and aligning them to the owner agenda can weaken managerial interest in the firm, other than as a source of short-term profit and personal cash incentives. It can indeed be argued that the rise of highly rewarded irresponsible managers has, in fact, posed a more serious challenge to sustainable growth than the classical agency problem (Boyer, 2009). Nonetheless, the direct effect of right-wing governments on unions is worth investigating closer.

Limits of rational hierarchical accounts

There are clear limitations to the above noted approaches in that they fail to take account of the nature of complementarity; the latter means that rules and practices can together yield better results than a scrutiny of their component parts would suggest (Crouch, 2005). Complementarity may build on systemic strengths, compensate for inherent weaknesses, and/or impart flexibility into apparently rigid systemic features (Crouch, 2005; Lane & Wood, 2009). Complementarity means that more than one party may win out: more rights or resources for one party does not necessarily mean fewer for others. In short, the relationship between shareholder and employee rights is not necessarily a zero-sum game; both sides may win, for example, via neo-corporatist arrangements that have often yielded very strong macro-economic benefits (Harcourt & Wood, 2003).

A second limitation is the assumption of hierarchy, that one specific dimension (be it law, politics, or electoral system) overrides others, imposing its effects on subsidiary institutions, corporate governance, and managerial practice. In practice, this may mean that the effects of, say, politics on what firms do will be mitigated – or exaggerated – through other institutional features, or, indeed, the role of associations in wider society. This does not mean that law and politics do not matter, but the effects may be less direct and more contingent – and open to contestation – than would be suggested by rational hierarchical approaches.

A third limitation is on the notion that only owners have sunk capital in the enterprise. In reality employees have at least as much to lose if the company underperforms: they may lose their jobs, and may not readily find others, especially during a time of recession (Goergen, Brewster, & Wood, 2009). And any job move poses transaction costs on the individual; a new job under similar terms and conditions of service can still leave the individual worse off (Marsden, 1999). In addition, a host of other stakeholders (suppliers, customers, and surrounding communities) are likely to have some interest in the prosperity of the firm.

Non-hierarchical approaches

In contrast to approaches that focus on the primacy of property rights, the burgeoning varieties of capitalism (VOC) literature conceives of institutions as centres of webs of social relationships; property rights are not the only thing underpinning a wide range of interlocking relationships that make social life possible. This would suggest that corporate governance and what firms do reflects the interactions of a range of rules, norms and practices, although much of the early literature in this genre (Hall & Soskice, 2001; Dore, 2000; Lincoln & Kalleberg, 1990) continued to place issues of governance at the centre of the analysis, as the primary interface between external pressures and internal organizational practices.

A common feature of this literature involves a key distinction between liberal market economies (LMEs) and coordinated market economies (CMEs). In the former, shareholder/owner rights are dominant, making for specific sets of organizational practices. This includes a strong focus on individual contracting, and a reliance on flexible external labour markets to resource skills as and when needed. Owners have a greater freedom to adjust workforce sizes and the terms and conditions of employment according to market needs. In practice, this has led to the growing bifurcation of the workforce between relatively well-paid generically skilled workers in "high technology" manufacturing and services, and a large unskilled workforce confined to low end and poorly rewarded work in the service sector (Wright & Dwyer, 2006). In LMEs employees in both these categories have a relatively high degree of individualization in contracting and – where applicable – representation. Within the latter category, unions would be seen as a natural impediment to labour repression. Meanwhile, in the former category, individual employees would be in a reasonably good bargaining position, using exit or the threat thereof as the primary means of securing improvements in wages and working conditions; given the generic skills base, employers may indirectly benefit from such a set up, in that organizational experience is diffused across the relevant sector (Thelen, 2001).

In contrast, in coordinated markets the power of owners is diluted through a range of other relationships and structural features. These would include strong industry-based employer associations, embedded traditions of collective bargaining and centralized neo-corporatist deals, interlocking ownership, and legally underwritten structures for collective representation at the workplace over issues of work organization (Hall & Soskice, 2001; Harcourt & Wood, 2003). This would make union power stronger at the workplace not only owing to greater formal legal rights – itself the outcome of centralized deal making – but owing to conventions of cooperation. In turn, such relationships would be conducive to incrementally innovative production paradigms founded on industry specific skills, high mutual commitment, and good human capital development (Lincoln & Kalleberg, 1990; Thelen, 2001). Reflecting this dichotomy between shareholder and stakeholder rights, stock markets are more capitalized in LMEs, and employment protection weaker; the converse is true in CMEs. Weaker employment protection makes union members more open to victimization, while the greater churn of employees would make union organizing drives more difficult.

Key propositions

This leads us to a number of alternative propositions:

Proposition 1: Union influence at the workplace has generally declined, overriding any national institutional effects.

Proposition 2: Union influence at the workplace is weakest in common law countries and strongest in French tradition civil law ones.

Proposition 3: Union influence at the workplace is strongest in countries with a high degree of proportionality in their electoral systems.

Proposition 4: Union influence at the workplace is strongest in countries with left wing governments.

Proposition 5: Union influence in the workplace is strongest in coordinated market economies (CMEs).

Measuring union influence

This chapter makes use of two measures of union influence. The first is penetration rates. Unions cannot succeed in their role if they do not represent people (Hyman, 2002, p. 55; Kelly, 1998, pp. 126–127). Quite simply, it measures the capacity of unions to recruit and retain members (Checchi & Visser, 2005). Nor can collective bargaining – or, for that matter, collective action – take place without a meaningful following at the workplace (Kelly, 1998, p. 61). The survey questionnaire makes use of an ordinal scale of union membership as follows: 0 = 0%, 1 = 1–10%; 2 = 11–25%; 3 = 26–50%; 4 = 51–75%; 5 = 76–100%.

The second measure of union influence we employ is managerial perceptions of this change; this may reflect objective facts or a point of view. Union power in the workplace is a dynamic thing, and reflects changes in capabilities and resources (Hyman, 2002, pp. 62–63). If managers see unions as weak, they are more likely to adopt union busting measures, or at the very least to push them back further (Hyman, 2002; Kelly, 1998; Kelly, 2002; Rigby, Smith, & Brewster, 2004). In other words, this variable is about changes in union strength, and/or the extent to which management takes them seriously and/or are more likely to be able to further marginalize them. Again, this is an ordinal variable scaled as follows: 0 = no influence; 1 = decreasing influence; 2 = influence has stayed the same; 3 = union influence has increased. The estimation technique employed is ordered logit modelling. Each regression contains year and industry dummy variables.[1]

Survey method

This chapter is based on the Cranet surveys, and makes use of longitudinal data from successive waves of surveys. This survey is centred mostly on closed ended questions, making for clear and unambiguous answers, and is aimed at HR managers or, in the absence thereof, the most senior manager with a responsibility for HRM. The survey takes place at three- to four- year intervals; we make use of survey data since 1994. It could be argued that those responding to the survey are representatives of firms that place a stronger emphasis on people management; nonetheless, very clear patterns emerge from the data, with more hard line approaches to HRM not being evenly distributed across space and place. The survey is focused at the firm rather than the worksite level (as policies as well as practices were being studied) and excludes smaller firms – those with less than 100 employees. As a consequence, the results differ from comparable employer surveys such as the Workplace Employment Relations Survey (WERS) in the UK and reflect a different reality. Shifts in responses over time were identified via the usage of time dummy variables. It was not possible to identify or match individual firms owing to the anonymous nature of responses; hence, this chapter focuses on overall trends, and is appropriate to its aims (see Bailey, 1987). The tables of results are available from the authors on request.

Findings

The results for the ordered logits for the proportion of employees who are union members confirmed that trade union penetration is indeed lower in common law countries, as suggested by La Porta et al. (1997; 1998). However, the differences between different civil law traditions are not on the lines predicted. Unionization is in fact highest in Scandinavian law countries, followed by German law countries. Lowest unionization in the civil law family is encountered in French tradition civil law countries, despite property rights being "weakest" in this category (cf. La Porta et al., 1997; 1998). Evidently, owner and union rights are not mutually exclusive, nor represent a zero-sum game. As can be seen from the figure, industry dummies were positive and significant; this would reflect industry variations in terms of bargaining practices and work organization (cf. Boyer & Hollingsworth, 1997).

More generally speaking, the proportion of workers who are union members has declined in many instances; this would reflect the weaker bargaining position of workers during a long period of volatility, mediocre growth, and periodic recessions. While there is no doubt that unions have done better in some cases than others, many have had to deal with the problem of membership losses and/or poor recruitment (Kelly, 1998; cf. Checchi & Visser, 2005).

Further, the industry dummies for sectors providing services to public institutions are highly significant and positive. This may reflect the privatization of central and local government services over the period of study. The private sector organizations taking over the provision of public services may then have inherited workers who have had traditionally a high trade union representation, and who would now have to fight for their collective rights (Dibben, James, Roper, & Wood, 2007).

We then went on to explore perceived changes in union influence over the past three years. Union influence was perceived as declining the most in common law countries. However, contrary to La Porta et al. (1997; 1998), union influence was seen as modestly increasing in Scandinavian civil law countries, in contrast to French civil law countries where it was seen as weakening. Again, this would demonstrate that owner and worker rights are not mutually exclusive; it is not where owners are weakest that unions are at their most influential. Again, we did encounter some industry effects with trade union influence being higher in sectors catering for public institutions.

We then explored the index of proportionality in electoral systems, derived by Pagano & Volpin (2005), as an indicator of union power. It does seem that union influence is strongest in those countries with more proportionally representative electoral systems. Similar to all the previous regressions there has been a particularly strong perceived decline in union power since after 1995 in first-past-the-post systems: again, however, it is not more pronounced than the portion of workers that are union members – this would seemingly confirm the argument that managerial assessments of changes in union influence do not represent wishful thinking – or a means of justifying harder line policies – but are a more realistic assessment of union power. Again, the level and evolution of trade union influence have been different across various industry sectors, and these patterns hold across various national systems.

We turn now to Roe (2003) on the effects of politics, based on the Cusack and Engelhardt (2006) index (RILE), which encompasses government orientations in a range of socio-economic areas. We found that the influence of unions is lower in countries with right wing governments. This provides support for Roe's (2003) politics thesis. Unions appear weaker in the workplace under right-wing governments; again there were industry effects.

How do VOC theories fit as a predictor of union power? A review of the regression results would confirm that LMEs (countries which are also uniformly common law based, and with a few notable exceptions low on the proportionality index) are rather different from CMEs. Within the former category, union representation is the lowest, the decline – and perceived decline – of unions the most pronounced. Clear sectoral variations – and the fact that law, electoral systems, and politics appear to have an influence – would highlight the complex effects of interlocking webs of relations at local and national level. Clearly, a single institutional feature such as law or electoral system does not override all other institutional effects. However, there are clear limitations to dichotomous approaches. For example, we found pronounced differences between Scandinavia and continental European countries. There is no doubt that the CME category is a very diverse one.

On the basis of the pseudo r-squares results, it is evident that electoral systems appear to have relatively good explanatory power of trade union penetration and perceived shifts in influence. This would suggest that the relative fortunes of unions in New Zealand, a LME that has undergone electoral reform, would be worse than, say, Australia, which has not. While it is evident that legal tradition matters, this is not along the lines predicted by La Porta et al. (1998); differences in property rights under the law cannot directly explain variations in union power, especially if the case of Scandinavia is considered.

A somewhat less strong predictor was the Cusack index of right- or left-wing governments; as suggested by both Roe (2003), and a significant body of the industrial relations literature (cf. Turner, 2004; McIlroy 1998), right wing governments are worse for unions and collective representation at the workplace. However, there appeared more to this relationship than a simple hierarchy: union strength varied on a sectoral basis, reflecting the operation of other dynamics, most notably, the relationship between work and unionization in the public sector, and the effects of unions on privatization and outsourcing (see Dibben et al., 2007). A further four caveats are in order.

First, the weakening of the traditional model of union-party relations encountered in social democracies (cf. Valenzuela, 2002; McIlroy, 1998) makes it difficult to conclude that a left-wing government will be consistently union friendly. This situation is particularly pronounced in the United Kingdom and the United States. In the latter, unions had little to show for their backing of the Democratic Party in the Clinton era (Moberg, 1999, p. 32). In the United Kingdom, international standards in workers' rights in a range of areas, from picketing to organizing are ignored, with legal rights of employees often being vague, and difficult to enforce, while ongoing privatizations and outsourcing of state functions have had long term consequences for union organization (Smith & Morton, 2006, p. 414).

Second, the role of right-wing governments may vary from concentrating on protecting investor rights, to a more active role in curbing the organizing and mobilizing activities of unions (Gamble, 2002). Third, governments may change within the time period under consideration and the effects of a new government of a different political slant may take time to be felt. Fourth, different state and institutional traditions may limit the powers of elected governments vis-à-vis a range of social collectives (Turner, 2004). These caveats may explain why electoral systems and the law are stronger predictors of union strength.

While there was insufficient evidence to confirm the dichotomous VOC model, it was evident that institutional arrangements operate in more than a simply hierarchical basis: more than one set of causal relations is apparent, with not only owners, but also employees actively intervening to reconfirm and reshape their respective roles within the organization, leading to conflicts and compromises, with long-term consequences for the specific nature of competitiveness that is sought.

Here a caveat is in order: while we need to take account of direct institutional effects on employees and their collectives (rather than simply in terms of managerial responses), this does not represent the only other set of relations at work: the role of other associations – of employers and civil society groupings – will also mould the manner in which the firm is being governed.

Conclusion

This chapter highlighted the complex relationship between societal institutions, legal traditions, political parties and electoral systems, corporate governance, and the relative strength of unions and collective representation at workplace level. The fact that all three impact on union strength, not always in the manner predicted – and that one may constrain the effects of another – would highlight the fact that there is more to understanding corporate governance than simply property relations. Law provides the basis not only for securing property rights, but indeed, for the rights of employees on a collective and individual basis, and these may overlap; more of one does not mean less of the other (Piore & Safford, 2006). While right-wing governments may be more sympathetic to property owners, different state traditions may limit or facilitate their capacity for active intervention on the side of the latter. Again, left wing political parties may vary in the strength and quality of their relations with unions. Again, proportional representative electoral systems lend themselves to centralization and coalition building, which may facilitate neo-corporatist arrangements, strengthening the hand of unions. Furthermore, such systems may be characterized by a "virtuous circle" between collective participation at the workplace, and a tendency by union members to take a more active part in national political life (D'Art & Turner, 2007). As Del'Aringa and Pangani (2007, p. 30) note, there is no concrete evidence as to a relationship between weak unions and strong macro-economic performance: indeed, a union presence may make for complementarities between high levels of participation, investment in human capital, and high quality incrementally innovative production (Thelen, 2001; Harcourt & Wood, 2007). In addition, while firms are clearly constrained by their institutional setting there is enough variation in the data to suggest that they are not entirely strait-jacketed – managers have and do make choices that vary across firms in similar institutional circumstances.

This might suggest that VOC approaches, which see the role of institutions in terms of multi-faceted socio-economic relations, rather than simply constraints or facilitators of certain paths of rational decision making (cf. Powell & DiMaggio, 1991), might be a valuable predictor of corporate governance and, hence, behaviour. Why, then, is the dichotomous VOC model relatively weak in their explanatory power? First, it tends to discount the effects of legal and electoral systems in Mediterranean economies as a driver of cooperation (and, indeed, gives little attention to such economies at all). In practice, right-wing governments have been constrained in countries such as Italy and Spain, on account of the relative strength of unions, both in terms of a corporatist tradition, and, in terms of the law (cf. Turner, 2004). Again, this model takes insufficient account of the important differences between Scandinavia and North Western continental Europe.

Second, the dichotomous VOC model is a relatively static one, assuming path dependence. Hence, it is difficult to account for the dynamic effects of governments of different political ideologies, nor for the ongoing process of experimentation at firm level in response to changes in the external political, and economic environment, encompassing both national and global trends (see Behrens & Jacoby, 2004). More recent multi-variety models (e.g. Amable, 2003) have attempted to redress these shortfalls. However, in doing so, Amable no longer places governance as the central dimension in his analysis; while this weakens the analytical clarity of earlier models, this can make for a more nuanced understanding of interlocking institutional effects.

Hence, we would argue for an approach that sees corporate governance and behaviour as more than simply variations in property rights, and institutions in terms of the operations of hierarchies making for specific isomorphisms. There is more to the role and effects of institutions than simply providers of incentives and disincentives for rational property maximizing individuals. The industrial relations literature's tradition of empirical rigour and pragmatism may provide valuable insights into understanding the nuances of the relationship between law, political parties, electoral systems, and union power. At the same time, a caveat is in order. It would take comparative survey evidence over a very much longer period of time to conclude a linearity to the practice of corporate governance and industrial relations. What evidence we have points to a degree of systemic dynamism but also discontinuity. While unions remain relatively stronger in countries such as Germany, and weaker in Britain, the general decline of union power since the 1970s may reflect both long-term global economic cycles (Kelly, 1998), and indeed, ruptures and discontinuities: new technologies and new global trading patterns may place unions under new pressures and open up new organizational opportunities (Kelly & Frege, 2004; cf. Behrens & Jacoby, 2004). This would suggest the utility of a non-linear approach to understanding the relationship between socio-economic context, corporate governance and practice, as suggested by contemporary regulationist thinking.

* Some of the points made in this chapter are also contained in Goergen et al. (2009). We wish to thank our colleagues in the Cranet network for their permission to use the data they collected and to acknowledge the role of the Cranfield School of Management in co-ordinating the network.

Notes

1. The industry sectors are based on the EU NACE classification. The sectors are as follows: Agriculture, hunting, forestry, fishing (IND1); Energy and water (IND2); Non-energy chemicals (IND3); Metal manufacture (IND4); Other manufacturing (IND5); Building and civil engineering (IND6); Distributive trades (IND7); Transport & communication (IND8); Banking & finance (IND9); Personal services (IND10); Health services (IND11); Other services (IND12); Education (IND13); Local government (IND14); Central government (IND15); Other (IND16); Other public (IND17).

References

Amable, B. (2003). *The diversity of modern capitalism*. Oxford: Oxford University Press.

Bailey, K. (1987). *Methods of social research*. New York: Free Press.

Behrens, M., & Jacoby, W. (2004). The rise of experimentalism in German collective bargaining. *British Journal of Industrial Relations, 42*(1), 95–123.

Boyer, R. (2009). *History repeating for economists.* Annual Conference of the Society for the Advancement of Socio-Economics, Paris, July.

Boyer, R,. & Hollingsworth, J. R. (1997). From national embeddedness to spatial and institutional nestedness. In J. R. Hollingsworth & R. Boyer (eds), *Contemporary capitalism: the embeddedness of institutions.* Cambridge and New York: Cambridge University Press.

Checchi, D., & Visser, J. (2005). Pattern persistence in European trade union density. *European Sociological Review, 21*(1): 1–21.

Crouch, C. (2005). Three meanings of complementarity. *Socio-Economic Review, 3*(2), 359–363.

Cusack, T., & Engelhardt, L. (2006). Parties, governments and legislatures data set. Retrieved from http://www.wz-berlin.de/mp/ism/people/misc/cusack/d_sets.en.htm#data

D'Art, D., & Turner, T. (2007). Trade unions and political participation in the European Union. *British Journal of Industrial Relations, 45*(1), 103–126.

Del'Aringa, C., & Pangani, L. (2007). Collective bargaining and wage dispersion in Europe. *British Journal of Industrial Relations, 45*(1), 29–54.

Dibben, P., James, P., Roper, I., & Wood, G. (eds). (2007). *Modernizing work and employment in public services.* London: Palgrave Macmillan.

Djankov, S., Glaeser, E., La Porta, R., Lopez-de-Silnes, F., & Shleifer, A. (2003). The new comparative economics. *Journal of Comparative Economics, 31*(4), 595–619.

Dore, R. (2000). *Stock market capitalism: welfare capitalism.* Cambridge: Cambridge University Press.

Gamble, A. (2002). The new right. In J. Kelly (ed.), *Industrial relations – Critical perspectives on business and management,*vol. 3. London: Routledge.

Goergen, M., Brewster, C., & Wood, G. (2009). Corporate governance regimes and employment relations in Europe. *Industrial Relations/Relations Industrielles, 64*(4), 555–574.

Hall, P., & Soskice, D. (2001). An introduction to the varieties of capitalism. In P. Hall & D. Soskice (eds), *Varieties of capitalism: the institutional basis of competitive advantage* (pp. 1–68). Oxford: Oxford University Press.

Harcourt, M., & Wood, G. (2003). Under what circumstances do social accords work? *Journal of Economic Issues, 37*(3), 747–767.

Harcourt, M., & Wood, G. (2007). The importance of employment protection for skill development in coordinated market economies. *European Journal of Industrial Relations, 13*(2), 141–159.

Hyman, R. (2002). What is industrial relations. In J. Kelly (ed.), *Industrial relations – Critical perspectives on business and management,*vol. 1. London: Routledge.

Kelly, J. (1998). *Rethinking industrial relations: mobilization, collectivism and long waves.* London: Routledge.

Kelly, J. (2002). General Introduction. In J. Kelly (ed.), *Industrial relations – critical perspectives on business and management,*vol. 2. London: Routledge.

Kelly, J., & Frege, C. (2004). Conclusions: varieties of unionism. In J. Kelly & C. Frege (eds), *Varieties of unionism.* Oxford: Oxford University Press.

La Porta, R., Lopez-de-Silanes, F., Shleifer, A., &Vishny, R. (1997). Legal determinants of finance. *Journal of Finance, 52*, 1131–1150.

La Porta, R., Lopez-de-Silanes, F., Shleifer, A., & Vishny, R. (1998). Law and finance. *Journal of Political Economy, 106*, 1113–1155.

Lane, C., & Wood, G. (2009). Introducing diversity in capitalism and capitalist diversity. *Economy and Society, 38*(3), 531–551.

Lincoln, J., & Kalleberg, A. (1990). *Culture, control and commitment: a study of work organization in the United States and Japan.* Cambridge: Cambridge University Press.

Marsden, D. (1999). *A theory of employment systems.* Oxford: Oxford University Press.

McIlroy, J. (1998). The enduring alliance? Trade unions and the marking of new labour, 1994–1998. *British Journal of Industrial Relations, 36*(4), 537–564.

North, D. C. (1990) *Institutions, institutional change and economic performance.* Cambridge: Cambridge University Press.

Pagano, M., & Volpin, P. (2005). The political economy of corporate governance. *American Economic Review, 95*, 1005–1030.

Piore, M., & Safford, S. (2006). Changing regimes of workplace governance, shifting axes of social mobilization and the challenges to industrial relations theory. *Industrial Relations, 45*(3), 299–325.

Powell, W., & Di Maggio, P. (1991) *The new institutionalism in organizational analysis.* Chicago: University of Chicago Press.

Prosser, T. (2006). Regulation and social solidarity. *Journal of Law and Society, 33*(3), 367–387.

Rigby, M., Smith, R., & Brewster, C. (2004). The changing impact and strength of the labour movement in Europe. In M. Harcourt and G. Wood (eds), *Tradeunions and democracy: strategies and perspectives.* Manchester: Manchester University Press

Roe, M. (2003). *Political determinants of corporate governance.* Oxford: Oxford University Press.

Shleifer, A., & Vishny, R. (1997) A survey of corporate governance. *Journal of Finance, 52*, 737–783.

Smith, P., & Morton, G. (2006) Nine years of new labour: neoliberalism and worker's rights. *British Journal of Industrial Relations, 44*(3): 401–420.

Thelen, K. (2001). Varieties of labor politics in the developed democracies. In P. Hall & D. Soskice (eds), *Varieties of capitalism: the institutional basis of competitive advantage.* Oxford: Oxford University Press.

Turner, L. (2004). Why revitalize? Labour's urgent mission in a contested global economy. In J. Kelly & C. Frege (eds), *Varieties of Unionism.* Oxford: Oxford University Press.

Valenzuela, S. (2002). Trade unions and political systems: some variations. In J. Kelly (ed.), *Industrial relations – Critical perspectives on business and management,*vol. 3. London: Routledge.

Wood, G., Harcourt, M., & Harcourt, S. (2004). The effects of age discrimination legislation on workplace practice. *Industrial Relations Journal, 35*(4), 359–371.

Wright, E., & Dwyer, R. (2006). The patterns of jobs expansion in the USA. In G. Wood & P. James (eds), *Institutions, production and working life.* Oxford: Oxford University Press.

Index